MAKING THE
AMALGAMATED

STUDIES IN INDUSTRY AND SOCIETY
Philip B. Scranton, *Series Editor*

Published with the assistance of the Hagley Museum and Library

RELATED TITLES IN THE SERIES:

John Bodnar
Workers' World:
Kinship, Community, and Protest in an
Industrial Society, 1900–1940

David A. Hounshell
From the American System to Mass Production, 1800–1932:
The Development of Manufacturing Technology
in the United States

John K. Brown
The Baldwin Locomotive Works, 1831–1915:
A Study in American Industrial Practice

Edward S. Cooke Jr.
Making Furniture in Preindustrial America:
The Social Economy of Newtown and Woodbury, Connecticut

Thomas R. Heinrich
Ships for the Seven Seas:
Philadelphia Shipbuilding in the Age of Industrial Capitalism

Mark Aldrich
Safety First:
Technology, Labor, and Business in the Building of
American Work Safety, 1870–1939

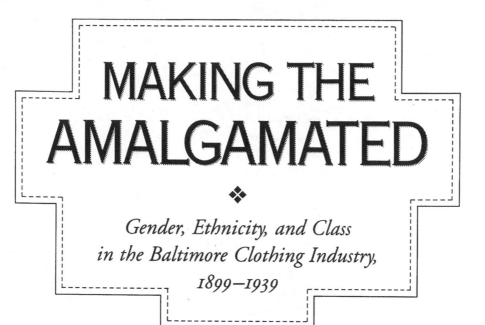

MAKING THE AMALGAMATED

❖

*Gender, Ethnicity, and Class
in the Baltimore Clothing Industry,
1899–1939*

JO ANN E. ARGERSINGER

THE JOHNS HOPKINS UNIVERSITY PRESS

Baltimore and London

© 1999 The Johns Hopkins University Press
All rights reserved. Published 1999
Printed in the United States of America on acid-free paper
2 4 6 8 9 7 5 3 1

The Johns Hopkins University Press
2715 North Charles Street
Baltimore, Maryland 21218-4363
www.press.jhu.edu

Library of Congress Cataloging-in-Publication Data will be found
at the end of this book.
A catalog record for this book is available from the British Library.
ISBN 0-8018-5989-1

For Peter

CONTENTS

Illustrations follow page 82

ACKNOWLEDGMENTS

Much time has passed since I began the research for this book, and there are many people to thank and many to remember. In 1988, the extraordinarily talented staff at the Walter P. Reuther Library and Archives at Wayne State University made my Rockefeller Fellowship there more profitable and enjoyable. Special thanks go to Phil Mason and Warner Pflug for their assistance at the library. While in Detroit, I benefited from discussions with Professor John Barnard of Oakland University and the late Bernard J. Firestone, secretary-treasurer of the Chicago and Central States Board of the Amalgamated Clothing and Textile Workers Union. In addition, I had the good fortune to become friends with the late Millie Jeffrey, a retired Amalgamated organizer and official who lived on Wayne State's campus and had organized in Baltimore in the 1930s. Her spirit and compassion inform this book.

Other officials of the Amalgamated have been instrumental in sharing resources and information; I want especially to thank Robert Gasior and Carmen Papale of Baltimore. The Amalgamated records housed in Cornell University's Martin P. Catherwood Library were essential, as was the assistance of the library's director, Richard Strassberg.

Several friends and colleagues either read parts of the manuscript or commented on papers at conferences. I only hope I incorporated fully their suggestions and insights, for I certainly benefited from them. I want to acknowledge the generous assistance of Kathy Peiss, Joan Cashin, Philip Scranton, and Linda Shopes. Other friends who just made my work more enjoyable include my colleagues in the Provost Office, Carole McCann, Debbie Mason, Robin Radespiel Sabatini, Diane Lee, Beth Pennington, Tony Moreira, and Linda Hatmaker.

In Baltimore, Virginia North, archivist at the Jewish Historical Society of Maryland, provided invaluable assistance in using oral history records and acquiring illustrations for the book. Before their deaths, Jacob Edelman

x   and Sara Barron, both longtime Baltimoreans and veterans of the Amalgamated, shared with me their vivid, and remarkably precise, recollections of the early decades of the union. I had the privilege to be invited to their homes on several occasions and to experience firsthand their dedication to their brothers and sisters of the Amalgamated.

Robert J. Brugger of the Johns Hopkins University Press made this project possible and the book better. His talents as a historian and an editor were evident in all his comments, and I genuinely appreciated his warm friendship throughout the process. Deborah Klenotic, the delightful and very able copyeditor for the Press, also deserves special recognition for the outstanding job she did on the manuscript.

Acknowledging the support of my family is always a special pleasure, but my heart still hurts when I think of the recent losses in my family. My father and grandmother passed away just over a year ago, and we lost my husband's father and my brother several years earlier. I know that my father, the late Buford C. Eady, with his humor and wit, would have been delighted to have seen this book *finally* finished.

Above all, my affection and appreciation go to my husband and colleague, Peter H. Argersinger. After all these years, he continues to amaze me with his intellectual rigor, his untiring scholarly efforts and breadth of knowledge, and his generous support of me and my work. His extraordinary contributions to this project (and his gentle nudging to complete my revisions) truly brought the book to fruition. I thank him for his kindness and dedicate this book to him with my love.

MAKING THE
AMALGAMATED

INTRODUCTION

In the 1990s, exposés of sweatshop conditions in clothing factories have repeatedly captured news headlines and public attention. As secretary of labor, Robert Reich reported that one-third of the garment shops in the United States were hazardous to the health and safety of workers. Investigators found five thousand illegal sweatshops violating wage, hours, and safety requirements in southern California and another two thousand in New York City. Congressional hearings revealed that clothing lines endorsed by celebrities were manufactured by child labor in sweatshops in both the United States and other countries. Macy's, Neiman Marcus, and other leading retailers were named as sellers of sweatshop products. Editorialists expressed their outrage, public officials their dismay. Unionists took to the streets in protest.[1]

AFL-CIO president John Sweeney led a march of thousands through New York's Garment District in a rally against sweatshop conditions. In Baltimore, hundreds of union members picketed the Hecht Company, demanding that the huge retailer stop purchasing "sweatshop suits" from Peerless Clothing Inc., a Montreal-based company that had become North America's largest manufacturer of men's suits. Some twenty other cities wit-

2   nessed similar protests denouncing manufacturers for paying substandard wages to immigrant workers and for constantly shifting production sites and subcontracting piecework in efforts to capture cheaper labor pools.[2]

In 1994 Baltimore witnessed another highly publicized dispute in the garment industry, centered on corporate plans to shift production from local to foreign factories to cut labor costs. London Fog company, founded in Baltimore in 1922, announced plans to shut all six of its domestic plants unless workers accepted deep wage concessions and surrendered rights secured by union contracts. Carmen Papale, Maryland's ranking official of the Amalgamated Clothing and Textile Workers Union, labored furiously to keep the "jobs from going overseas," offering counterproposals to address company concerns while protecting workers' interests. Papale had already earned praise from business leaders for his "realistic" approach to industrial issues and his commitment to a cooperative partnership between management and labor. Executives of both the English American Tailoring Company and Jos. A. Bank Clothiers noted appreciatively that such cooperation brought benefits to both sides: "They stepped up to the plate and helped us out when we needed help. [Papale] has been fair and we have gone overboard to be fair with him." Papale himself explained his labor-management philosophy when he insisted on mutually respectful negotiations. Papale's efforts, however, were rebuffed by the unyielding managers of London Fog, who insisted that domestic workers had to learn to accept wages similar to their foreign counterparts. Only when public officials promised the company financial assistance and the union accepted drastic wage reductions did London Fog agree to keep open a single factory in northwest Baltimore, with a sharply reduced workforce. All other production was transferred to foreign countries, eliminating the jobs of nearly eleven hundred workers, mostly women.[3]

These developments reproduced a pattern familiar to organized clothing workers. A volatile, competitive, and seasonal industry, the making of men's suits has long been characterized by manufacturers who search relentlessly for the cheapest labor pools. Sweatshop labor conditions have been a regular feature of the industry, provoking repeated and explosive investigations and constituting a target for social reform and a major source of union concern. The Amalgamated Clothing Workers (ACW) from its inception in 1914 has sought to create a process of labor-management relations that emphasizes cooperation and negotiation. Union officials have insisted throughout this century that by working with employers, they can save jobs and the

industry, thereby bringing economic stability to union members and owners alike.

These labor and industry patterns provide the broad outlines of Baltimore's history as a major national center for the production of men's clothes.
In the late nineteenth century, the city exploited its geographic position as
well as its workers to claim first regional, and then national, prominence in
garment manufacturing. By World War I, its production—ranking third in
the nation—was dominated by five major manufacturers. These firms, all
of German Jewish origin, had modern, multistory "sky-scraping factories"
that by 1915 accounted for three-fourths of the city's production of men's
clothes and employed more than half of Baltimore's fourteen thousand men's
garment workers. These large, mechanized factories were equipped and
arranged so that all the steps of production occurred under one roof. The
striking growth of these "inside shops" took place in the loft district west of
the central business district, producing a concentration of wealth and business productivity unparalleled by the other industries in Baltimore.[4]

The garment industry also included, across town in East Baltimore,
hundreds of petty entrepreneurs, who moved in and out of business with remarkable frequency and who indeed alternated between employer and employee status themselves. They operated out of tiny rowhouses, hiring young
boys and girls to repetitively perform fixed tasks with bolts of cloth and piles
of scraps. Known as "sweaters," these precarious capitalists were particularly vulnerable to market swings and to the larger manufacturers, who contracted them for piecework tasks. Sweaters barely eked out a measure of profit even as they exploited family and neighbors. It was in these grimy
workrooms that the garment industry had been born in Baltimore, and
sweatshops would remain a durable part of the city's clothing industry. Indeed, these two seemingly disparate segments of an unintegrated industry
were economically linked. The large, modern manufacturers often found it
cheaper to lay off their own workers and contract out one or two steps of the
production process to the small shops, pitting sweaters against each other in
search of the lowest bid.

World War I and the recession in its aftermath permanently altered Baltimore's garment industry; never again did large manufacturers dominate
the industry. The recession of the 1920s, dramatically reinforced by the Great
Depression of the 1930s, also diminished the city's place in the ACW. Like
Chicago, Baltimore had been among the earliest battlegrounds in the forming of the ACW, and its importance in the union's founding was matched by

4   its privileged position in the composition of the ACW's national leadership
and as a focus of union policy. As sweatshops displaced the large manufactories, however, union interest in the city's industry waned, for organizing
hundreds of primitive workshops, each employing only a small group of
workers, was costly and unpredictable. Moreover, union contracts were difficult to enforce in such settings.

The Amalgamated saw its future in a different context, linked to modern factories and major entrepreneurs with long-term commitments and in-
vestments. ACW leaders sought a partnership, even if an unequal one, with
leading manufacturers who could engage in long-range planning, influence
market shares, and respond to public tastes and fashion trends. Accordingly, as Baltimore's garment industry increasingly shifted back to the sweatshops in the 1930s, the ACW refocused its organizational energy on other
cities, where major manufacturers still dominated the market. Baltimore's
ACW membership declined, and Baltimore became, in the words of one
Amalgamated leader, merely an irritant in the industry, its scale and cost of
production threatening to undermine union control in such centers as New
York City and Rochester.[5]

The ACW's practice of supporting larger manufactories at the expense
of small shops collided with the industrial trends in Baltimore and often imposed hardship both on the union's members there and on the industry itself. Only after World War II did more medium-sized firms emerge, and the
ACW attempted to recapture some of its earlier strength by organizing those
firms.

Baltimore's prominence in the garment industry and the ACW makes it a
valuable focus for the study of the transformation of this industry and union.
Strikes in the early twentieth century heralded the beginning of the Amalgamated, and the local industrial transformation anticipated the subsequent
national decline of both the union and the garment business. In this book I
portray the women and men who worked to form a new union, and the employers who resisted and those who embraced unionism. I depict also the
union itself, from its national leadership in New York to local activists in Baltimore. Though I focus on the union's evolution in the industrial context, I
also link unionism to the interplay among politics and reform, regional market shares and economic policy, and community building and political mobilization in an urban setting. In doing so, I draw from the strengths of both
the old-style labor history, emphasizing institutional aspects of the union
movement—organizations; leadership; and strikes, bargaining, and con-

tracts—and the insights of the new approach to labor history, which stresses labor's social context and issues of ethnicity, gender, and culture.[6]

The story I present is, in some ways, familiar, reminiscent of other industries and unions in twentieth-century America. In other ways, the story is not familiar, for I examine all the processes attendant upon building a union even as it unravels the complex connections affecting the workplace and the market. Both a labor and a business history, this book is about the role of power, particularly its shifting and sometimes conflicting dimensions and applications. The idiosyncracies of employers and their insistence on managerial prerogatives often confounded the business and labor communities alike. Garment workers, union officials, and business leaders, all carrying their own personal lessons of the past, often distorted each other's perceptions, reinforced old prejudices, and focused efforts on winning old battles and reclaiming lost triumphs rather than on encouraging effective responses to significant new economic issues and industrial trends. The cultures of both business and labor too often militated against making necessary changes.

This examination of the garment industry and the Amalgamated also points up in full force the power of gender and ethnicity in shaping the cultures of work, the policies of union leaders, the processes of industry, and the national clothing economy itself. Women wage earners dominated the workforce in the men's clothing industry in Baltimore in the twentieth century. Yet the making of garments had strong links to a tradition of male domination in craft skills, work culture, and union activism. Accordingly, the role of power at the workplace often emerged as an issue of gender relations— even when social, political, and economic forces combined to mute a discussion of women and the workplace.

My intention in this book is to shed new light on the role that gender and ethnicity played in the ACW, the political arena, and the manufacturing process, especially including the definition of jobs and skills on the shopfloor. My research challenges those studies that suggest that all women responded similarly to inequality in unions or that limit women's aspirations to fantasies of mass culture or visions of home and hearth. Many women garment workers eagerly sought to learn new skills and took great pride in their accomplishments on the shopfloor and the picket line. Moreover, leadership and activism were not confined to the traditional arenas most often identified by labor scholars. Although women were marginalized in such settings as union meetings and local elections, they assumed primary responsibility

6 for politicizing the union, firmly linking it to the Democratic Party, and for starting and leading the union's important educational movement. Notwithstanding the outspoken ambivalence of key national leaders about the value of educational activities, in nearly every major Amalgamated stronghold, from Philadelphia to Chicago, women members established and drove the educational agenda.[7]

Not surprisingly, given their leadership in the educational arm of the union movement, women took seriously the ACW's language of "industrial democracy" and spent a good deal of time translating it for the rank-and-file. Guided by the union's exhortation to act as "equal citizens in an industrial democracy," Amalgamated women took up various causes and initiatives to promote that goal. Although the union's directive focused more on class than on gender—emphasizing that workers and bosses should both be respected—women members expanded the mandate and even crossed class lines to fulfill their own vision of equality. To the shock of more than a few ACW men, the sisters of the Amalgamated joined arms with middle-class women, embracing woman suffrage and other reforms as necessary steps to achieve industrial democracy for all citizens, "union brothers and sisters alike."[8]

Similarly, in this book I refine the findings of those studies that perhaps unwittingly position ethnic hierarchies among men workers and, as a consequence, too narrowly define activism in male work culture. Just as women workers observed and challenged the traditional boundaries of gender, men used both gender and ethnicity to define their place in the community and the union. Forms of resistance to the rules of the workplace, for example, varied among ethnic groups, and this book illustrates that diversity of responses. Some scholars' perception of certain types of responses among male workers as docility and elevation of other types of responses because of traditional notions about aggressiveness and male leadership distort male workers' own ideas about manliness. Men's search for "manly respectability" at work and in the union drew specific features from ethnic ties and alternately led to cooperation and conflict with their union sisters, their bosses, and each other.[9]

Although labeled "radical greenhorns," the men of the ACW labored under familiar notions about work and family, even when circumstances failed to reinforce those views. Tied to traditional definitions of skill and yet influenced by the limited availability of work, men who were forced to work alongside women—performing the same jobs—always expected higher pay and usually found enhanced status within the union. Still other union brothers, shaped by the concept of "the man's right to earn a family's wage," never fully accepted the permanence of wage-earning women, and that resistance resonated in their work culture and informed their expectations in policy priorities for the union. For them, "equal citizens in an industrial democracy" might include male Jews, Italians, and Lithuanians—but not women. Still, such strong views, especially among workers who were also challenging power, authority, and business tradition, were never so firmly formed as to be immune from other influences and perspectives, and even their resistance to welcoming women as equal citizens could never isolate male workers from periodic encounters with their union sisters or the "women's issue."[10]

Reminders of gender-based differences were commonplace and structural, from the company's definition and allocation of jobs to the union's definition and recognition of the "successful shop chairman." Sex-segregated jobs based purportedly on differing skills placed men at the top of the occupational hierarchy and also affected the ways in which men defined their own respectability on the shopfloor. Employers effectively used gender baiting to divide workers, threatening to hire women for "men's jobs" and to pay them lower wages. The ACW attempted to defuse such issues by protecting men's jobs at the expense of women's and by sanctioning gender-based differences in the wages paid for the same work.

Of course, neither all women nor all men accepted these inequalities. Both the union and the workplace offered them genuine opportunities to challenge conventional wisdom. Ethnic loyalties could simultaneously reinforce and challenge gender-based divisions, and women's efforts to win an equal voice in the union could—and did—both reaffirm and threaten manly respectability among their union brothers. Despite deeply ingrained prejudices and unequal practices, a certain elasticity still characterized gender roles and ethnic barriers. It was this characteristic that enabled all workers to reach points of solidarity; to bridge differences; and, at certain moments, to embrace collectively the Amalgamated.

Overall, in this book I examine the forces for unity and the factors that led to division in the industry and the union while underscoring the role of power in both the Amalgamated's search for "industrial democracy" and the garment industry's rise and decline. The ACW in Baltimore never regained its early prominence, and the garment industry became, after World War II, an international one. The record offered by the union and the city's industry remains complex; ultimately, neither succeeded in fulfilling its potential or preserving its achievements.

1

Toilers and Sweaters

The Rise of the Clothing Industry

In the late nineteenth century, a number of significant changes promoted Baltimore's transition from a commercial to an industrial city. Between 1870 and 1900, its population nearly doubled to more than half a million and its spatial configurations adapted to reflect that growth and attendant economic specialization. Residential segregation joined industrial developments to give the city new shape and identity, as ethnic enclaves emerged and nascent industries redrew Baltimore's boundaries of opportunity and economic growth. Fashionable neighborhoods sprang up along Charles Street, and wealthy residents left such older areas as Fells Point to the working classes who labored on the port and in factories and workshops. The city could also now boast of new department stores—emporiums of consumer elegance such as Hutzler's and Hochschild, Kohn & Co. The 1890 census reported that for the first time, the total value of the city's manufacturing exceeded that of its trade—a significant development for the great port. Improved transportation combined with the addition of electric power to ensure greater industrial development. Baltimore's industrial advancement was preeminent in the state.[1]

Still, the city lacked many features of more advanced industrial centers.

The social services available were quite limited compared with those provided by other large cities. There was no sewage system, and only after the
massive destruction from the Great Fire of 1904 did Baltimore provide a water system. Especially significant, Baltimore's manufacturing base, even after the dramatic growth of the late nineteenth century, had not yet met the
hopes of city boosters. Indeed, the 300 percent increase in manufacturing
establishments and in industrial workers that occurred between 1870 and
1900 represented only a 1 percent increase in the percentage of the population engaged in manufacturing. Growth had characterized all sectors during
that period, and when transportation was added to trade, the two easily
eclipsed the role of manufacturing in the city's economy.[2]

The city's port served as the entry point for thousands of immigrants at
the turn of the century. However, Baltimore's limited manufacturing base
and its ample supply of African American laborers, along with thousands of
wage-earning women and children, encouraged most immigrants to move
on to other cities. Known as a "blue-collar town," Baltimore also had a reputation for low wages, and several surveys conducted after the depression of
1893 confirmed that view. Many male workers suffered from underemploy-
ment, and few enjoyed either sufficiently regular employment or high
enough incomes to support families. Low wages especially characterized the
experiences of women and African Americans. This meant that several members of the family had to work just so the family could buy groceries and pay
the rent. In 1900, for example, about forty of every one hundred women in
Baltimore worked in wage-earning jobs. That year, the average annual income for all industrial workers was only $360. Moreover, although wages
had increased by about 10 percent since 1892, the cost of food had gone up
35 percent for the same period. Life for Baltimore's laboring classes was dependent on the entire family's income, and finding paid work was a family
occupation.[3]

THE CLOTHING INDUSTRY: FROM "SWEATERS"
TO LARGE MANUFACTURERS

The city's industrial base depended on certain critical areas, including
foundries, machine shops, and canneries; producers of fertilizers, boots and
shoes, and straw hats; and copper and iron processing plants. No industry,
however, mattered as much to the city's industrial growth as did the manufacturing of ready-to-wear clothing, particularly men's garments. The rapid
emergence of ready-made clothing reflected the shift from home manufac-

10 ture to large-scale commercial production that characterized economic change after the Civil War. Baltimore quickly gained prominence in the industry, ranking sixth in the nation by 1890 and fourth by the turn of the century in the production of men's garments. Capitalizing on the city's well-established commercial and financial ties to the South, the clothing industry was ideally suited to further Baltimore's reputation as the "Gateway to the South." A series of good crops in the postwar South enabled that region to purchase more than one-third of the clothes produced in Baltimore. In the 1880s the city's clothiers challenged their New York counterparts for the southern market; by 1895, Baltimore dominated it, and city manufacturers steadily increased their marketing reach into the Midwest as well.[4]

With modest capitalization requirements making entry relatively easy, the clothing industry attracted a variety of manufacturers, from petty entrepreneurs to owners of large factories, employing thousands of Baltimore's workers by the end of the nineteenth century. Even as early as 1860, when the manufacture of clothing was the city's single largest source of employment, with more than six thousand workers, about two-thirds of Baltimore's 119 men's clothing establishments were small shops that averaged fewer than ten workers; most of the remainder employed about thirty workers each. A few companies already employed several hundred workers, and the trend toward larger garment factories was well underway. Also gaining momentum was the growth of the contracting system and the proliferation of sweatshops, which assisted the advancement of the industry primarily at the expense of labor.[5]

By the turn of the century, Baltimore's garment district comprised two distinct areas of the city, and as the industry matured, two systems of production emerged that not only characterized the manufacturing process, but also reflected that spatial segregation. Searching for cheaper space, large manufacturers and wholesale dealers producing men's clothes set up shop in the area west of the central business district, forming what became known as the "loft district," around Paca and Redwood Streets. Most of these large and midsized entrepreneurs owned "inside shops," where workers completed all the steps of production—from laying out and cutting the cloth to finishing the garments. Often modern in organization and construction, inside shops adopted technological innovations easily and endorsed "scientific" approaches to increased efficiency at the workplace.[6]

On the other hand, petty entrepreneurs—also called "sweaters," petty contractors, and "Boss Tailors"—operated "contract shops," where only a few functions could be performed. Whereas the inside shops resembled factories, the contract shops operated more as workrooms. Typically, the contractors collected bundles of cut cloth from wholesale manufacturers and took them to their own small rooms, where their employees performed the various tasks necessary to complete the suit, coat, or vest. The *Baltimore Sun* described the process in 1895:

> After the cutters finish their work and the pieces of cloth and lining go out to the tailor shops to be sewed and finished they go first to the hands of the operators or machine sewers. Basters fit the parts together and finishers complete this part of the work, when the garment goes to the presser with his heavy hot irons. Back again to the finishers, this time women or girls, and then into the hands of the bushelers, who put on the final touches. This completes the garment save the button holes, which . . . are done by a separate set of workers, who do only this one part of making coats, vests, or trousers.

The contractors then returned the finished garment to the manufacturer for a fixed price.[7] The contractors' profits depended on the difference between their production costs and the contracted price. Under this sweating system, male garment workers made $6 to $10, and women only $3 to $6, per week—working typically six 10-hour days—or usually about 20 percent less than workers in the larger clothing factories for the same hours. Resistant to technological change, petty contractors appeared and disappeared with considerable frequency and in direct response to market demand. Less efficient and more economically vulnerable, contractors operated in an intensely competitive environment. They were pitted against each other by the large manufacturers, who, in trying to cut their own operating costs, sought the lowest possible bids for their piecework. Attempting to still make something of a profit under these conditions, the contractors turned their workshops into sweatshops. Forming the second center of the garment industry, these sweatshops clustered in the cramped and grimy rowhouses to the east of Baltimore's central business district, particularly in the area bounded by Lexington Street, Eastern Avenue, Caroline Street, and Jones Falls.[8]

The two production systems of the industry not only coexisted but were mutually dependent, for large manufacturers used contractors and even started their own contract shops. After the turn of the century, however, the trend was toward the factory system; manufacturers of men's furnishings averaged 126 workers per firm and the number of manufacturing establish-

12   ments declined despite the increase in the number of workers employed. More than ten thousand workers labored in the production of men's garments as Baltimore approached the twentieth century, and the large manufacturers who would dominate the market in the new century were also in place: the Henry Sonneborn Company, Strouse & Brothers, L. Greif & Brother, Schloss Brothers, and J. Schoeneman, Inc. By 1915, these firms, all established by entrepreneurs of German Jewish descent, would account for two-thirds of the total value of men's clothes produced and fully half the workers employed.[9]

Other trends were at work that permanently altered the city's social and industrial landscapes. Creating and responding to market forces, Baltimore's industry carved out specialty niches in the production of men's garments. Advertising assumed a critical new role in the production and distribution of men's garments, as manufacturers tried to establish consumer loyalty to specific brands and even particular cities. The summer clothing trade was especially important to Baltimore, whose manufacturers sent thousands of summer suits South. The production of men's shirts and overcoats also gained national recognition, and a few entrepreneurs focused exclusively on work clothes, especially the production of men's overalls. Although less seasonal and volatile than the production of women's garments, the men's clothing industry still responded to cycles of production and wear, leaving manufacturers with slack periods and workers without steady work.[10]

Technological change furthered economic specialization; the division of labor became more complex and the workforce more diverse. The steady improvement of the sewing machine since the 1850s meant that by 1900 the foot-powered machines capable of making eight hundred to nine hundred stitches per minute were outmoded by mechanically driven machines able to deliver four thousand stitches a minute. Various attachments enabled less-skilled workers to duplicate what had once been very skilled work, and the introduction of the cutting machine also challenged artisanal traditions. Every feature of the manufacturing process, including buttonhole making and garment pressing, experienced some modification as a result of new technologies. By the early twentieth century, the production of one man's overcoat involved about 150 separate operations. As the need for certain skills declined, employers often preferred to hire younger women for the lower-paying jobs. Even the men (as tailors) and women (as buttonhole makers) who performed skilled work saw changes that increased the pace and quantity of their work.[11]

City officials pointed with pride to the success of the garment industry.

It was the centerpiece of the city's industrial development and brought Baltimore national recognition as well as affording the city a strong position in regional competition, with local manufacturers vying against their counterparts in Philadelphia, Rochester, and Boston. City boosters delighted in the clothing industry's advertising campaigns, repeating its commercial slogans in public and private brochures alike. Of major significance, moreover, the striking growth of the garment industry stood in stark contrast to Baltimore's otherwise merely respectable position as an industrial center. Since 1880, other cities had been edging past Baltimore in total value of manufacturing, number of wage earners, and total population. In part, this development reflected a statewide trend toward decentralization of industrialization that put Maryland in the small minority of states in which the average manufacturing establishment was smaller in urban areas than in rural ones. Such a sluggish performance did not go unnoticed, prompting the organization of key groups such as the Merchants' and Manufacturers' Association as well as a variety of state and local political efforts—all determined to accelerate the pace of development. The garment industry stood apart from this; in 1900, the production of men's clothes seemed poised for a new era of growth, ready for the challenge of the twentieth century.[12]

"DARK, SWELTERING HOLES FILLED WITH VILE ODORS": THE SWEATSHOPS ROUSE INDIGNATION

As the industry expanded, capturing new markets and offering new products, its dependence on the contracting system grew, and the number of sweatshops increased in the 1880s and 1890s. The rise of the clothing industry and the use of the sweating system were inextricably linked to immigration to the city.

In the late nineteenth and early twentieth centuries, Baltimore attracted significant numbers of Germans, Irish, and Russians to its immigrant piers in Locust Point. Although not a major center for the new immigration of southern and eastern Europeans, Italians, Poles, Bohemians, and Lithuanians also entered the city. Of special significance for the garment industry, the number of Russians increased substantially, from 5.9 percent of the foreign-born residents of the city in 1890 to 15.3 percent by 1900—second only to the number of German immigrants. Many were Jewish immigrants who had left the shtetls—the small towns in eastern Europe where millions of Jews made their homes—because of the economic and political dislocation wracking eastern Europe and the accompanying acts of anti-Semitic vio-

14 lence that threatened their survival. Accustomed to migration for economic and religious reasons and traditionally linked to the needle trades, these Jewish immigrants often turned to the clothing industry to start their new lives in America.[13]

Many impoverished Russian "greenhorns" settled in East Baltimore rowhouses and operated workshops that doubled as living quarters. Six families lived in Simon Schapiro's house on North Exeter Street, with eleven persons laboring in a single small room as if "their very life depended upon the speed they exerted while at work." Outside such houses, noted one newspaper reporter, "there is little, if anything, to indicate the destitution within." But "a large proportion of these people are upon the verge of starvation, and were it not for the well known benevolence of the Hebrew people, many would be constantly slipping over it. They have reduced their standard of living to such a point that any further reduction involves death." Also in search of economic opportunity, smaller numbers of Bohemians, Lithuanians, and Italians congregated in East Baltimore and began working in the clothing trades. The newcomers' arrival attracted increasing attention. In a 1907 survey of housing conditions among the poor, even an observer sympathetic to their plight stereotypically lamented the ethnic transformation of East Baltimore: "Fifty years ago this section was the home of many old Baltimore families of high social standing," she noted, but their houses "are now occupied by the dark-eyed Jewish mothers with their babies."[14]

As the clothing industry expanded and the contracting system turned homes into sweatshops, the emergence of a visible concentration of poor immigrants living and working in squalid conditions stirred public concern. Hundreds of workshops existed in East Baltimore, and their clothing scraps spilled out into the streets, carefully dodged by immigrant children scurrying back and forth with new and completed work. These workshops were hot in the summer and cold in the winter, noisy, dimly lit, and filled with workers, sewing machines, pressing boards, stoves and irons, and piles of cloth. Contractors who observed the Jewish sabbath, Friday, worked on Sundays in violation of city law and, to escape detection, kept the doors and windows shut, making conditions inside still worse for the workers. Labeled a public nuisance, the sweatshop district was denounced in the press and the pulpit. Comparing it to "the regions of his Satanic majesty," one newspaper reporter detailed the district's "dark, sweltering holes filled with vile odors, hot-beds of disease, rank and foul smelling, filthy attics crowded with perspiring workers, and close stifling garrets."[15]

Investigations led by inspectors from the state Bureau of Industrial Statistics (BIS) confirmed the fears of a middle-class public concerned about the welfare of children and women, unnerved by the dense concentration of immigrants, and alarmed that the unhealthy environment would lead to widespread disease in the city. In its annual reports the BIS described houses serving as workrooms as full of "dirt and filth," plagued by inadequate ventilation, and "swarming with half-clothed children, the imprints of [whose] unclean hands are found everywhere." The "malodorous" alleys, pools of stagnant water, and other unsanitary features of the congested neighborhood added to the squalor. The terrible depression that began in 1893 made conditions still worse by increasing the economic pressures on the sweatshops. Of a shop where portions of letter carrier uniforms were made, for example, the BIS claimed, "it would be difficult to conceive of a more filthy and unwholesome place in which to manufacture clothing . . . The entrance is through a dirty side-alley . . . . It would be miraculous if the inmates escaped disease to say nothing of communicating it to others." Finally, BIS inspectors found that the "general depression" had reduced the already paltry wages paid to workers in such shops by more than one-third.[16]

Singled out for most of the criticism, the sweater, or petty contractor, became the symbol of the evils of the clothing industry: "the petty contractor has made possible the sweating evil and he is inseparable from it." Labeled greedy and unscrupulous, the sweater offered a convenient target for critics of the system, who more often than not condemned him in anti-Semitic terms. Sweaters were described as deeply sinister and shadowy creatures with "swarthy complexions," who crowded men and women together without proper regard for decency and privacy. To be sure, these contractors notoriously exploited their workers, cheating them when competition against fellow contractors became especially intense. But few sweaters managed to save money; like most of their workers, they lived and worked on the edge. Paying for rent, fuel, and thread and providing the sewing machines, which they purchased by weekly installments, the contractors were "little, if any, better off," reported the BIS. "It is only by constant self-denial and hard labor that they can even live." The contractors carved out their role, despite public hostility, regulatory legislation, and high rents, precisely because they served larger wholesalers and manufacturers. Just as mechanization and the factory system in the garment industry accelerated the dilution of craft skills, the contract system structurally complemented the continuing process of the subdivision of labor.[17]

In the 1890s, most of the contractors and their workers were Russian Jews, who had traded the repression and limited opportunities of their

16   homeland for the sewing machines and squalor of city sweatshops. Attempting to win a measure of independence and prosperity as small entrepreneurs, these contractors exploited members of their own and other ethnic communities and overworked their own daughters and sons. Usually specializing in the production of one garment, they employed the "task system," hiring as many as ten workers, each performing a separate task: basting, stitching, finishing, making buttonholes, sewing on buttons, or pressing. Squeezed by the manufacturer, contractors continually forced workers to produce more units in order to maintain income, effectively eliminating regular working hours and wages. As a result of the 1893 depression, Baltimore contractors were by 1896 setting production quotas so high that at least two 12-hour days were necessary to complete what was called "a day's work." The garment workers, according to one reporter, "toiled on with an energy born of desperation."[18]

"FEMALE OPERATORS"

Female Operators
O men, with sisters dear!
O men, with mothers and wives!
It is not linen you are wearing out,
But human creatures' lives!
Stitch, Stitch, Stitch
In poverty, hunger and dirt,
Sewing at once with a double thread
A shroud as well as a shirt.

More than half of Baltimore's ten thousand men's garment workers were women or teenage girls. Difficult living conditions for working-class families required all members to contribute to the family income, and most families tied to the garment industry shared a "family culture of work": each member was expected to help sustain the whole. Yet the employment of women and especially young girls in factories and sweatshops aroused considerable public opposition. The city's hallmark of industrial progress—the men's clothing industry—was also an emblem of industrial shame, and publicized accounts of women working in the garment factories and shops pointed up that disparity.[19]

The task system and the contract system imposed particular hardship on the least-skilled workers, and female wage earners often fit that category.

Although sewing had traditionally been considered "women's work," the art of needlework, like the skill of tailoring, fell prey to the division of labor, and in the clothing industry the highest paying and most skilled jobs—cutting, trimming, and pressing—went to men. Still, women had been employed in the men's garment industry from its inception, not just in Baltimore, but also in the other cities that were the major centers of the industry. The young women who entered shops and factories in the late nineteenth century, however, did so as operatives or as thread pullers, the lowest-paying, least-skilled positions. Even when a woman performed the same job that a man performed, she earned less than he. These differentials prompted one woman to dress and pass as a man: "I am a tailor and can make $3 as a man where I could get only $1 for the same work as a woman." Other women also labored on men's garments in their own homes, confined by cultural tradition, family obligation, or both. They simply set up shop in their kitchens, punctuating their daily household work rhythms with piecework—stitching hems or seams and finishing collars or buttonholes. Theirs was the homework system, and they too were extraordinarily vulnerable to the "chiseling" practices of contractors and manufacturers.[20]

Women especially dominated the workforce in the production of men's and women's shirts and undergarments. Seen as an industry distinct from men's clothing, this sector was characterized by extremely low pay and an intense division of labor. Fourteen different steps were required to make a shirt, and the "girls," as they were called, each performed but one repetitive task for ten to twelve numbing hours. Organized in teams, they were paid by the piece—but only after their team met its quota. At week's end, women earned on average $3.50 to $4.00, and even the most skilled sleeve makers could not go home with more than $4.00—wages described by the press and the BIS as "ridiculously small." The BIS solemnly noted that city leaders had kept in "ominous silence" the "subject of wages for work done in the city of Baltimore by an army upwards of 10,000 women and girls." Conceding that "the making of a shirt has always, it seems, been an illy paid and distressful trade," the BIS nonetheless concluded that Baltimore's women garment workers "toil without just recompense" and face "hardships innumerable."[21]

BIS investigators were of course influenced by Progressive Era reform sentiments as well as culturally prescribed notions of appropriate female behavior. Consequently, they struggled with the very idea of women participating in the workforce and found especially abhorrent working conditions for women that seriously diverged from the home environment and the homework system that challenged the sanctity of the home:

How many a poor woman is there who toils throughout the entire day in her poor home with insufficient food and warmth, until the midnight hour, to add to that pittance which will be doled out to her on pay day. She knows nothing of the luxuries of life.

Those who work in the factories have not a much happier lot. They are principally girls and they labor in season and out, in summer or winter, rain or shine. While other more fortunate mortals are still snug and warm in their downy beds, these girls are seen wending their way from all sections of the city, towards the factories in which they are employed. They all carry a small lunch and walk. It matters not how far they have to come, it would make too big a hole in their pay for car fare. Once inside the walls of the factory a weary day's work of ten hours is begun, with an intermission for lunch at noon. Once home, they swallow a hasty supper and soon retire to a needed and well deserved rest with no pleasant anticipation for the morrow.

What lives are these for future wives? Future generations will answer.[22]

For some women labor leaders, however, the issue was not that working would threaten women's femininity, but that women who worked felt ashamed of the fact. They worried that some working-class women too closely identified with the values of middle-class culture, which deemed it beneath a woman to work. As Leonora Barry reported to the Knights of Labor in 1886, "If there is one cause more than another that fastens the chains on Baltimore working-women, it is their foolish pride, they deeming it a disgrace to have it known that they are engaged in honest toil." It was this social attitude that employers were able to exploit, Barry maintained, and, unless women workers challenged their bosses, they would continue to receive inadequate wages and work in miserable conditions.[23]

The Knights master workman for Baltimore's District 41, J. G. Schonfarber, professed to see evidence of that foolish pride and its consequences in the course of the Myrtle Assembly. Established in 1886 by women garment workers as a Knights local assembly exclusively for women, the Myrtle Assembly proved especially active. It held discussions entitled "The Condition of the Working Women," sponsored lectures on public issues and classes in reading and history, provided sick benefits to members, lobbied for women factory inspectors and woman suffrage, and even pledged to wrest "the full share of the wealth they create" from "the hands of selfish employers, who

. . . care not how hard we battle for bread." But as middle-class women reformers increasingly cooperated with the Myrtle Assembly, Schonfarber
claimed, the "charity ladies" had "captured" the working girls, imbued them
with "aristocratic pretensions," and weakened their identification with the
working class and organized labor.[24]

Although most immigrant wage-earning women did not identify with
the exalted notion of domesticity held by members of the American middle
class in the nineteenth century, neither did they regard themselves as victims
of industrialized society. They behaved in ways that both challenged and reinforced traditional notions about gender, femininity, and women's public
roles. And their cooperation with middle-class women resulted less from for-
getting their class than from pursuing new educational and political opportunities. To be sure, women garment workers, like their male counterparts,
fancied well-made clothes and fashionable hats. But that vanity, Sara Barron
later confided, was a "hazard" of the trade.[25]

"To work not as beasts but as human beings": Reforming the Clothing Industry

Baltimore's garment trade early became a target of public scrutiny; it was an
industry unusually susceptible to economic and social reform initiatives.
Characterized by both small and large manufacturers, by intense competition, by modern factories and cramped, dirty sweatshops, the clothing industry represented for many reformers the ideal candidate for economic rationalization and industrial improvement. Yet those same features that
allowed easy entry, ensured seasonal fluctuations, and resulted in organizational chaos also provided considerable resistance to reform initiatives. Still,
concerns about health and disease and about women and sweatshops led a
variety of groups to join forces in preunion organizational activities in the
early 1890s to protest the "rag trade" and the sweating system. On their own
behalf, the garment workers themselves took to the streets to protest their
wages, their treatment at the workplace, and a series of employer practices,
especially the use of the blacklist. These preunion strikes proved instrumental both in attracting public attention to their work conditions and wages
and in galvanizing support for needed reforms. In conjunction with the lobbying efforts of union leaders, the garment workers thus managed to secure
some minor legislative achievements, particularly passage of the modest
sweatshop laws beginning in 1894.[26]

Clothing workers were a mixed lot, much like the industry itself. Some

20   very old, some very young, both men and women labored in shops small and large, speaking different languages and practicing diverse skills. More women and children were concentrated in men's garment manufacturing than in any other industry in the city, with the periodic exception of canning. Notwithstanding the long tradition of men's tailoring, few garment laborers could count themselves among the city's craft workers. Moreover, the persistence of long hours and low wages served as a poignant reminder of the effects of the steady dilution of skills caused by mechanization and the relentless division of labor. Not even the industry's most skilled—the cutters and pressers—were valued commensurate with the city's other craft workers: when both the carpenters and the clothing workers struck in 1892, for example, the former demanded an eight-hour day and the latter a ten.[27]

In addition, no other industry provoked the degree of public sympathy and outrage that garment making did. The subject of regular investigations, the object of pity, disgust, and even fear, and the focus of legislative and legal reform, the clothing industry illustrated the paradoxes of progress, as poor immigrants labored in grimy rooms to produce the latest in fashionable attire for a seemingly insatiable consumerism. The irony was not lost on the workers or their advocates. The chief result was a constant, but unsuccessful, struggle to abolish the sweatshop.[28]

Garment workers in sweatshops, larger contract shops, and inside shops often went on strike to protest their conditions and improve their prospects. Small strikes occurred in the 1880s, usually lasting only hours or several days and attracting minor attention. In 1889, a 10 percent wage cut drove women workers at the Chesapeake Shirt Factory to the street. Other work stoppages and protests were far larger, but still they were essentially brief dress rehearsals for the more protracted battles to come in the twentieth century.[29]

The strike of 1892 was the first major strike by men's garment workers in the city's history. One thousand workers turned out in July to protest the sweating and task systems. "The greatest objection," observed the *Baltimore American,* "seems to be the system of tasks, whereby a man receives a certain sum a day—say $3—and is given a certain number of coats to make, which the men say ranges from ten to sixteen, and that whilst it is called a 'day's work' that it often takes a man two working days to complete his task." Although the newspaper referred repeatedly to the workers as "men," at least half of the strikers were women, who had walked out of fifty-four shops to protest hours and wages and who, contrary to what the lopsided press coverage indicated, actually held leadership roles in the strike. They had originally organized under the leadership of Rosa Schuchat as the Ladies' Protective Association, which subsequently became Local #33 of the United Garment Workers (UGW). Calling for a ten-hour workday and weekly payment of wages, the strikers vowed not to return until the contractors signed letters of agreement: "We have never been paid for our work weekly; sometimes we are paid once in two weeks or three weeks, as the contractor pleases. Now we demand a workday of ten hours and weekly payments. This seems to be a fair proposition."[30]

As the strike dragged on, workers faced deteriorating conditions. One union leader had warned, "They are poor and some may have to starve a little to win," and this prediction had proved true. To secure some income, the strikers opened fifteen cooperative shops, but Cilea Stott, secretary of the Women's Branch of Local #33 of the UGW, promised that members would not work as finishers on garments made by nonunion workers and that women would remain on strike without drawing benefits from the union. Some assistance came from the Baltimore Federation of Labor (BFL) and from garment workers in New York, and several East Baltimore merchants contributed food and cash. Still, by late August, the mayor received what the *Baltimore Sun* termed a "pitiful letter" from the strikers: "We are all starving. The grocers and the butchers will not trust us any more, and if the strike continues any longer you will find us starved to death." Even an outspoken critic of the strike noted uncomfortably that "the unfortunate Hebrews have been striking and starving."[31]

The contractors, themselves organized as the Monumental Tailors' Beneficial Association, stood fast. They defended the piecework system as "the only practicable way of working" and rejected "having the union dictate to them" on wages and hours. To ensure their own solidarity and coordinate their resistance to the strike, the contractors met daily on Lexington Street in East Baltimore, only a short distance from the strikers' meeting place.[32]

The 1892 strike was complicated by a bitter contest between unions and thus represented a preview of the struggles that would accompany the founding of the Amalgamated Clothing Workers (ACW) in Baltimore in 1914. In 1892, however, the fight focused on the newly formed UGW's attempt to displace locals already organized under the banner of the Knights of Labor. For the UGW, which had affiliated with the American Federation of Labor (AFL) shortly after its founding in 1891, the emergence of sweatshops signaled primarily the demise of the long-venerated tailoring craft. Unconcerned with the predicament of the trade's less skilled workers, the UGW mirrored—and indeed, in Baltimore, magnified—the AFL's policy of disdain for the unskilled. At the same time, although the Knights officially ad-

22   vocated a policy of inclusion, its local assemblies were not always receptive to diverse constituencies. Most of the UGW tailors had been Knights but were now "suspended, expelled, or withdrawn," largely because, as the Knights saw it, "we would not countenance just such a strike or were too conservative for them."[33]

Petty contractors, eager to exploit the division among organized workers, tried to undermine the UGW by making overtures to the Knights. Two contractors, for example, signed an agreement with UGW strikers contingent on their joining the Knights. Eager for the ten-hour day and weekly payment of wages, the strikers promptly applied for a Knights of Labor charter. However, when they returned to work, the contractors repudiated the agreement. The UGW, in turn, proposed labor agreements requiring all employees to be members of its organization. The Knights, with three local assemblies engaged in the garment industry, forcefully denounced this "conspiracy to extinguish them from the labor field" and countered with the unusual step of actually organizing seventy employers—contractors—into a fourth assembly: the Monumental Coat Contractors Assembly. Knights master workman Schonfarber vigorously defended the new assembly, illustrating perfectly the peculiar status of these petty entrepreneurs who alternated between employer and employee: "While the Contractors are really the 'sweaters,' they are also men, with families, who, as individuals, are not to blame for the system they work under . . . . Indeed, it is a question whether they are not more sinned against than sinning." The BIS aptly noted of the UGW and the Knights: "No sooner would one side obtain a temporary advantage then the other would strive to neutralize it." Ethnic differences further complicated the conflict, with Polish and Russsian Jews aligned with the UGW against the Lithuanian Catholics organized in the Knights' tailor assembly.[34]

The confused and bitter struggle continued for months. The UGW claimed victory at a small number of shops, but divided allegiances among workers and internecine warfare between unions left permanent scars that often obscured labor's few gains. The unprecedented scale of the 1892 strike did invite public inquiry, however, and the city's daily newspapers extensively covered the dispute, even printing the names and locations of the sweaters and their shops. The prolonged disruption in business also led wholesale clothiers, eager to receive their new stock, to enlist the services of an arbitration committee. That effort also failed when contractors refused to yield on the issue of weekly payment of wages. As one contractor explained, "We proposed to let the strikers remain out as long as they please, we have no proposition to offer." Dealing with a new and unfamiliar union especially troubled some of the small contractors, and they resisted cooperating with the UGW. One discredited the union's leaders as "outside agitators" from New York, who "know about as much about the tailoring business as I do about shoemaking." Several other attempts at arbitration met with similar failure, and ultimately many of the strikers returned to work with no more than modest concessions and a good deal of disillusionment.[35]

The strike of 1892 did alarm the public about unsanitary conditions in the contract shops, and the BFL used that concern to lobby for legislative reform. Even more critical to this effort was the work of a newly established reform organization called the Union for Public Good in Baltimore, a local chapter of the short-lived Union for Practical Progress. The BFL joined with this group of representatives from charities, churches, and synagogues to form a nonsectarian organization dedicated to urban social reform. Motivated by religious principles of social justice, many of its members were women, who were otherwise excluded from political reform organizations springing up in the city. In response to the strike, the Union for Public Good conducted an investigation of sweatshops in the fall of 1893. Its report cited the evils and dangers of the sweating system, emphasizing the damage done to overworked women and children in unsanitary shops, and sternly warned middle-class citizens of the perils of wearing clothes made in dirty, disease-ridden environments.[36]

The state legislature responded to these fears in 1894 by prohibiting the manufacture or sale of garments "whereby disease may be transmitted" and by setting minimum space, temperature, and sanitary standards for workrooms or apartments. Guided by the new legislation, the BIS then conducted its own investigation, publishing the results in its annual report of 1895. The BIS confirmed the widespread fear about "the possibility of contagion spreading through infected clothing, coming from filthy shops," and reported that "prominent physicians [have] acknowledged this to be an imminent danger." Significantly, it also specified that the owners of the large factories were complicit in the persistence of the sweating system, while noting as well that work conditions in the "sky-scraping" factories were also less than satisfactory.[37]

The depression of 1893 had worsened conditions for workers in small shops and large factories. Even with subsequent economic improvement, only the amount of available work increased—wages remained nearly the same, and the failure of the new law to provide for inspections meant that working conditions continued as before. In late 1894 one appalled Baltimore

24   minister asserted, "The garment workers are oppressed by their employers as bad as the Israelites were oppressed by the Egyptians in the time of Moses . . . . The sweating system is the greatest evil of the age." As large manufacturers dominated more of the market, moreover, they continued to rely on contract shops for certain steps in the production process and organized themselves to meet the growing challenge of unionization. Their Clothiers' Board of Trade took pains to defuse the public's fears about the clothing industry by attempting to disassociate their modern factories from the squalid workrooms of the sweating system. They also cooperated in pitting the UGW and the Knights of Labor against each other, an effort practically unnecessary given the animosity between the two unions.[38]

Labor protests broke out against these developments. In 1895, for example, persisting sweatshop conditions prompted locals of the UGW to strike against the contractors, again demanding an end to the task system, a uniform ten-hour day, increased wages paid weekly, and a union shop. A UGW circular issued in Polish, Lithuanian, and Bohemian urged garment workers to "come to your senses and join together to make a decent living. We want to work not as beasts but as human beings." To enforce the work stoppage, strikers blocked the delivery of cut cloth from the manufacturers to their contract shops. Several dozen contractors soon accepted the union proposal on the condition that the manufacturers increase the rates they paid to them, illustrating the interdependence of the sweaters and the manufacturers. The UGW achieved only limited success, for the manufacturers only slightly increased the rates. Moreover, ethnic and organizational conflict again impeded labor's efforts. Bohemian tailors early proposed returning to work, and when Lithuanians vigorously objected, the Bohemians withdrew from the UGW and met at the Bohemian Hall on Broadway to affiliate with the Bohemian Tailors Assembly of the Knights.[39]

A larger strike that occurred the following year in February began at an inside shop and drew attention to problems in the factory system as well. Led by the UGW, the strike resulted from a concerted effort by the city's clothiers to reduce union influence and the bargaining power of the highly skilled cutters. Schloss Brothers, one of Baltimore's largest manufacturers, took the initiative by sharply reducing wages (by 35 percent) and firing two cutters who had joined the union. The company took the further step of refusing to provide the discharged cutters with written recommendations, without which they could not obtain employment from any member of the Clothiers' Board of Trade. The cutters, who regarded themselves as craftsmen and not merely laborers, protested this "black list" as a "condition equal to the servitude of the slave" and anathema to the rights of the skilled worker. The

UGW called out the workers at Schloss Brothers, but the struggle had only begun.[40]

Strouse & Brothers, another major firm in the loft district, widened the attack by calling on its female employees to renounce the UGW. The women, undeterred by the union's conventional emphasis on skilled men, turned instead on their employer, declaring, "We will stick to the union." Walking off the job, the women of Strouse & Brothers vowed to stay on the picket line until the company recognized the UGW. Their action inspired still other workers to follow their lead. Within days, the *Baltimore Sun* reported that some five thousand garment workers were on strike, including "Bohemians, Lithuanians, Russian Jews, and German-Americans, both men and women." The strike continued to spread until it affected nearly every clothing manufacturer in the city, including the contract shops.[41]

Women played a prominent role in the strike. Several had taken advantage of the competition between the UGW and the Knights to secure leadership roles among garment-making women in the city; and UGW officials, although always more committed to the "laboring man," welcomed the support and the numbers women workers could deliver. Indeed, "companies of the girls," reported one paper, formed part of the demonstration march on March 10, 1896, from the union hall on East Baltimore Street to the loft district on the west side. The parade, they explained, was designed "to show the public that the members of the United Garment Workers' Union are orderly citizens and that their ranks are not thinning as the fight goes on." Their parade banners proclaimed, "Starvation wages are not conducive to promote happiness" and "This strike will disclose whether we mean to be blacklisted." A week later, women were also leaders in more disorderly actions as well. Fifty rioting strikers, half of them "women and young girls," fought police and nonstriking workers to prevent the delivery of cloth from manufacturers to homeworkers.[42]

Manufacturers were equally determined. Samuel Rosenthal of Strouse & Brothers, the president of the Clothiers' Board of Trade, firmly stated his company's resolution to resist union influence: "We are determined not to allow our help to run the shop through their union." Schloss Brothers, in particular, objected to the control over the production process exercised by unionized cutters and hoped to eliminate the UGW once and for all. "For some time the union has been coercing us, dictating to and defying our foreman, and we have concluded that it is about time for us to put a stop to this. We have dismissed some of our people because [they] have been unruly, and have led in the agitation which causes dissension." Employers even attempted to pit the declining Knights of Labor against the UGW, some promising not to lock out members of the Knights, others actually importing Knights-affiliated cutters from other cities.[43]

In public, the Clothiers' Board of Trade dismissed the strike as a "dispute" not "between employers and employees, but between the rival [labor] organizations." The board's statements convinced neither public observers nor striking unions. Even as they worked to undermine each other, the two unions agreed on the origins of the strike: "No matter what the firm may claim," the UGW announced, "this [35 percent wage reduction], with their unjust 'black listing,' is the cause of our trouble, and it is not a fight against the Knights." Nor was the board particularly successful in addressing the issues of wages and working conditions, both of which received much attention in the press. Details of the economic interdependence between the inside shops and contract shops further tarnished the image of the major clothiers. Their resistance to calls for arbitration prompted the BIS to lament the absence of conciliation and diplomacy.[44]

After five weeks, the UGW finally called off the strike. The cutters' local wanted to persevere, but the poorer Lithuanian tailors could hold out no longer and voted to return to work. The union feebly tried to claim victory when a few inside shops abandoned their blacklists and rehired UGW members, but the strikers' final public resolution pointed to a different outcome: "For the present our struggle for independence, for justice, must be discontinued until such time as circumstances are more favorable." Even that promise was mostly bravado, for in the coming years the UGW would become less interested in representing all the garment workers, particularly given the steady influx of newer immigrants, and would narrow its appeals, constituency, and activism. The Knights of Labor all but disappeared with the 1896 strike, never again to lead garment workers to the picket line. The Board of Trade termed the strike a failure, as workers returned to their jobs under the previous conditions.[45]

The additional attention attracted by the clothing industry did, however, produce further legislative reform. Modifications in the language of the 1894 law made it easier to identify sweatshops. Still, inadequate funding meant too few inspectors to carry out the law, and few contractors actually felt its effects. Indeed, in 1896 the BIS observed that, despite the law, sweatshops were still "flourishing."[46]

"MANUFACTURERS MAY WELL BE PROUD OF THE PROGRESS"

On the eve of the new century, Baltimore's clothing industry offered the city its best hope for economic growth and industrial expansion. Enthusiasm for that possibility could scarcely obscure serious problems, however: workers divided among themselves along lines of skill, ethnicity, and gender; labor and management locked in stances of hostility and suspicion; a chaotic and seasonal industry with managers uncertain how to reduce that volatility and expand their market regionally; and a public alarmed by sweatshops and eager for greater regulatory control. In the nineteenth century few employers had to contend with that level of intervention—and precisely at a time of intense competition. None of the city's business leaders liked what they regarded as inappropriate interference with private enterprise. They joined with the major clothiers to challenge the campaign against sweatshops, warning that if it continued it could "drive [the industry] elsewhere, where worse conditions exist, but no great publicity of the fact is made." The message was heard. In its annual report for 1900, the BIS uncharacteristically noted that the city's "business people . . . *rightly claim that Baltimore has less of the objectionable [sweatshop] system*" than most other cities.[47]

A year later, the message resonated still louder. The BIS began its annual report for 1901 by citing the value and growth of the men's garment industry, noting that it was "easily the greatest [industry] in the state" and adding, "Baltimore manufacturers may well be proud of the progress they have made and the position that Baltimore clothing holds in the markets of the country." Significantly, for the first time, the BIS also carefully distinguished between the contractors and manufacturers. Asserting that "of late years the manufacturers of clothing have taken much more interest in the conditions under which the contractors work than ever before," the BIS also praised the large clothiers for "do[ing] away with 'sweatshops' by establishing factories in their own buildings," where "cleanly conditions exist, ample conveniences for work and air space, with regular hours, and a change of location to home as soon as the day's work is done."[48]

Gone were the earlier indictments of the factory system, now replaced by interest in industrial progress and economic growth and focusing of concern onto the sweatshops. This was the changed environment that would confront labor's new voice and the new unionism in the twentieth century. The ACW would regard these changes as opportunities for shared labor-management control, whereby the union could help discipline both the industry and the workforce in exchange for genuine improvements in wages and conditions and a greater role on the shopfloor. Some manufacturers would accept the Amalgamated's offer; others would not.

2

Forming Labor's New Voice

A Union for All Garment Workers

"We didn't get the union so easy," recalled Sara Barron of Baltimore's Amalgamated Clothing Workers (ACW). The struggle, she added, was a "bloody thing." There were strikes and sweatshops, blacklists and brickbats, and even workers battling among themselves.[1] The problems of the garment workers and the clothing industry proved durable; yet the new century brought important changes in the industry and a new voice for workers who produced men's garments.

In 1900, Baltimore, the sixth largest city in the United States, ranked fourth nationally in the production of men's clothes. Over ten thousand workers, more than half of them women, annually turned out about $17 million worth of clothes. Each of the major clothiers had begun to consolidate its manufacturing operations under one roof, constructing "sky-scraping" factories in the city's loft district where thousands of workers could cut, stitch, sew, and press. When Henry Sonneborn Company opened its factory at the corner of Paca and Pratt Streets in 1905, it was the world's largest clothing manufacturing building, with more than 250,000 square feet of space. An imposing, elegant ten-story structure, "fireproof and durable" with many windows for natural light, the new factory was carefully designed so that all work could be performed "easily, economically, and in a sanitary fashion." The twin themes of efficiency and economy characterized the new factory and its production system. Railroad cars running on tracks on Pratt Street moved directly into the shipping department. To avoid delays from relying on elevators to transport cloth and discard scraps, a scientific "arrangement of chutes" efficiently moved the men's suits through the building and conveyed all the scrap material gathered from each floor to a plant where it was converted into material for padding in clothes. Sonneborn also introduced new machines to reduce labor costs: a die-cutting machine supplanted ten workers; an electric cutting machine "made it possible for one man to do the work of six"; and buttonhole making, once an art, could now be accomplished by a machine "in a wink," leaving to the human hand only the sewing of buttons. The pace in the sewing room was breathlessly fast, according to a *Baltimore Sun* reporter: "The eye and the ear are assailed by the rush and clatter of hundreds of machines and girls, young men, and boys are in a frantic race with these machines." Employees were paid by the piece, their work "automatically registered by little clock devices attached to each machine." This modern system enabled four thousand workers to turn out three thousand men's suits every day. Most important, the new system avoided the "sweatshop evil" by creating separate departments under one roof and by ensuring high standards of cleanliness for the consumer.[2]

Yet, the contract system and sweatshops persisted in Baltimore's garment industry. In a survey conducted in 1900, the Bureau of Industrial Statistics (BIS) counted some four hundred sweatshops and estimated that they produced about half of the men's clothes manufactured in the city. Furthermore, Baltimore's industrial expansion continued to lag; the average amount of capital invested in the city's clothing manufacturing firms figured about 30 percent less than the national average of the leading urban centers, and workers—both men and women—could expect periods of unemployment lasting at least a few months every year.[3]

Reform legislation had not been able to eliminate the "sweatshop evil," although in 1902 new BIS inspectors received authority to enforce the antisweatshop legislation passed in 1894—a major step in challenging the sweatshop system. The city's large manufacturers joined the chorus of opposition to the contract shops, and the largest among them pledged to stop sending out garments to the smaller shops. Inspectors began to issue contractors citations for violations, and in retaliation contractors organized to

30 challenge the "legality of the sweatshop law." When this proved unsuccessful, they attempted to point out the unsatisfactory work conditions in factories and questioned the BIS's narrow focus on the smaller shops. But that, too, failed. Large clothiers had recognized by the turn of the century that the public outcry against the threat of disease-ridden clothes required either performing all the work under one roof or creating their own contract shops, in which the contractor would be an employee of the company and the shop would be regarded by the public as simply an extension of the well-known larger manufacturer. Most of all, the larger companies recognized the need to advertise, and all the major clothiers launched significant advertising campaigns designed to establish their name brands and create customer loyalty. In 1904, the BIS proudly proclaimed that it was performing "great work" by "correcting this [sweatshop] evil and keeping Baltimore-made clothing on the high plane it now occupies." The BIS added that the support of the large companies was essential to the effort, for "it will now be possible for our manufacturers to proclaim to the world that all their goods are made under sanitary inspection."[4]

In important ways, then, the effort to reform sweatshops corresponded to other Progressive reforms driven by not just a genuine compassion for the predicament of immigrants, especially women and children, but an even greater commitment to ensure the safety of middle-class consumers. It also satisfied more fully the needs and interests of larger manufacturers at the expense of small ones unable to afford the increased costs imposed by the new regulatory legislation. As the petty entrepreneurs who joined together to form the Brother Contractors explained, they were more like employees themselves and the "sweatshop law" would force them to "vacate our Old Shops and go to the large expense of building or renting large shops, outside of our homes"—something they could ill afford to do. By focusing on sanitary conditions, the legislation also permitted the issues of the clothing workers' wages and hours to escape notice. And as the "sky-scraping" factories took a larger share of the market, sweatshops decreased in number. But the contractors had been correct in charging that working conditions in these new factories also merited concern. Moreover, the large manufacturers, not under the scrutiny of either the BIS or the health department, also opened their own contract shops, hiring former contractors and paying them for the goods they produced in their workrooms.[5]

"Aristocrats," "Squareheads," and "Girls":
Ethnic and Gender Divisions among
Baltimore's Garment Workers

The New Immigrants' Challenge to the United Garment Workers

Despite its earlier activism, the United Garment Workers (UGW) did little either to eliminate sweatshops or to improve working conditions in the industry. No longer challenged by the Knights of Labor, the UGW after the turn of the century directed its attention primarily to the workers most skilled in the trade. In keeping with a traditional emphasis on craft, the UGW followed a program of exclusivity that derived its strength from the support of the "aristocrats" of labor—the cutters, trimmers, and pressers who enjoyed a privileged position at the workplace. These workers, according to the UGW, were critical to the production process and not easily replaced by employers, which gave the union some leverage in dealing with management. Like the Baltimore Federation of Labor (BFL), with which it was affiliated, the UGW focused on workers who possessed the most marketable and valuable skills and was less concerned with the semiskilled and unskilled workers, a policy that operated to the detriment of women and newer immigrants.

The 1908 records of one large manufacturer, employing nearly one thousand workers, indicate how ethnicity and gender intersected with skilled-labor status in Baltimore's clothing industry. No women were employed in the several "skilled" occupations in the firm's cutting departments. Most of these skilled workers were German American men, and 90 percent of the foreign-born workers were German men. In the many "unskilled" occupations in the tailoring departments, both women and men worked, and almost all were foreign born. Forty percent were Russian Jews, 40 percent were Lithuanian, and the remainder were Italians, Bohemians, and Poles; there were virtually no Germans in these unskilled positions.

In 1911 two concurrent federal investigations of Baltimore's garment industry filled in the details about the roles of ethnicity, gender, and "skill." Employment of workers, even in the inside shops that predominated in Baltimore, tended to be "along the lines of one race [i.e., ethnicity]," matching the ethnicity of the foreman or contractor. Given the division of labor and specialization of garments by departments or contractors, "different classes of work have become identified with different races," with the lowest positions filled by the most recent arrivals. In turn, "differences in work reflect themselves in earnings," noted the investigators, who added pointedly that

32 the "marked differences in earnings among the workers of different races" were often independent of the actual "capacity or skill of the employees." One salary survey, for instance, found average weekly earnings of $14.55 for German Americans, $10.68 for Russian Jewish men, and $6.23 for Russian Jewish women.[6]

In the context of the significant technological innovation in the clothing industry, along with the diversity of skills and workers in the factory system, the UGW's limited approach to labor organization did not always provide effective bargaining power. Indeed, the entire notion of identifying the skilled workers was, as will be discussed more fully, subjective and inconsistent, and even the cutters and trimmers hardly acknowledged a kinship or brotherhood with each other in the UGW. Rather than inculcating a sense of union culture or developing strong ties to the union among the workers, the UGW relied on the threat of the boycott for its leverage on the shopfloor and required employers to buy union labels. It even sold the UGW label to companies that negotiated only with cutters and trimmers, without regard to the other clothing workers in the same factory. When competing with the Knights for members, the UGW had adopted more aggressive and inclusive strategies, encouraging, for example, the organization of a local of skilled women garment workers in 1895. In the early years of the twentieth century, with the Knights defunct, the UGW resisted overtures from the newest immigrant clothing workers, adopted a policy of benign neglect toward its women members, and emerged primarily as a cutters' union.[7]

The UGW was only slightly more receptive to newer immigrant tailors, those men possessing the requisite craft skills. Although the union was founded in 1891 to unite Russian Jewish tailors with American-born cutters, many of Irish and German descent, persistent ethnic divisions impeded craft solidarity. The influx of more immigrants from eastern Europe, Italy, and Russia at the turn of the century further stressed this fragile alliance. In particular, the rise of Russian Jewish contract shops turned latent anti-Semitism among some garment workers into overt, vitriolic attacks on those they described as "greenhorn tramps" who sweated and cheated their workers. At the national level, according to one historian, the UGW quickly "became patently corrupt, nativist, elitist, and anti-Semitic," and, as a union of skilled cutters with no or only distant ethnic ties, it "affected a castelike sense of superiority and indifference toward the mass of immigrant tailors."[8]

At the local level in Baltimore, the UGW generally conformed to the national pattern, though the disparities and hostilities within the organization were not quite so stark. To a large extent, the progressive leadership of the BFL lessened conflict and division. BFL president Edward Hirsch, a German Jewish typesetter, deserved the respect and recognition he received from the city's reform elite. A leader in the movement against sweatshops, Hirsch also campaigned against child labor and in favor of women's suffrage as well as an array of reforms for the city's working class. However, he, too, found limits to his tolerance for cultural diversity and was unable to disguise his occasional embarrassment at the newer Jewish immigrants, with their thick accents and peculiar Old World habits, such as their attachment to the *mivke,* or public steam bath.[9]

It was not merely the newer immigrants' fondness for the *mivke* that confounded even sympathetic observers and challenged the UGW,[10] but also another Old World trait: their ardent socialism. The immigrant clothing workers who would embrace the Amalgamated in 1914 shared certain beliefs that promoted greater democracy at the workplace and in the economy, that decried the practices of both the sweaters and the manufacturers, and that fostered an idealism dictating militant action. Of course, not all these beliefs were foreign born, for the tradition of reform and unionization in the United States also figured prominently in shaping both the garment workers' critique of industrialization and their dream of industrial democracy.[11]

The UGW's focus on cutters eventually caused growing concern among the city's tailors. By 1912 even one of the UGW's own officials had declared that Baltimore had become "the poorest organized city in the country in that [tailoring] craft." The practice of blacklisting labor activists, he added, had become increasingly common among the large manufacturers in the Clothiers' Board of Trade. Newer immigrant tailors organized their own locals and began to challenge openly the UGW's complacency, using the weapon they thought most effective: the strike.[12]

In one of their earliest efforts, they struck at one of the contract shops of Henry Sonneborn Company, the largest clothier in Baltimore and the fourth largest in the nation. In October 1905, the contractor, responding to what he claimed was attempted dictation by unionized immigrant tailors, "laid off" three "union men," saying there was "no work for them as union men." When the entire shop complained, he locked the doors, declaring that no work whatsoever was available. The local, led mostly by Jewish tailors, immediately called for a strike against all of Sonneborn's contract shops. The UGW leadership, chiefly unsympathetic sons of Irish or German immigrants, vacillated, forcing BFL president Hirsch to intervene and arrange a meeting with Sonneborn. The UGW then accepted Sonneborn's offer to "re-

34   open these shops and re-employ the men now on strike, and not discriminate against them on account of being union men." Sonneborn steadfastly refused to bargain collectively with the union, however, declaring, "We reserve the right to dispense with the services of anybody whom we consider not a good workman or inimical to the interests of our firm, and replace him by whomever we see fit." Sonneborn confirmed his commitment to "open shops," or nonunion shops, claiming that they were essential to economic progress. The BIS noted that the settlement of the strike was "disastrous" for all clothing workers, for they lost "the principle for which they have been working continually, viz., the employment only of Union men and women."[13]

Despite this disappointment, immigrant tailors persisted in their efforts to improve their wages and working conditions. In 1909 the *Weekly Bulletin of the Clothing Trades* reported, with some exaggeration, on the "continuous strikes in Baltimore." Women workers were frequently in the forefront of these actions. In December, for example, when Sonneborn introduced "a new system of work" based on further mechanization and labor displacement, the "girls" initiated a walkout and persuaded the tailors and pressers, if not the cutters, to follow them. At Schloss Brothers, four hundred women garment workers struck in protest of an abusive foreman who had "grossly insulted" them with "many names unfit to print." The actions of the foreman and the reactions of the women workers illustrated fully how both the workplace and the UGW marginalized women. Whereas the UGW might defend the "manhood" of its traditional skilled male workers, it felt no obligation to uphold the dignity of working women. Ethnicity also provided important cues for workers' decisions. In the Schloss Brothers strike, for example, after delaying several days, 175 Italian workers went out together to join the other women strikers. As in earlier incidents, BFL president Hirsch intervened to resolve these disputes, but the UGW leadership provided little support. Regarding all forms of immigrant activism, among both men and women, as threatening to union policy and governance, UGW officials renounced the new militancy. Indeed, thereafter, union officials insisted that the new locals avoid actions that disrupted production among other organized garment workers.[14]

The new locals of immigrant tailors included Russian and eastern European Jews, Lithuanians, Italians, and Bohemians, and they all encountered indifference, if not hostility, within the UGW. Jacob Edelman, a Russian-born tailor who became one of the ACW's first members, recalled that UGW leaders "were not interested in the improvement of conditions of the immi-

grant workers who came from eastern and southern Europe. Indeed, they
held most of these people in utter contempt. They referred to the Italians as
the 'wops and the guineas,' the Jews were the 'kikes,' and the rest were known
as 'square heads.'" Ridiculed for their inability to speak English and ignored
at meetings, the immigrant tailors remained isolated and divided within the
union. Even their skills went unrecognized, for the UGW prohibited them
from moving up to positions as cutters and trimmers, refusing to send them
to companies in need of workers in those positions and reserving these high-
est-paying jobs for the American or Americanized members. Indeed, when
the UGW learned that a shop had hired an immigrant tailor as a cutter, the
union protested to the company and fined the worker.[15]

The UGW's disdain for immigrants, and its particular objection to the
independent actions of the immigrant locals, provided an opportunity for
the struggling Industrial Workers of the World (IWW) to gain a foothold
among Baltimore's garment workers and led to a fierce battle between the
two organizations in 1913. The *Baltimore Sun* declared that the IWW had its
appeal to "the unorganized elements among the Poles, Italians, and Lithuanians and especially of the more ignorant of these." Abe Gordon, Baltimore's
representative to the General Executive Board of the UGW, also ridiculed
the local IWW members as "ignorant and illiterate" immigrants. New BFL
president John Ferguson denounced them in similarly nativist terms, sin-
gling out the many immigrant women who had listened to speeches "in foreign tongues" and paraded in white shirtwaists and red sashes to welcome
IWW national organizer William D. Haywood to Baltimore. But Ferguson's
condemnation of Baltimore's Wobblies as "anarchists and the scum of the
industrial world" also reflected his commitment to trade, rather than industrial, unionism.[16]

Perhaps three thousand garment workers joined the IWW in Baltimore,
and the UGW leadership consistently strove to undercut their rival in what
the *Baltimore Sun* called a "labor war." Indeed, when the IWW called a strike
in the city, Gordon promised that the UGW would stand by the employers:
"We haven't a particle of grievance against a manufacturer in the city and we
don't want to raise any trouble. We are absolutely contented." In fact, members of one UGW tailors local, predominantly Russian Jews, were even then
on strike for higher wages and shorter hours, and Gordon's contentment was
reported in the same newspaper story recounting police arrests of their "girl
pickets." UGW leadership continued to place its priority on the fifteen hundred male members of the cutters and trimmers local, described by a sympathetic manufacturer, Michael Schloss of Schloss Brothers, as "the most in-

36   telligent part of the American trade." The cutters already boasted shorter
hours and better wages than the tailors, but the UGW viewed their importance much as the *Baltimore Sun* did: "persons employed in other lines of the
business of manufacturing clothing would be helpless unless furnished work
by the cutters and trimmers."[17]

Angered by those who dismissed and demeaned them, Baltimore's Jewish tailors continued their own organizational efforts and also began looking for allies in other cities. A few of them, as Edelman recalled, traveled to
New York City to work in shops with "more radical" tailors. Their politics
and principles fortified, they returned to Baltimore to press the UGW to
challenge the trend toward open shops among the major clothiers and to organize tailors throughout the city. In 1911, they joined with New York tailors
to call a conference in Philadelphia, at which they formed the United Tailors Council of U.S. and Canada, an association dedicated primarily to organizing tailors in a massive union movement. The UGW initially denigrated this venture but, under rank-and-file pressure, reluctantly sanctioned
the new council and appointed two organizers to lead the effort.[18]

Labor stirrings in other cities excited and inspired Baltimore's garment
workers and reinforced their commitment to act. Guided by a few organizers who would later become prominent in the ACW, the union movement
among immigrant garment makers began taking new shape, with greater
force, definition, and clarity.

Immigrant Women's Deepening Involvement: The 1913 Greif Strike
The actions of one young woman in 1909 not only advanced the cause
of unionism, but pointed up the inadequacies of the UGW. Born in Zemel,
Latvia, in 1894, Dorothy Jacobs settled in Baltimore with her parents and
three sisters in 1900. Her father found work in his trade as a tailor, and when
her mother died, Dorothy also joined the ranks of the garment workers, leaving school at age thirteen. Within a year, she was working among the most
skilled women as a buttonhole maker, for which she drew a paltry $3 per
week, despite her arduous ten-hour days. From her father and their community, she gained knowledge of the tailors' grievances and an awareness of
the principles of industrial justice. In 1909, she responded eagerly to the "Uprising of the 20,000" in New York and Clara Lemlich's call to young garment
workers to "Strike, Strike, Strike." Just fifteen years old, Jacobs organized
Baltimore's first immigrant buttonhole makers local of the UGW. By doing
so, she ensured that her local would be an integral part of the Amalgamated's new union movement.[19]

A convulsive strike in 1913 dramatically revealed the tensions within Baltimore's clothing industry and among its garment workers. Believing that the large clothier L. Greif & Brother had agreed to do scab work for New York companies under strike, some three hundred workers spontaneously struck the firm's factory at German (later renamed Redwood) and Eutaw streets on January 17. Leonard Greif denounced "a certain set of local agitators" for instigating the action, and the company's cutters tried to discourage the strike, but it spread quickly, especially among women workers. Just as quickly, the *Baltimore Evening Sun* reported, "the point at issue changed suddenly and radically." The strikers demanded union recognition, a nine- rather than ten-hour day, and increased wages (a 5 percent increase for pieceworkers and 10 percent for vest makers). Rousing mass meetings of strikers virtually forced UGW leaders to belatedly endorse the strike for these goals, but even then they refused to order a citywide walkout in the industry, which the strikers saw as necessary to their success. Nevertheless, hundreds of workers from other companies in the loft district soon joined the Greif strikers on their picket lines.[20]

Although the UGW named a committee of five men to oversee the strike, Lena Schlossberg immediately emerged as the dominant figure in the crisis and was "unanimously accepted" as the strikers' leader. The city's daily newspapers took note of the strikers from "across the falls"—the immigrant communities in East Baltimore, on the other side of Jones Falls—and lamented the behavior of the city's foreign element. A local reporter, at once fascinated and repulsed by the "black eyed, black-haired beauty," managed to combine the twin themes of sexism and ethnocentrism as he declared of Schlossberg, "She can blarney a policeman with diabolical ingenuity, hurting his vanity and taming the fierceness of his mustaches with gentle sarcastic torture. She is a whole inquisition in herself and a past mistress at verbal cruelty." In addressing the workers, she had a "dramatic power" that alarmed him but made her the "Joan of Arc, as they call her, of the garment workers who want more pay, more lunch hour, and more liberty." Schlossberg visited newspaper offices to get out the strikers' side of the story, negotiated with the police over strike conditions, and rallied the pickets, shaking "a defiant fist at her former foreman and shriek[ing] 'We fight to the last blood; labor always wins!'"[21]

Women and girls usually made up at least half of the strikers and their sympathizers from other shops, and by all accounts they were the most enthusiastic and the most "determined to exact the last tithe of their demands before consenting to return to work." Their "grim determination," accord-

38   ing to the *Baltimore Evening Sun,* bolstered "the courage of the weak-kneed among the strikers."[22] It also won them considerable middle-class reform support. Prominent women endorsed their demands for shorter work days, joined their picket lines and parades, commended their "pluck and courage." Margaret Carey, daughter of one of Baltimore's leading attorneys, rushed to the Labor Lyceum to tell the "girl strikers" that "you may expect the sympathy and support of every good woman in Baltimore." East Baltimore merchants organized to provide food and to extend credit for strikers. Church and social service clubs offered to arbitrate the conflict, but Greif officials flatly rejected their offers.[23]

Indeed, Greif took a hard line. The company refused to negotiate with representatives of the union or the strikers, insisting it would deal only with individual workers. It also kept its shops operating, importing tailors from New York and Philadelphia to join the loyal workers still on the job, and threatened not to take back the strikers. To maintain production and protect the strikebreakers, Greif employed a private detective agency, hired a number of retired police, and, according to Edelman, ran "an espionage system" within the shops to deter union talk. Baltimore's regular police ringed the factories and attempted to limit pickets and demonstrations.[24]

The daily confrontations brought frequent arrests, but these often merely steeled strikers' determination, especially when "girl pickets" were arrested or roughly handled. Police sought out leaders like Schlossberg, and Edelman was repeatedly arrested during the lengthy course of the strike. Russian Jews appeared most commonly on the arrest lists, but newspapers also recorded Poles, Lithuanians, and others uncategorized beyond "speaking in foreign tongues." Well before the strike peaked, police reported that they had made more arrests on a single day than they had during an entire protracted stevedore strike the previous year.[25]

As the strike dragged on and police intervention accelerated, real conflicts occurred, culminating in a three-day period in mid-March when, as the *Baltimore Evening Sun* reported, "all Baltimore was a battlefield" for "wandering bands" of strikers, strikebreakers, supporters of both, and hundreds of police. Another newspaper reported that "disorder extended over an area of 20 city blocks" and three police districts, adding that the police touched off the three-day "riot" when they roughly seized a woman picket and attempted to take her away in a police wagon. "Shouting men and screaming women," reported one observer, then "hurled themselves against the police." Police fought back with clubs and drawn pistols until Baltimore Street in the loft district "was jammed with a fighting mass." Seven blocks away, on Charles Street, combatants fought with scissors, knives, and clubs. By the time police finally restored order, all sides had suffered numerous injuries.[26]

At the height of the crisis, on March 13, Frank White, chief of the state labor bureau, volunteered to mediate the strike. This time Greif accepted, and the strikers agreed to approve any settlement reached by a committee containing a member from each "nationality" among their ranks. After lengthy negotiations, White secured an agreement when BFL president Ferguson, one of the mediators, pressured the strikers' committee to accept the terms. These provided for a fifty-four-hour workweek—a reduction of one hour for Greif workers—no change in wages, and no union shop, but a promise from Greif to negotiate future disputes with an employees committee. The district council of UGW immediately endorsed the agreement, and Ferguson and UGW officials defended it as "a decided gain for the workers and a liberal concession on the part of the Greif firm." At a mass meeting, strikers expressed their deep disappointment in the terms, especially in abandoning the goal of a union shop, but Ferguson and UGW officials refused to support a continuation of the strike to achieve that objective. After "hours of argument," the strikers reluctantly voted to stand by their pledge to accept the terms agreed to by their representatives; however, what the *Baltimore Sun* called the "radical element" voted against ratification.[27]

Radical or not, many of the immigrant garment workers regarded the deal as a betrayal, and resentment over the terms of the agreement festered. Edelman recalled that the strike had "electrified me—here was a struggle of various ethnic groups—Italians, Poles, Lithuanians, Bohemians, and Jews, and some Americans—all unified together" and that he had been furious that the UGW leadership had "sold out" the strikers. When Greif subsequently violated the agreement and refused to allow strike leaders to return to work, even employees who were glad to get back to the job after such a violent strike openly scorned the union.[28]

"As we fight, so shall we make history": The Amalgamated Secures Its First Contract

The division between the UGW's leadership and its immigrant members ruptured the union movement in other cities besides Baltimore. A series of spontaneous strikes combined to seem like open rebellion, directed not only at manufacturers but at shattering the UGW itself. A climax came at the 1914 national convention of the UGW, held in Nashville on October 13. In-

40   surgent locals from Chicago, New York, Baltimore, Rochester, and Boston attempted to reorganize the UGW, proposing industrial unionism, increased organizational activity, and a new leadership sympathetic to those goals. Resistant UGW officials, however, arbitrarily unseated the "progressive" delegates though their locals contained fully two-thirds of the union's membership. Infuriated, and convinced that they legitimately represented the organized garment workers, the insurgents promptly met separately, called their movement the New United Garment Workers Union, and elected national officers. They summoned to the presidency Sidney Hillman, then the leader of the International Ladies' Garment Workers' Union in New York City but formerly a prominent UGW progressive in Chicago. Two of the UGW's largest locals in Baltimore along with the buttonhole makers local bolted the union in favor of the insurgents at the national convention.

The sides were clearly drawn at Nashville as they were in Baltimore: skilled, semiskilled, and unskilled immigrants, both men and women, joined the new industrial movement, whereas skilled, native and Americanized, and mostly male workers remained loyal to the more traditional craft union. It was this division that led the American Federation of Labor (AFL), meeting in November, to refuse to recognize the "secessionist" union and instead to side with the old leadership of the UGW, an important constituent of the craft union structure to which the AFL remained committed. Hillman accordingly called a delegate convention of the progressive locals to meet in New York on December 26, 1914. This convention founded the Amalgamated Clothing Workers of America, adopting the name to symbolize the organizers' conviction that all clothing workers should be combined into one industrial union.[29]

Before the Amalgamated could fully establish itself, it had to deal with a major crisis in Baltimore in order to demonstrate its ability to organize and protect the clothing workers, deal effectively with large manufacturers, and withstand the hostility of rival labor groups. In early October 1914, at about the very time the Nashville convention ruptured, more than three thousand clothing workers walked off their jobs in Baltimore at Sonneborn's main factory. The strike settlement emerged as the first test of the new union against the old order. It also represented a workers' struggle against the city clothiers' efforts to institute changes in their shops and factories based on theories of scientific management and designed to combat what they regarded as worker unruliness and inefficiency. The recent activism of immigrant tailors had given employers all the incentive they needed to assert their authority on the shopfloor by controlling how jobs were performed and by ensuring that only the fittest performed them. Often loosely referred to as Taylorism, the movement for scientific management among employers was never as systematic or as reciprocal as Frederick Taylor himself would have preferred. Still, Henry and Siegmund Sonneborn had incorporated their vision of scientific management into the company's policies and had taken the lead in the subdivision of labor and piecework payment plans, all in an effort to increase efficiency and control by diluting the skills necessary for the completion of specific tasks. Now in October, during the slack season, they intended to dismiss the workers, close the plant, change the machinery, and then rehire a much reduced workforce, who would have to "pass" medically supervised physical examinations before returning to work.[30]

United in their opposition to Sonneborn's plan but divided in their union loyalties, the workers struck under two rival sets of leaders and organization committees. The cutters, numbering about 250, remained faithful to what John Ferguson called the "constructive trade unionism" of the UGW. Ferguson had replaced Hirsch as president of the BFL and had neither the sympathies nor demeanor of his predecessor. The flamboyant Ferguson preferred acid quips to compromise and never held the respect of the reform community. A longtime foe of the immigrant garment workers, he barely disguised his nativist sentiments, promised generous strike payments to the loyal cutters, and blasted the "unaffiliated" for dividing the union movement.[31]

On the other side stood the representatives of the new union movement coalescing into the Amalgamated. The riveting voices of immigrant leaders Dorothy Jacobs and Hyman Blumberg rallied new members to the new union. Blumberg, like Jacobs, had left the Pale as a child and settled in Baltimore with his family. Lacking the financial resources of the BFL, these leaders instead offered emotionally charged speeches promising "industrial democracy," counted on cultural solidarity and pent-up hostility against the UGW, spoke of what they saw as a history of betrayal and ridicule by the old union, and called on all immigrants to demand the respect and recognition they deserved. The intensity of their organizational work reflected the transforming power of a new movement; as converts and leaders, they held a special place in the minds of the city's immigrant garment workers, and they drew fresh inspiration from the leaders at the national level. Stirring visits by Hillman and the Bellanca brothers connected the Baltimore workers to those in New York and Chicago. When Hillman dramatically held up before the Baltimore strikers the hard cash donated by their Amalgamated sisters and brothers from distant cities—from people they had never met—the re-

42   sponse was overwhelming. This generous support contrasted vividly with
the position taken by the loyal UGW members. These people, with whom
the immigrants had worked and shared a union identity, denigrated them
publicly and seemed to resent their very presence. As Sara Barron noted of
the immigrant workers, "for the first time, we mattered, too."[32]

Tailors and operatives found irresistible appeals for the union cause
made in their own language. Although an "outsider" from New York, August Bellanca rallied Italian tailors as never before. Blumberg and Jacobs gal-
vanized their Jewish comrades, and Jacobs, more than the other ACW leaders, was also able to cross ethnic boundaries, despite her gender and youth.
Although more than a few men winced at the sight of a young woman speaking passionately in public, she captivated the majority. At the first meeting
of the Sonneborn strikers, waving a telegram from Hillman, she captured
the significance of the historical moment by predicting that "a new era is beginning for the people of the clothing industry. As we fight, so shall we make
history. Our example will be followed by our brothers and sisters in other
cities."[33]

To derail the new union movement and deflate the excitement it generated, Ferguson attempted to strike a deal with Sonneborn. He promised that
the cutters would return to work if they received minor wage adjustments
and were exempted from the Taylorite reforms. The remaining workers, he
predicted, could not remain on strike for long. Upon learning of these negotiations, Hillman countered by urging Sonneborn to accept an arrangement similar to that adopted in Chicago at Hart, Schaffner & Marx, a company much admired by Sonneborn and one that had achieved national
recognition for the quality of its men's suits. The plan proposed arbitration
through an advisory committee and permitted the return of striking workers "without discrimination." Sonneborn agreed, provided that the ACW
accepted a reduction in the workforce to eliminate the inefficient. Without
notifying the rank-and-file, Hillman tentatively accepted the proposal,
though restricting the number of planned dismissals under the Taylor system to 240. Hillman's action smacked too much of the UGW's practices,
and he faced certain repudiation by his new followers. Blumberg, supported by August Bellanca, warned Hillman against finalizing the agreement.
Reluctant to risk alienating the new union's members by imposing an unwanted settlement on them, Hillman decided to continue the strike and even
contributed $200 to the strike fund.[34]

With the apparent settlement arranged by Ferguson, however, the
UGW cutters returned to their jobs, confident about the supremacy of their

union and their privileged position in the workforce. As they entered the Sonneborn factory, they even taunted the strikers, ridiculing them, their politics, and their "greenhorn union." Outraged and now feeling empowered by their new union movement, nearly fifteen hundred workers surrounded Sonneborn's, vowing not to allow the "scab" cutters to leave the building. Hundreds of police officers swarmed the crowd and began thinning its ranks, arresting hundreds of strikers. The cutters didn't budge from the factory; despite the police actions, they remained fearful of the hostile crowd and ate their dinners inside, rather than risk leaving the building. Only the personal escorts offered by police convinced the cutters that they could safely depart. The UGW's gambit had failed; Ferguson had assured Henry Sonneborn that the other strikers would follow the cutters back to their jobs. Instead, the workers were united more than ever behind the ACW, and a highly irritated Sonneborn instructed the cutters not to return to work. Humiliated and dispirited, the cutters learned that despite their important position in the production process, they did not hold sway over the less skilled. They were no longer the automatic leaders of the garment workers at the workplace or in the union movement.[35]

Now fully convinced of the power of the Amalgamated, Sonneborn moved toward the new union for a settlement. Further compelling him to reach an agreement was the union's appeal to him on the basis of the Jewish culture and religion he shared with the striking workers. Sonneborn, as Jacob Edelman later explained, "was given the choice of cooperating with Socialist Jews or anti-Semitic tailors." Strikers accompanied by their visibly impoverished children picketed both the synagogue where Sonneborn worshipped and his nearby home, revealing their hardship to his family and affluent German Jewish neighbors.[36]

Embarrassed, Sonneborn quickly settled the strike, agreeing to keep the 240 workers earlier targeted for dismissal and calling for the selection of "workers' representatives" to oversee the new arrangements. With the assistance of Jacobs and Blumberg, Sonneborn agreed to an arbitration system largely devised by the ACW; Judge Jacob Moses, a German Jewish lawyer, Progressive reformer, and author of the 1902 sweatshop inspection law, would serve as the impartial arbiter. Sonneborn also abandoned many of his Taylorite reforms, including the dreaded physical examinations designed to determine the "fittest" workers for the "Taylor Efficiency System" but regarded by workers as "degrading." Finally, Sonneborn introduced a pension plan, improved safety features, including periodic fire drills, and a medical department staffed with a trained nurse. In return, the ACW promised pro-

44 ductive and disciplined workers, who would not engage in spontaneous strikes but would turn to shop chairmen and chairwomen and the established arbitration procedures to resolve all grievances. Hillman and Blumberg also agreed that the Amalgamated would provide Sonneborn much needed information on the marketing practices of major firms in New York and Chicago.[37]

The Amalgamated's victory over Sonneborn and the UGW was especially important for the new union. Both the strike and the settlement suggested the broad outlines of the union's philosophy and its approach to labor-management relations. It articulated a brand of unionism that called for the organization of workers along quasi-industrial lines and emphasized cooperation between labor and management, governmental intervention in the affairs of business and unions, collective bargaining, rational industrial policies, increased efficiency in all aspects of production, and substantial concessions from management for the welfare of the workers. To be sure, the founding rhetoric of the ACW had promised the emancipation of the working class and delivered more blows to the wage system and capitalism than the strike settlement at Sonneborn's suggests. The critical strike in 1914 and the establishment of a new union for all garment workers served to make the promises seem real and the goal of industrial democracy achievable. Of special importance to the immigrant workers in Baltimore locals was the ACW's recognition of the need for the "organization of labor along industrial lines" and the attendant disappearance of the "old craft demarcations"; no longer would their skills be degraded and no longer, they believed, would they have to tolerate a diminished role in their own labor movement. As Dorothy Jacobs explained when asked why they needed a new union when they already had one, "the difference" between the UGW and the Amalgamated "is between the dark night and the smiling dawn."[38]

The new union officially became the Baltimore District Council of the ACW in early 1915, when it received a charter to represent the city's founding locals as well as one small local recently organized in Washington, D.C. The District Council was constituted by a proportional representation of delegates elected by the locals, which were organized along lines of ethnicity, skill, or both. New locals could receive charters only through the council, which voted on all issues concerning membership. The District Council in Baltimore represented the counterpart to the ACW's Joint Boards in other cities. In 1919 the District Council became the Baltimore Joint Board when Washington had a sufficient number of locals to have its own Joint Board.

The District Council—and later the Joint Board—was responsible for collecting dues, dealing with management, promoting collective bargaining and the "collective welfare of its members," and ensuring "aid and protection to all its members, irrespective of their race, color, or creed." The council also elected an executive body called the Board of Directors, which dealt with all budgetary matters and all issues of enforcement of union regulations. The chief officer of the union, elected by majority vote of the District Council delegates, was the general manager, who represented the wishes of the council to the national union's General Executive Board and who dealt personally with management on all bargaining issues.

The goals of the new union as set out in its constitution were as follows:

to ensure the "betterment of human, social, and economic conditions for the many thousands of working men and women connected to the clothing industry,"
to "bring new life where the sweat shop destroyed the daily spiritual life of a human being,"
to promote "a better understanding and a better relationship among all workers," and
to bring about "industrial peace, industrial harmony, industrial freedom, and industrial democracy."[39]

"To extend our control in the factories"

The Amalgamated held its national founding convention in December 1914, and Baltimore's Hyman Blumberg and Dorothy Jacobs received special recognition for their roles in the ACW's "glorious victory" at Sonneborn's. Blumberg advanced rapidly in the union, gaining a position on the General Executive Board, and Jacobs, too, took a seat on the board in 1916. They remained loyal to Baltimore, however, and worked extremely hard in the Amalgamated's early years to ensure their union and hometown a firm place in the clothing industry.[40]

When the ACW began its campaign in 1915 to unionize Baltimore's clothing industry, significant changes had occurred since the turn of the century. Already well known for producing medium- and high-priced garments, Baltimore had gained wider recognition for its men's clothes. Contract shops, except those owned directly by the major manufacturers, had diminished sharply in number. The city's largest clothiers—Sonneborn, Strouse, Greif, and Schloss Brothers—accounted now for about three-

46   fourths of all the men's clothing produced in the city, up from half at the turn of the century. They all had "perfectly equipped" factories, each employing from one thousand to more than four thousand workers; they had modernized their marketing techniques, attempting to establish their own brand names and consumer loyalty; and they had extended their merchandising sophistication to the standardization of garments and patterns. They held special ties to city department stores, supplied clothes to mail-order houses, and still catered to the southern market, especially the market for summer suits. They all had also adopted some features of scientific management, mainly relying on piecework and the division of labor to ensure productivity and efficiency. The ACW was well aware of these changes and generally supported them, for the sweatshops and homework system, union leaders believed, too often defied industrial organization and undermined unionization.[41]

Beginning in 1915, the ACW attempted to secure union contracts with these major firms and their contract shops and to remove the UGW's influence from the shopfloor. But on the shopfloor the ACW organizers encountered other obstacles: gender, ethnic, and cultural divisions; a strong tradition among workers of resistance to labor-management cooperation; and the presence of other unions, not only the UGW but the IWW, which held the loyalty of a number of Italian and Lithuanian tailors. Ethnic animosities had been exploited by employers and unions alike. At John Ferguson's direction, for example, the UGW routinely inflamed ethnic hatreds, pitting Italians and Lithuanians against Jews and leading to a violent outpouring of anti-Semitism. Even some of the Italian tailors who had endorsed the new union as a necessary alternative to the UGW approached the ACW warily. Fearful of dictation by its Jewish leadership—a fear fed by the UGW and the IWW—Italians and other immigrant groups also remained suspicious of any union that openly called for arbitration and labor-management cooperation. One ACW organizer observed that "the people here are so distrustful and discouraged." Having been betrayed by the UGW, they "are afraid when the representative of the Union talks to the superintendent that he will surely sell [them] out."[42]

Winning their trust proved easier than reconciling their ethnic divisions. Yet the ACW, at Sidney Hillman's insistence, initially followed a policy of cooperation with the IWW. "Brother Hillman said to me," August Bellanca reported, "to try my best to let the STATUS QUO about the rule between the Amalgamated and the I.W.W." He and other organizers, even while conceding that it was "proper to work in harmony" with radical unions

like the IWW, still regarded the Wobblies as "a permanent danger" to the
ACW. "The IWWs," Bellanca noted, "are vociferously anti-semitic."[43]

Throughout 1915, ACW organizers held shop meetings in the contract
shops of the major clothiers, insisting in each instance that the negotiated
settlement occur with the manufacturer and not merely the contractor. Success was uneven; victories were often transitory, and workers were rarely
ready to trade their weapon of spontaneous strikes for arbitration. Still, the
Amalgamated made headway, and the UGW's influence was increasingly
limited to the cutters and trimmers employed in the large factories. One
UGW official suggested the union's decline in his statement that "at present
the fairest firm to the United Garment Workers" was the adamantly antiunion L. Greif & Brother. In 1915, Sonneborn agreed to a new ACW contract
that reduced the workweek from fifty-four to fifty hours and increased wages
slightly. The Strouse company followed suit. Even these small settlements
required "constant attention"; ACW organizers discovered that both managers and workers could sabotage negotiated settlements. Employers, they
believed, "chiseled" at every angle, and some workers preferred spontaneous
strikes to lengthy arbitration. The "IWW problem" also persisted, as did the
ACW's failure to direct its organizational efforts toward women workers,
who constituted more than half the workforce. The founding convention
had endorsed a resolution from Baltimore's women buttonhole makers local, #170, eloquently presented by Dorothy Jacobs, calling for the ACW to
hire at least one woman organizer for the city, but the union did not appoint
one full-time until 1917. Of course, Jacobs still worked to bring "the girls"
into the fold, but, unlike her male counterparts, she did so not as a paid organizer.[44]

At the end of 1915, the male ACW organizers in Baltimore decided that
they could no longer do without a woman organizer or follow a hands-off
policy toward the IWW. Bellanca continued to make progress "among the
Italians," visiting their homes and meeting their families. Charismatic and
tenacious, he drank wine with garment worker families and friends and
talked until the early hours of the morning. His visits to different homes
night after night became legendary, and word about the new union and "industrial democracy" spread throughout their neighborhoods and helped
weaken their ties to the IWW. Some of the Lithuanian tailors, too, abandoned the IWW for the Amalgamated, prompting organizer Harry Madanick to comment that "whilst the Italians and Lithuanians are coming along
very slowly, I feel that we will have them with us in the long run." Madanick and Bellanca agreed, however, that the ultimate victory would not come

48   without a fight with the IWW. Even then, it would not be easy: as Bellanca explained, "I see the necessity to work very hard to extend our control in the factories."[45]

In early 1916, the Amalgamated claimed to have nine thousand members in Baltimore, but it probably had several thousand fewer. Still, it had transformed the union movement among the city's garment workers in a remarkably short time, winning new recruits, converting others, and spreading the gospel of industrial unionism. Full of promise and guided by energetic and idealistic organizers, the ACW accelerated its campaign to organize the city. As a result, the year proved decisive for the union locally as well as nationally. Two cities—Chicago and Baltimore—commanded the Amalgamated's attention and energy in its early years. Both were important centers of production, and both were expanding their regional and national markets. Most important, from the ACW's perspective, both held the promise of citywide unionization, because of the predominance of large manufacturers in both.[46] The year 1916 in Baltimore brought to the fore all the problems and possibilities anticipated in the victory and defeats of 1915.

The *Baltimore Sun* likened labor's tumultuous strikes to the war raging in Europe, and the "labor troubles," as they were called, affected not only every major clothing firm, but nearly every industry in the city. By the summer of 1916, the newspaper was warning that "strike fever is spreading," and that workers were prepared more than ever to conduct "sympathy walkouts" as well. Police met strikers with clubs and wagons, and hauled hundreds off to jail. Despite judges' injunctions against unions, strikes continued to break out. Yet demand for workers continued to rise. Enjoying what the *Baltimore Sun* termed a "record era of prosperity," Baltimore benefited from the war in Europe, producing needed items for war-ravaged countries. Bethlehem Steel issued a full-page appeal in the *Baltimore Evening Sun* for "the names and addresses of persons who would accommodate Sparrows Point workmen as boarders," explaining that the workforce had exceeded the company's capacity to house them. To meet their own unprecedented demand, the major clothing companies rented additional buildings throughout the city, setting up new shops and hiring scores of new workers, most of them women, to make clothing and uniforms for the market abroad. One employer complained that he, too, would have to begin hiring women, for the city "was outgrowing its labor market" of "able-bodied men."[47]

Between 1914 and 1919, Baltimore reclaimed its position as the nation's seventh largest industrial center, moving up from the eleventh place, where it had languished for several years. Its total value of manufacturing tripled, the workforce increased by more than one-third, and investment in manufacturing doubled. The city itself expanded dramatically in size; the annexation of surrounding environs in 1918 increased its area from thirty to ninety-two square miles. Some asserted that finally Baltimore was becoming a "modern city," that its manufacturers had become more enlightened, and that labor-management cooperation was becoming more common. Developments in 1916 would strain the credibility of such observations, and even U.S. entry into the Great War would not foster a long-term trend in union-management cooperation.[48]

"Riot Call": The 1916 Greif Strike

Having won a major victory at Sonneborn's, the ACW turned in 1916 to another of the city's largest clothiers, L. Greif & Brother. Conditions among Greif workers were still far from harmonious in the sour aftermath of the great 1913 strike: bitter divisions between cutters and tailors persisted and overlapped with important issues of ethnicity and gender. Early ACW organizational efforts at Greif produced few significant results, except to harden the company's resistance to unionization. The strategy that the ACW had used successfully at Sonneborn's failed from the start at Greif's. Appeals to a common Jewish heritage met little response; Greif managers preferred dealing with a small group of unionized cutters in the UGW rather than a union of all garment workers committed, they believed, to "dictation" at the workplace. Nor were the union's promises of a more reliable and regular workforce effective: Greif flatly rejected the Amalgamated's notion of "shared control" in the factory.[49]

Anxious to avoid both an organized workforce and a permanent arbitration system, Greif claimed the right to manage its workers and to hire and fire them without union interference. But Greif also recognized the particular importance of the cutters, at least temporarily, and, significantly, was one of the first companies to train women workers as cutters, hoping thereby to eliminate ultimately any union presence in its shops and factories. A major firm with operations in a number of states, Greif uniformly followed an antiunion stance. The ACW, committed as it was to nationwide unionization as well as control of regional markets, threatened Greif's policies. The company found the UGW's limited goals far more appealing than a new union movement calling for "industrial democracy." Consequently, Greif responded vigorously to the Amalgamated's challenge, exploiting the split between the UGW and the ACW and continuing to pit men against women and to arouse ethnic animosities.[50]

Under fire in his own union for negotiating an unwanted settlement in a streetcar strike, John Ferguson eagerly took his cue from Greif. Indeed, Greif apparently put the BFL president on its payroll, and it certainly contributed money to the UGW's fight against the Amalgamated. These odd instances of cooperation were only the beginning of a strange, tortuous tale of unions competing for authority among workers, companies seeking to deter all unionization, and workers anxious for significant improvements in a traditionally low-paying industry. Greif even flirted with aspects of welfare capitalism, despite its opposition to that program. At Ferguson's request, moreover, Greif agreed to negotiate with two IWW locals of Italian and Lithuanian tailors. With the BFL's assistance, the UGW attempted to displace the emergent ACW by using the Wobblies to appeal to Italian and Lithuanian tailors, who were told they should resent the "Jew domination" in the Amalgamated.[51]

Hurling anti-Semitic epithets against the Amalgamated "greenhorns," the UGW forged an unlikely alliance with the IWW in order to halt the expansion of the ACW. The Amalgamated responded swiftly, dispatching to Baltimore organizers who could speak the various immigrant groups' native languages. This step was imperative. A third of Baltimore's immigrant garment workers, a 1910 government study found, did not speak English. Among some groups, such as Lithuanian women, the figure rose to half. Now Lithuanian tailors heard appeals for unity in the ACW in Lithuanian, and Italians and Bohemians also received separate organizers. August Bellanca, who already had a sizable following among the city's Italian workers, returned to recharge their spirits and cement their loyalty. Still, the UGW's divisive tactics had some success, and the ACW found the process of establishing union loyalty fitful, characterized by daily setbacks as well as victories.[52]

Greif further divided the workforce by appealing to ethnic and gender differences among the workers. At one of its factories, where more than five hundred of the seven hundred employees were women, many of them very young daughters from Bohemian families, Greif warned against the "advances" of strange men, that is, the labor leaders. Company foremen even visited the workers' homes, cautioning their parents not to be duped by men who pretended to be labor organizers and used the guise of unionization to lure unsuspecting "girls" into their fold. The danger, they said, was real and

imminent; it had happened at other factories, with the result that young
women had become tied forever to illicit houses of prostitution. Their
daughters, they reassured the parents, could count on Greif for assistance.
To provide protection, the foremen announced, the company had started a
mutual aid society "just for the girls." On nights when the so-called union
meetings were held, moreover, the company promised to offer safe and attractive Bohemian folk dances.

The few women who rejected the company's overtures in favor of the
Amalgamated's met with swift punishment. Foremen assigned them less
work and sharply criticized what they produced. Under the piecework system, these women's wages depended on both the quantity and the quality of
their work, and, accordingly, ACW members suffered substantial decreases
in their week's pay. The message was clear and unmistakable: the cause of
unionism could even mean the loss of your job. To emphasize the point,
Greif fired some twenty women after they joined the Amalgamated at a mass
meeting in January 1916.[53]

To counter these efforts, the Amalgamated enhanced its organizational
campaign and called a strike in February 1916 at two of Greif's major factories. On February 2, some thirty-five hundred clothing workers crowded
around the Greif plant on Milton and Ashland Avenues in East Baltimore.
The police commissioner issued a "riot call" against the strike, reported the
Baltimore Sun, and seventy police officers arrived to break up the strikers and
the "sympathy workers," who had left work early from Sonneborn's to offer
a show of strength. Residents from the ethnic neighborhoods that surrounded the factory also began to swell the crowd's ranks, and police soon
began arresting both strikers and their neighbors. More police and wagons
arrived to shore up the first contingent.[54]

Of the thirty-five hundred workers, more than two thousand were
women and girls, and the overwhelming majority of the ninety-five arrested were also women. Charged with "disorderly conduct" for refusing to
"move along," young female unionists taunted and ridiculed the police. Collective jeering brought more punitive responses, and the women workers often responded in kind. Scuffling broke out, whereupon the police captain
shouted, "Don't stand any guff; if anyone kicks, run her in." The crowd, still
expanding in size, soon stood at ten thousand, and many of its members
openly castigated the police for arresting daughters of their neighbors. The
police carted those protesters off to jail as well. According to reporters, these
actions merely stiffened the strikers' resolve, and by the end of the "riot,"
having been arrested represented a badge of honor. Documenting the strik-

52   ers' exclamations, one reporter wrote, "That's all right, Betty; we'll get you out soon. Don't worry, Agnes; Don't worry. See you later Josie.' These and similar cries of encouragement, multiplied a hundredfold, were shouted to the prisoners. They injected stubbornness into the crowds, and the press toward the Greif plant increased." ACW organizers from New York also were incredulous at finding "the crowd so big" and the "excitement so intense." One exclaimed, "I assure you that I have never seen a sight of this kind. People that pass through the neighborhood, inspectors of the Gas Co. and other people of this class who know nothing of the strike, were locked up. There is no station house big enough to keep all of the people who are arrested." August Bellanca, despite being hauled to jail, found the demonstration "exhilarating" and praised the "splendid spirit of our strikers" for refusing to be intimidated by the presence of hundreds of police officers. All agreed that "whatever the outcome will be, one thing is assured and that is that Mr. Greif will surely not forget today."[55]

The spectacle of such a massive strike along with threats from the ACW of a citywide strike prompted the head of the BIS to act as mediator and arrange a meeting with Greif and the Amalgamated. Greif officials attended, but they vociferously objected to what they regarded as union coercion, pure and simple. After considerable discussion, the company signed an agreement with the ACW, nearly identical to the one Sonneborn's had signed. The *Baltimore Sun* reported that the "firm grants all demands of [the] clothing workers' union" and that Greif had been unable to obtain any concession.[56]

The agreement was shortlived, for despite the ACW's progress in organizing Greif's women workers, the company sought new means of unraveling the armistice. On the shopfloor, Greif foremen blatantly discriminated against workers who wore ACW buttons. They sent some of those workers home, claiming there wasn't enough work to keep them busy, but then sent the garments to be finished in a contract shop. One Amalgamated organizer reported that "since the settlement" at Greif's "many difficulties" had arisen, but the company categorically refused to negotiate. Greif again sponsored dances and other social activities to attract the support of its women workers and held weekly meetings in which the women were promised that "if they stick to the firm, they will have plenty of work." Some members, especially among those young women whose families depended on their wages, did trade in their union cards for the assurance of steady work.[57]

Despite the significant presence of women in the factory, the local ACW had done too little to organize them. The union's sensitivity to ethnicity and language was not matched by a similar appreciation of the importance of gender, and its organizational campaign—unlike the company's strategy—contained no special efforts directed at women. Because many of the ACW's male members were comfortable with the subordination of their daughters and wives in the home, they were certainly averse to women's intrusion into the Amalgamated's world of work. A few male unionizers sent to Baltimore early on recognized this liability in their organizational campaign: "It is absolutely necessary for our organization to have a woman organizer near [Greif's] factory daily in order that we get them to join the union." Their warning fell on deaf ears, however. Without women's leadership in the ACW and with constant pressure coming from the company to abandon the union, workers' spirits sagged and commitments wavered in the weeks after the February "settlement" with Greif. Moreover, the company continued to send agents to workers' homes to persuade parents of the impropriety of union activities. This tactic did have some effect, for even during the strike, Bohemian mothers arrived on the scene "to take their daughters home," fearing that they might "be molested in some way."[58]

Shortly after the settlement, Greif and Ferguson announced that the company had signed an agreement with the UGW that would last a year and serve "to insure peaceful conditions" at the Greif shops. Some six hundred workers, most of them cutters and trimmers, and nearly all of them male, supported the agreement. Ferguson explained that unlike the "lawlessness" of the union of "non-citizens," the UGW was for "American men and women," who "are law-abiding and industrious, and prefer to be associated with a safe, conservative organization, building up, rather than tearing down." The *Baltimore Labor Leader,* the BFL organ edited by Ferguson, heralded the agreement as "the beginning of the end" of the ACW in Baltimore.[59]

The Amalgamated denounced Greif for deceiving its members with the earlier agreement, now no more than "a scrap of paper." Late in February, the union issued another strike call, which immediately brought nearly one thousand workers to the picket line. Significantly, this time the ACW put Dorothy Jacobs on the payroll temporarily, placing her in the Greif factory to "take care" of the women there. Believing that women were at once more difficult to organize and more disposed to take the lead in strikes, the local ACW leadership finally conceded that a woman organizer was necessary to make women more durable members. This time, however, the strikers encountered not only police, but two hundred members of the BFL "patrolling" the plant, and Ferguson vowed that there would be no repeat of the

54   earlier demonstration. Dismissing accusations that the BFL was "bullying the girls," Ferguson countered by denying the strikers status as ladies and denouncing them as a "disreputable band of hooligans." To endorse the UGW's efforts, Samuel Gompers, president of the AFL, arrived in Baltimore amid fanfare.[60]

The strike dragged on for months. Production declined slightly at Greif's, but the company steadfastly refused to negotiate with the Amalgamated. Under Jacobs's direction, several hundred women also stood firm, picketing daily under the ACW's banner. To keep up their morale, she visited their homes, held parties and picnics, and delivered a series of weekly lectures titled "Labor Problems in the United States." The ACW's New York Joint Board sent $1,000 for the strike fund, and Jacobs also sought support from individuals and associations throughout Baltimore. Still, for the striking women, donations of food and cash remained meager and times hard. Jacobs appealed to prominent women in the city for assistance, pointing out the hardships daily faced by wage-earning women and citing city police for their "uncivilized" treatment of women workers. She also turned to the Socialist Party, which endorsed the ACW in its paper, *Public Ownership,* and took the unusual step of denouncing the Wobblies for collaborating with the BFL. At an open forum held at the Academy of Music, social workers and "society women" joined together to register their support for the Amalgamated, denounce the working conditions at Greif, and condemn the police for gross "brutality" and the use of "language which cannot be repeated in dealing with girl strikers." They closed the meeting with a unanimous resolution for the BIS to investigate the strike, working conditions, and the treatment of working women.[61]

The ACW had predicted "a long fight" at Greif's, but it hadn't anticipated other features of the strike or their consequences. Because Ferguson had persuaded Greif to recognize the IWW, for example, Lithuanian and Italian workers replaced striking ACW members. Initially, the ACW was reluctant to repudiate the Wobblies as scabs, but after a few months it rebuked them for "still scabbing." More serious, local ACW members resisted acknowledging the need for a permanent woman organizer. Only belatedly did they accede to the urgings of the national-level organizers and use Dorothy Jacobs to recruit and mobilize Greif's women workers. Finally, the ACW's strike fund could not support a long strike. Most of Greif's workers were "among the struggling poor," noted one ACW member. "The class of people that we have out [on strike]," the organizer explained, "must be paid from the very first minute," for they had no resources to fall back on. Eventually,

even Jacobs recognized that the strikers could no longer postpone the needs   **55**
of their families: swallowing their pride and apparently switching their loyalty, some "women with tears in their eyes" returned to Greif's by late May.[62]

THE BATTLE OF THE SCISSORS

After its defeat at Greif's, the Amalgamated hatched new plans to displace
the UGW, while the latter looked to repeat its success at another factory. For
the ACW, it was painfully clear that appeals to ethnicity had been only partially successful, especially among Italian and Lithuanian tailors. Reaching
out to new constituencies required additional efforts, which the ACW now
set out to undertake. Narrowly interpreting the failure at Greif's not as a failure to organize women workers but as a result of Italian Wobblies' "scabbing," the local ACW began a campaign to attract more Italians into the
union. Frank Bellanca wrote and reproduced a pamphlet in Italian, detailing the importance of industrial organization, the strike at Greif's, and the
unfortunate alliance between the Wobblies and the nativist BFL. All local
officials agreed the pamphlet was "very good for propaganda work." The
ACW also ordered from Chicago bundles of the Italian paper *La Parola Pro-
letaria* for distribution in Baltimore's Italian neighborhoods. Finally, to
counter the UGW's contention that the ACW was "only for Jews," the local Amalgamated relied increasingly on the rallying talents of its Italian
members. In particular, a young worker named Ulisse DeDominicis
emerged as an ardent advocate of the new union. He spoke with eloquent
indignation at industrial inequities and blasted all those who would divide
workers among themselves. His role and stature in the union grew, as he effectively promoted the cause of the Amalgamated in the city.[63]

By the end of the year, Baltimore's ACW had sanctioned the establishment of an Italian local, whose members included former Wobblies. Maintaining that they had been "forced" to join the IWW and cooperate with the
BFL, the Italian workers now pledged themselves to an industrial labor
union and to "stay solid and fight for this organization." They expressed their
concurrence, moreover, that "all members must respect one another in spite
of nationality."[64]

The UGW, meanwhile, sought to duplicate the success it had achieved
at Greif at another of the city's clothiers. By promising a union of the few
and minimal interference at the workplace, the UGW reaffirmed the employers' right to manage. According to Ferguson, only skilled workers held
the right to bargain, and no union should take part in the production deci-

56 sions of the factory. In stark contrast to the ACW's calls for sophisticated arbitration systems, greater governmental involvement in the affairs of business and labor, union participation in all phases of manufacturing and distribution, and not only a totally unionized factory but an entirely organized industry, the UGW promised employers much by requesting less. In the summer of 1916, the UGW moved its battle with the Amalgamated from Greif's to Strouse & Brothers, instructing this company's cutters to strike in an attempt to undermine a contractual agreement signed earlier between Strouse and the ACW. Without the cutters and trimmers, Ferguson again argued, production would have to stop, forcing the company to recognize that it could not deal with a union that did not have the support of those skilled workers. As for the ACW, Ferguson appealed ominously for its destruction. This "revolutionary" and "anarchistic" organization, he announced, "must be silenced, if not by public opinion, by public force," and its members—"the scum of the universe, gathered on these shores, who have no knowledge of American ideas"—"must be driven from the city."[65]

Union positions were now reversed. The Amalgamated instructed its workers to ignore the strike, cross the picket line, and abide by its contract. Shouting obscenities, the members of the UGW's all-male local of cutters and trimmers directed their attacks particularly toward the women workers, who refused to join them on the picket line. Arm in arm, Dorothy Jacobs daily escorted the ACW women to and from the building. They marched forcefully to their workplaces, confident of their new union. The women, Jacobs reported to the ACW's general secretary, Joseph Schlossberg, had taken the lead in the fight against the BFL; they had "contributed morally and financially" and had always been "the first in line." "This affair," Jacobs proudly proclaimed of the UGW harassment, "has brought more spirit into the girls than I expected. It seems as though nothing can frighten them out of the building."[66]

To preserve the authority of the ACW and to reassure Strouse of union control, the Amalgamated turned to tactics hardly in keeping with traditional union practices. First, it brought ACW cutters and trimmers in from Chicago and New York to work in the Strouse shop, training some of the tailors for the positions vacated by the UGW cutters and trimmers and ensuring uninterrupted production. Unable to halt production, Ferguson then issued a call for retail shops and mail-order houses to boycott Strouse's garments, claiming they had been produced by "scabs." Strouse appealed to the ACW to remedy the situation, whereupon the Amalgamated undertook the unusual step of writing to firms throughout the country, explaining the

city's peculiar labor situation and urging them to place orders with the
Strouse company. All of this "un-unionlike behavior" on the part of the
ACW underscored its determination not only to fight the UGW, but also to
be an integral part of all phases of the clothing production process.[67]

These cooperative efforts, which allowed production and distribution
to continue, persuaded Eli Strouse personally of the ACW's value. The
Amalgamated's agreement with Sonneborn along with Strouse's own bonds
with the city's Jewish community further tied the company to the union. In
August 1916 Strouse publicly announced that he would continue to honor
his agreement with the ACW. More significantly, he also declared that despite Ferguson's demand, he would not necessarily rehire the striking UGW
cutters or fire the ACW cutters. This announcement served to legitimize the
role of the Amalgamated and erode sharply the power not only of the UGW,
but also of the skilled native-born cutters in the workplace. The strike facilitated the movement upward of a number of Jewish tailors, who rapidly assumed positions as cutters and thereby altered the traditional ethnic composition of the elite level of the city's garment industry workforce. One
UGW supporter exaggerated the importance of ethnic conflict only slightly when he observed, "The fight between the two clothing working organizations in this city had developed into a purely racial one."[68]

Strouse's announcement struck at the heart of the UGW, threatening its
very existence by challenging its authority among the skilled workers. The
entire BFL rallied behind one of its constituent unions. At a mass meeting
of member unions, amidst chants of "General strike" and "Strikebreakers are
making Strouse & Bros. clothing," the BFL unanimously resolved to make
the fight against the ACW a national one. At the local level, it resolved to tax
every member to support the struggle and to patrol all clothing factories to
prevent scab cutters from working in the city. In another reversal of its behavior in the Greif strike, the BFL lambasted city police for protecting strikebreakers and for restricting the numbers of pickets. Boasting of their past
fights with ACW "cowards," BFL members crowed that the Amalgamated
workers "would flee at the mere knowledge that the police were absent." A
more radical faction of the BFL, long dissatisfied with what they regarded as
Ferguson's "no-strike policy," called for a general strike: Baltimore, they asserted, was "in need of an industrial shaking up." The no-strike policy prevailed, however, and the BFL continued its guerrilla warfare on the picket
lines.[69]

The ACW had early on recognized its limited attraction to native-born
skilled cutters; after all, the union was a product of both craft and ethnic ten-

58   sions. Amalgamated organizers had even told the UGW they would not vi-
olate its jurisdictional authority over the cutters and trimmers and, accordingly, had made no efforts to organize them. (Any effort to do so would've
met with certain rejection, anyway.) By the summer of 1916, things had
changed; the Amalgamated was beginning to appreciate the prerogatives of
power. Emboldened by its victory at Strouse, the union determined to advance along a new front, abandoning its policy of conceding control of the
cutters to the UGW. It was a risky venture and liable to transform the already
bitter rivalry into all-out warfare.

Starting in the safer environs of the Sonneborn factory, where the union
had secured its first contract and the arbitration system was winning national
acclaim, the ACW persuaded Sonneborn to hire 4 Amalgamated-affiliated
cutters, placing them on the same floor with 250 UGW cutters and trimmers. With this, the *Baltimore Sun* suggested, "the war for supremacy" had
begun. Claiming their right to "maintain a closed shop"—a call that mus-
tered little support from the thirty-five hundred other workers—the UGW
cutters appealed to Sonneborn for redress. He refused to fire the four cutters, thereby providing the managerial cooperation necessary for the ACW
to displace the UGW among skilled workers. A few of the UGW cutters bolted their union, believing, as the Amalgamated explained, that the ACW "has
secured the upper hand in the war for factory control."[70]

Ferguson vowed that the "American Federation of Labor is going to fight
the Amalgamated Clothing Workers until every member is driven out of
town" and declared that his men would not work alongside the ACW cutters. Determined to maintain control over their floor in Sonneborn's factory, the UGW cutters turned to direct action. Early Saturday morning, August 26, 1916, they physically attacked the four Amalgamated men. Workers
from other floors joined the fracas, and the Amalgamated called on members from other factories for help. Armed with clothing shears and knives,
UGW cutters and ACW tailors fought ferociously, first in the hallways and
stairwells, but soon out in the street.More than a hundred police officers, "all
wielding clubs," according to the *Baltimore Sun,* "and some with drawn re-
volvers, charged into the mob, striking right and left." It took over an hour
to stop what became known as the "Battle of the Scissors." Four workers, all
of them Amalgamated members, suffered serious injury; at least another
twenty received cuts and bruises. Police arrested twelve workers, all of them
members of the Amalgamated.[71]

"This is only the beginning, unless those gunmen leave the city," Ferguson warned at the end of the battle, but as he suspected and the ACW lead-

ers knew, the events at the Strouse and Sonneborn factories had permanently altered the struggle for union control. Significantly, Moses Strouse helped the Amalgamated pay the fines imposed at the hearings of the ACW members who had been arrested, and State Senator and attorney William Ogden officially represented the ACW. The "greenhorn" union had made new friends, and the show of economic and political support suggested its strength and legitimacy in the city's clothing industry.[72]

By the end of 1916, the Amalgamated was firmly established in Baltimore's men's garment industry. It had organized about 75 percent of the clothing workers and had challenged the UGW's control over the cutters at Strouse and Sonneborn. Although Sonneborn agreed to create another floor of cutters for the ACW and allowed some of the UGW members to stay, the ACW had fundamentally shifted the locus of power. Cutters and trimmers soon joined to form a new local, #15, in the ACW. The struggle for control of the factories would still occur on contested terrain, but the sides were no longer as clearly drawn.

Having secured its place, the ACW turned to disciplining the industry. It consolidated its gains by campaigning for the eight-hour day, seeking to institutionalize its arbitration system citywide, and enhancing its cooperative efforts with "enlightened" employers. At the same time, it worked to strengthen its membership and educate and unify the workers—although hierarchies based on gender, ethnicity, and skill would continue to divide the union.[73]

3

To Discipline an Industry

Workers, Employers, and the Amalgamated

Citing the success of the Amalgamated Clothing Workers (ACW) in Baltimore, the local socialist newspaper, *Public Ownership*, praised the union in 1918 as an example of "industrial democracy in the making." The ACW had sharply reduced the power of the "clothing capitalists," it declared, and now exercised a "firm hand on [their] business." In fact, the ACW had managed to win the support and cooperation of both the "clothing capitalists" and their detractors, and through its distinctive brand of unionism the ACW would continue to cultivate those disparate groups. For those who believed there was an inherent conflict between labor and capital, the ACW fully acknowledged that the interests of the two were "not identical" and called for industrial unionism, which in essence meant "class unionism." For those who wanted stability and greater predictability in a seasonal and chaotic industry, the ACW promoted "agreements with employers" as long as each agreement "is made with the organization of all the workers involved, is of benefit to them, and it is done with the authority and consent of the organized workers."[1]

Later dubbed the "new unionism," the program of the ACW departed in important ways from traditional trade unionism. It was the union's responsibility, as ACW president Sidney Hillman explained, to "bring in a reign of real law and order into the [clothing] industry." Employers might occasionally cooperate with one another, especially against the interests of labor, but, as competitors in an intensely competitive industry, they would not be able to provide the "rule of law" necessary for the survival of the industry itself. Anticipating the industrial unionism of the later Congress for Industrial Organization era, the Amalgamated not only organized along quasi-industrial lines, but operated on the premise of the inevitable demise of traditional craft divisions. Its goal was industrial democracy, wherein union-management cooperation resulted in shared control of the workplace, ensuring the welfare of the worker, and the union movement enabled its members to exercise their rights as worker-citizens in the political arena as well.[2]

At the same time that the Amalgamated's experiment in industrial democracy attracted attention throughout the nation, some business leaders developed plans of their own to improve the image of corporations and enhance worker loyalty while eliminating the threat of unionization. In their efforts, known collectively as "welfare capitalism," they also spoke the language of labor-management cooperation, efficiency, and the rationalization of industry and promised concessions for (unorganized) labor. The ACW encountered a number of these employers, usually with mixed results. The Greif company in Baltimore, for example, which persistently eluded unionization under the ACW, strengthened its mutual aid society for workers and expanded its public relations program in order to portray its labor policies as attractively enlightened. Repeatedly, the company claimed that it offered workers more than the unionized factories, even using misleading photographs to suggest that its factories included modern cafeterias and gyms. Although the ACW sarcastically pronounced "welfare capitalism" as "hellfare camouflage" and charged that it was designed to "hypnotize the workers," the union was not always successful in combatting the corporate message.[3]

Still other employers, even those who participated fitfully in collective bargaining, had already begun to dabble in the new research area of personnel management. Although this approach emphasized labor-management cooperation, it stood in stark contrast to the ACW by focusing on the individual worker as a means of defusing collective action or the development of a class-based solidarity. Genuine labor-management harmony, personnel managers argued, could never be achieved if workers viewed their company loyalty through the lens of a collective identity or if unions determined the

62   conditions of work on the shopfloor. Management could motivate workers and ensure productivity by extending individual recognition while remaining discreet about personal wages and rewards; public negotiations of wages and hours with a union, the argument went, would only result in adversarial relations between labor and management. Whereas the ACW used shared control of the workplace to win wage increases and working reforms, thereby mediating the dehumanizing effects of scientific management, personnel departments called for personal counseling of workers to humanize the management process.[4] These goals, though similar, were not identical, and the ACW was quick to point out the distinctions. It waged its own public relations campaign, promising workers industrial democracy, employers a productive and reliable workforce, and the nation a cooperative and patriotic union.

Industrial developments during World War I along with government-supported arrangements between labor and management perfectly suited the Amalgamated's new unionism and certainly enhanced its growth. Nationally, membership jumped from 48,000 in 1916 to 138,000 in 1919; in Baltimore, it grew from about 7,000 to 12,000 for the same period. Government contracts expanded economic opportunities for manufacturers, and such government initiatives as the Board of Control of Labor Standards provided the ACW with the kind of state intervention it needed to prod intransigent employers. In Baltimore, the alliance between the ACW and the Sonneborn and Strouse companies grew stronger. As part of its goal to ensure a modern, efficient, and profitable garment industry, the ACW worked to provide them with a stable workforce, win substantial improvements for union members, and coordinate marketing and manufacturing decisions. Both firms, although occasionally lapsing into moments of noncooperation, relied considerably on the ACW to perform a variety of industrial functions. For example, they routinely or, as their workers believed, reflexively reported labor and production problems to the union leadership, and they even consulted the Amalgamated on the best means of winning additional government contracts.[5]

"100 PERCENT UNION": SCHLOSS BROTHERS SETTLES

The Baltimore District Council of the Amalgamated continued its organizational campaign during the war years, vigilantly supervising its gains in the large factories while steadily expanding its efforts in the midsized firms. The task was not an easy one, for as business boomed, many firms opened new shops overnight to meet the demand for uniforms and other war-related clothing. The ACW also won major wage increases at the Sonneborn and Strouse companies, although soaring inflation muted worker enthusiasm for the adjustments. Pants makers, for example, long underpaid and over-worked, scored a victory when the ACW launched a brief strike and then in-sisted on negotiating with a number of firms simultaneously in order to ar-rive at an agreement "across the board." As Hyman Blumberg, Baltimore's ACW manager, explained, the strike represented an effort to "reorganize" the industry.[6]

The ACW also conducted a general strike against the small shops that produced custom-tailored clothes and garments for mail-order houses, not merely to gain a reduction of hours and an increase in wages, but to "make it impossible for the small contractor to remain in business so the work will go to better class shops." Sounding more like a capitalist than a unionist, Blumberg detailed the ACW's plans: "An effort will be made to combine a number of the small shops into large shops where the overhead expenses will be reduced and better working conditions will be assured the members of the Amalgamated Clothing Workers of America." The union, then, would facilitate economic concentration among the city's larger manufacturers, bringing together petty entrepreneurs who survived only precariously and enabling them to have a more secure profit margin, if less independence. Af-ter all, as Blumberg noted, the economic reorganization was essential for the union to maintain its control of the contract shops and necessary for the members as well. The small shops were particularly susceptible to the de-structive effects of inflation and "will not be able to grant many further [wage] increases if [they] are not combined." Within about a week, the ACW had won the strike and secured the agreement for "uniting the small shops." The manufacturers, Blumberg exulted, "have agreed to [our] plan for the es-tablishment of larger and more sanitary shops for the coming season."[7]

Throughout 1917 and 1918, the Baltimore District Council monitored the proliferation of shops, led brief strikes to unionize them, and won sig-nificant wage increases for the Amalgamated members. Both the Sonneborn and Strouse companies profited handsomely from this policy, which allowed them control—and a share of the profits—of many of the contract shops. Schloss Brothers, another of the major clothiers, had only reluctantly en-dorsed the ACW and had consistently tried to undermine unionization in its factory and shops, but in 1918 the ACW brought Schloss into line with two sharp strikes. About 50 percent of the workers at its major factory be-longed to the union, but fully 90 percent of the workers struck under ACW

64 leadership in early April to demand that the company fire an objectionable superintendent. Unable to continue production on its government contracts, Schloss, and not the union, immediately requested a conference and agreed to discharge the unpopular manager. Thanks to the quick success of the strike and the company's obvious willingness to settle, hundreds of workers in the factory eagerly joined the Amalgamated. "The victory," according to Dorothy Jacobs, who was on hand to ensure that the "girls who went out on strike join the union," had created a "new spirit of enthusiasm which has been felt in every Baltimore factory."[8]

Building on that enthusiasm, three weeks later the ACW struck Schloss again, demanding a 10 percent wage increase and a union shop. With the stakes higher, Schloss fought back, using United Garment Workers (UGW) members in an attempt to maintain production and relying on the aggressive actions of Baltimore police to keep strikers several blocks away from the factory. Nonetheless, disorder broke out frequently between the ACW strikers, predominantly Italian women, and the scabs. The *Baltimore American* carefully described the repeated "hand-to-hand fights" that brought police intervention. "Women and girls gathered in groups in the middle of the street and fought fiercely. Purses, bundles, and any sort of convenient weapons were used to batter their opponents, and but few escaped being scratched or bruised." In one "free-for-all fight," Baltimore Federation of Labor (BFL) president John Ferguson attacked several strikers and was himself arrested for disorderly conduct and assault, but most of those arrested in what the ACW's paper, the *Advance,* excitedly called a police "campaign of terrorism" were Italian women picketing for the ACW. Their determination was fueled by Frank Bellanca, editor of the ACW's Italian-language journal, *Il Lavoro,* who arrived from New York to address the strikers at the Garden Theater. "You are soldiers in the army of liberty, fighting today to win for your children a world where all will be free."[9]

Unable to find enough strikebreakers, Schloss sent agents to individual strikers' homes, urging them to return to work on generous terms. When that effort likewise failed, the company accepted the ACW's terms for a settlement. The agreement paralleled that which the ACW had already made with Sonneborn and Strouse, providing for a forty-eight-hour week and increased wages, recognition of the union and acceptance of the rights of ACW shop chairwomen and chairmen, and a permanent arbitration system. With the new agreement, Schloss joined the other major clothiers in promoting labor-management cooperation. Judge Jacob Moses, the longtime champi-

on of "enlightened labor and management," endorsed the settlement and
agreed to serve as the union's arbiter with Schloss, as with Strouse and Sonneborn. An erstwhile Progressive reformer, Moses had won a prize in law
school for his thesis, titled "Laws Applicable to Strikers," and had recently
joined the War Department's Board of Control as a mediator.[10]

The settlement with Schloss was not without costs. Jacobs was so exhausted by her relentless efforts that she had to leave Baltimore for several
weeks of rest. But the victory solidified the ACW's control over the Baltimore clothing industry and welded the loyalty of the city's garment workers
to the union. One ACW organizer, although overlooking the Greif company, claimed proudly that Baltimore's clothing industry was now "100 percent Union."[11]

"THE RULE OF LAW": MOVING FROM CONFRONTATION TO COOPERATION

Within a few years, the ACW had unionized most of the city, established a
system of labor-management arbitration, and begun to restructure the industry itself. Although sweatshops persisted, they were far fewer in number.
While wages remained low and conditions numbingly harsh, the ACW received and deserved no small credit for these significant changes.

Union rivalries had also subsided, with only occasional skirmishes and
periodic blasts in the press. In 1917, for example, the UGW attempted to
counter the ascendancy of the Amalgamated and especially attack its special
relationship with city clothiers by having Samuel Gompers of the American
Federation of Labor use his influence in Washington, D.C., to persuade the
Council of National Defense to cancel Sonneborn's government contracts.
Although unsuccessful, this effort underscored the interdependence of the
ACW and the large manufacturers. A few of the city's medium-sized firms
also continued to play on union divisions, prolonging the practice earlier followed by the larger manufacturers. The clothier Philip Kahn, also known as
the "Overcoat King," cooperated with the UGW, for example, and fired a
cutter who had joined the ACW. When four hundred Amalgamated tailors
picketed his shop, denouncing the "coalition between the firm and the United Garment Workers," Kahn relented, rehiring the cutter. "This was a test
case," boasted the ACW tailors, and it "has proven to the Baltimore cutters
that the Amalgamated is the Organization of all garment workers that pro-
tects its members." The ACW's cutters local also cheered the outcome, pre-

66   dicting a "100 percent cutters' organization in the near future." Soon the UGW was completely supplanted at the Kahn company, which came "under the A.C.W. of A. banner."[12]

The Amalgamated's other union rival, the Industrial Workers of the World (IWW), similarly lost influence. Indeed, after it failed in an organizing strike at another medium-sized shop, Frank Bellanca declared the IWW "dead in Baltimore" and attributed the ACW's success to "the honest management" of Hyman Blumberg. "Less than a year ago," Bellanca wrote in the Italian edition of the *Advance*, "the Amalgamated Clothing Workers of America were facing a fight against the American Federation of Labor and the I.W.W. in Baltimore. These two bitter enemies forgot their fight to join hands to crush" the ACW, but "the plot failed." Ferguson, the Amalgamated's old enemy in the BFL, was also brought low when he was no longer able to escape the scandals and allegations that had long dogged his career. To the delight of most ACW members, in 1918 the BFL's own *Trades Unionist* carried a feature story railing against him as a "traitor" and a "double dealer" who allied with "employers against workers."[13]

Not only was the ACW winning its struggle to "extend our control in the factories," but it also was making modest advances toward its goal of industrial democracy. At the urging of the rank-and-file, for example, Sonneborn agreed to establish a cooperative store, and the ACW sanctioned the arrangement only after receiving assurances that the store would be "thoroughly under the control" of the union. To promote the notion of the union as an organization of all garment workers and to help blunt the sharp edges of craft-based divisions among the workers, the ACW took pains to make the cutters' local an integral but not privileged part of the union. In part, and with no small dose of irony, the ACW was assisted in this effort by the durable, but much reduced, presence of the UGW among the city's cutters. Thus the ACW's cutters, unlike its tailors, had competitors. Moreover, the tailors, who had been among the founders of the union, continued to exercise an important role in the organization. Accordingly, the Amalgamated's Local #15 of cutters and trimmers cooperated more fully with other ACW locals than the UGW cutters had ever cooperated with other UGW locals. The cutters, after all, had depended on the support of the tailors to protect their position at the Kahn clothing shop. To celebrate its first birthday in the union, Local #15 remodeled its headquarters and held an Amalgamated picnic, inviting "all clothing workers to make merry." Under the banner of "labor solidarity," the cutters cosponsored with the tailors a "labor ball," which owed its "financial success to the brotherly spirit that exists between the cutters and tailors."[14]

From the perspective of the shopfloor, few things mattered as much in promoting industrial democracy as securing the position of shop chairmen and chairwomen, the union's representatives in the workplace. In this area, too, conduct at the workplace changed significantly with the arrival of the ACW. Although ACW leaders ignored shop chairwomen, they likened shop chairmen in union pamphlets to the "line sergeants" on the battlefront in France and contended that the "real battle" on the shopfloor depended on them. When the Socialist Party praised the Amalgamated for advancing the cause of industrial democracy, it focused on the increased power of the shop chairmen as critical to the progress. Noting that shop chairmen now "have all the power that the foremen once had," the party proclaimed, "the old argument that a man can do what he pleases with his own does not hold true here, as the chairmen in the shops have a great deal to say in how the business of the firm shall be run."[15]

Nonetheless, industrial democracy, Hyman Blumberg reminded his brothers and sisters in the ACW, rested on the "rule of law" in the workplace, and both employers and workers had to observe that dictum. The Amalgamated, from the shopfloor to the General Executive Board, recognized that enforcing the new codes of industrial conduct required by contracts and systems of arbitration often collided with past worker-management relationships, built on inequality and animated by distrust. Implementing the rule of law in the workplace demanded not only constant union vigilance against employer transgressions, but also reeducation of workers more accustomed to solving their problems through direct action. Confrontational actions in the daily operations of the garment industry offered workers, particularly skilled ones, opportunities for disruption and possibly immediate victory. They relinquished those opportunities only reluctantly, and the ACW's imposition of order and discipline was neither sudden nor complete.[16]

The enthusiasm for the union generated by strikes and mass demonstrations often foundered in the face of the new dictates of restraint and cooperation. Hostility between workers and their bosses buffeted the ACW's experiment in cooperation; even more vexing were the rivalries and divisions among workers that too often dissolved their unity. The vicissitudes of the Great War further hampered the ACW's efforts. To be sure, the war enhanced the union's legitimacy, advanced its reputation as "enlightened," and furthered its expansion in a growing industry—simply put, the war increased the demand for clothing workers and made the union seem more necessary. Still, these changes occurred within the context of rising inflation and accelerated production quotas, which meant longer hours for workers, some of whom were not fully persuaded of the advantages of the legalistic approach to labor-management relations.[17]

As a consequence, all too often garment workers engaged in disruptive actions that aggravated both employers and union officials. At Sonneborn's, for example, managers complained of workers' habit of "chiseling." After the company, at the union's insistence, had agreed to grant extra pay for over-time work, managers claimed, workers shirked their duties during regular hours in order to "coerce us into working overtime." At Strouse's main factory, owner Eli Strouse found the situation "almost unbearable" and charged that "the agreement which we have with the union seems to be worth only the paper that it is written on." The ACW, he maintained, had failed miserably in disciplining its members; workers with grievances ignored the arbitration process and cavalierly walked off their jobs, engaged in departmental slowdowns, or even initiated spontaneous strikes. The finishers and joiners, Strouse claimed, regularly fought among themselves and left their workplaces. The ACW itself conceded that shop chairmen and chairwomen were sometimes thwarted by other union members who "won't play the game square." Plagued by "petty" divisions among workers, the shop chairwomen and men sometimes failed in their enforcement duties or neglected them altogether. Indeed, some even encouraged the "uncooperative" behavior, sanctioning "slow-downs," "loafing," and "mishaps."[18]

Frustrated by what they regarded as chaos on the shopfloor, Strouse and Sonneborn appealed directly to Hillman to "get matters straightened out" and devise "some means" to "discipline these workers." Strouse was solicitous in his appeal, noting Hillman's busy schedule—"I know that you have your hands full and are going from morning until night"—but maintaining that only Hillman's personal intervention could make a difference, Strouse requested that he "visit the different factories and join in a few meetings with us for the betterment of conditions in *our* market." Hillman, who had become personal friends with the Sonneborns, felt obliged to address the problem. The day-to-day affairs of the Sonneborn company had passed from the hands of the owner Henry Sonneborn, who had started the company in 1853, to those of his brother-in-law with the same surname, Siegmund Sonneborn, who followed more carefully the literature on scientific management and who counted on unions to provide the stability he believed necessary for modern industry to progress. When Henry Sonneborn died in December

1917, Hillman served as a pallbearer at the funeral and spoke of the ACW's special relationship with the Sonneborn company. Still, even Hillman's personal involvement did not always prevail over the will of the workers. During one work stoppage that forced his intervention, for example, he publicly sided with union members, urging the reinstatement of a popular and militant worker, even though privately he complained that industrial production should not be halted on account of one worker, saying "I realize more and more that the system where the discharge of one man might cause a strike of thousands is very dangerous."[19]

No less than Hillman, the Baltimore District Council of the ACW attempted to instruct its members in the new ways of the workplace, the reciprocity mandated by "industrial democracy," and the "value of our organization." Its goal, only partially achieved, was to combat the slowdowns, work stoppages, and general "spirit of dissatisfaction" among garment workers that resulted from both the production demands of the war effort and the earlier, antagonistic nature of labor-management relations.[20]

Industrial habits informed by traditions of craft and ethnicity further complicated the Amalgamated's efforts to discipline its workers. Tied by culture and religion, many of the Jewish tailors and cutters loyally followed the able leadership of Hyman Blumberg, who staunchly defended the interests of the city's garment workers. Yet a few of the older Jewish tailors found the "new ways" disagreeable and expressed genuine confusion at cooperating with former enemies. The scars from deals gone sour and inadequate rewards for long hours and "good work" left these workers with deep-seated distrust toward their bosses. Others dismissed owners as capitalists without knowledge of the trade or due respect for the craft. They looked down on both their bosses and other workers. On rare occasions some even challenged the leadership of Hillman himself. Such actions horrified August Bellanca, who sharply criticized "several demagogues" who condemned Hillman for signing an agreement with Sonneborn. Strouse, too, angrily rebuked the recalcitrance of some ACW members. Insisting that he wanted to "do good for our people," Strouse nevertheless vigorously objected to the independence asserted by the "Jewish shop chairmen" at his main factory: "they seem to want to run things their own way, disregarding our executives entirely." They were, he believed, "almost as bad as the rank and file themselves."[21]

Nor had non-Jewish members of the Amalgamated fully abandoned the anti-Semitism earlier promoted by the UGW and the IWW. Such members complained that the union and the manufacturers favored Jewish workers, and they often expressed resentment at the ACW's Jewish leadership. Local

70   #15 of cutters and trimmers, known in the ACW as one of the city's "Jewish locals," provided many of the Amalgamated's leaders, including Blumberg. Local #36, the original Jewish and founding local of the Amalgamated, also exercised considerable authority in the union. Critics also perceived excessive Jewish influence in several locals' practice of holding their meetings in Baltimore synagogues. Local #117 of vest makers met regularly in B'rith Sholom Hall, and, on occasion, entire factory meetings were also held there.[22]

The increasing concentration of both skilled workers and the union's leadership in Local #15 and the not always latent anti-Semitism of some of the other locals strained relationships in the union. Conflict particularly flared between the Lithuanian local and the Jewish leadership. The Lithuanians who had left the IWW for the Amalgamated initially resisted the union's arbitration and labor-management policies; even as late as 1918, the ACW's Lithuanian organizer in Baltimore declared that there "is plenty of work to do in Baltimore until these traitors become loyal members of the organization." Their recalcitrance did not discourage him; once educational work began in earnest and the Lithuanian trimmers and tailors were persuaded of the need to join the union and pay what they regarded as "exorbitant" dues, he boasted, "we will have the biggest and strongest organization among Lithuanians of all tailor centers in the U.S."[23]

In some measure, the persistence of ethnic factions within the ACW reflected not merely historically embedded cultural divisions, but the union's conscious efforts to reach out to new constituencies by appealing to ethnic—as opposed to class—interests. Given the significance and resilience of those ethnocultural ties, perhaps the ACW had few choices when trying to gather new recruits and galvanize support. Still, its tactics had important consequences for its efforts in building the union movement. To counter the anti-Semitic diatribes of the UGW and the IWW, local ACW leaders felt it necessary to broaden their appeal by highlighting the role of other ethnic groups in the making of the union. In 1917, Hillman himself singled out the "younger Italian element, filled with enthusiasm and with a spirit to do things," as "becoming the leading part of the organization." Locally, not only did Italian organizers such as Ulisse DeDominicis and Mamie Santora emerge as important activists, but so did others from among the Polish and Bohemian tailors. The establishment of Polish and Bohemian versions of the *Advance* drew special praise from Baltimore's separate ethnic locals. Frank Bartosz, who organized Baltimore's "Polish local," commended the editions as necessary to organize the unorganized, to "enlighten our fellow workers and show them the right path": "In our union in Baltimore we have about five hundred of them [Polish members] and there is a great number outside the union. To organize them is the next thing on our program, and I believe that our papers will be most effective agencies in our work." The secretary of Baltimore's Local #230 of Bohemian tailors even told its membership, albeit incorrectly, that the ACW's constitution required nationalities to organize into separate locals.[24]

At the same time ethnic solidarity served as an effective recruitment tool, it also impeded the achievement of a larger unity within the union. Respect for ethnic diversity, although officially promoted by the union, could not always overcome the realities of ethnic differences and generations of prejudice. For example, even while some Amalgamated leaders praised the organizational role of some Italian officials, they fretted about the distinctive problems posed by Italian members. Both Italian and Jewish organizers described Italian workers as generally submissive to employers and as having a concept of unionism that rarely extended beyond the explosive drama of a short, successful strike. Making them durable union members proved a challenge. As Frank Bellanca argued, Italian workers were easy to convert but difficult to maintain as active union members, and Italian men frequently balked at their wives' and daughters' assuming public or militant roles in the union. The "Italian problem" for the ACW, according to historian Steven Fraser, "was more often one of inactivity rather than hyperactivity. . . . [The] mass of Italian operatives behaved more like subjects than citizens" in the Amalgamated's new experiments in industrial democracy.[25]

The ACW, then, worked simultaneously to energize its membership and rein in its troublesome and independent workers on the shopfloor. The rebellion at Strouse and Sonneborn's, which had forced Hillman to intervene personally, resulted from the actions of the most skilled and highly paid workers. However, the complaints of employers also suggest another way to interpret the problems on the shopfloor. To be sure, Italian operatives, who had not inherited the tradition of craft shared by Jewish and Lithuanian tailors, did not subvert the production process or challenge management authority in the same fashion as the other groups often did, but their industrial inexperience and their inaction should not be confused with submissiveness. Efforts to exert control at the workplace must be understood in forms other than those traditionally recognizable to skilled workers, union leaders, and historians as well. In order to appreciate the varied dimensions

72   of workers' behavior at the workplace—to more fully unravel the complexities of gender and ethnicity—alternative frameworks must be explored and new questions examined.[26]

At Sonneborn's, Italian workers behaved differently from their Jewish and Lithuanian counterparts. Although less overtly hostile to managers, the "Italian group" still garnered their share of the owners' criticisms of the workforce. Siegmund Sonneborn himself complained to the Amalgamated about Italian workers who secretly adopted a "contrary stand" by "laying down deliberately during the day-time in order to force us to work [them] overtime." Although, unlike their Jewish union brothers, they rarely engaged in open displays of militance, they simply worked at a more leisurely pace and quietly refused to meet daily production quotas. Despite the irritation they provoked in the management and the economic consequences of their inaction, they appeared far less threatening to managers than did the more vocal and animated Jewish cutters and tailors. Bosses on the shopfloor dismissively stereotyped Italian workers as "lazy," while reserving their harshest indictments for Jewish tailors and cutters. Moreover, language barriers also precluded Italian workers from engaging in public displays of criticism or overtly expressing their grievances. In this respect, too, Jewish workers held both the advantage and the disadvantage of sharing cultural similarities with their bosses; they derided managers openly and stood firm against them, placing their protests into more traditional masculine forms of worker culture.[27]

Interethnic factionalism, according to both Strouse and Sonneborn, compounded the "loafing" problem, for Italian workers often expressed their hostility toward Jewish tailors on the shopfloor and scarcely disguised their resentment at Jewish prominence in the ACW's leadership. Mamie Santora, an Italian member of Local #170 of buttonhole makers organized by Dorothy Jacobs, explained the problem to Hyman Blumberg. Decrying the ethnic separatism in the union as anathema to Amalgamated unity, Santora allowed that her Italian union brothers were jealous of the Jewish members' educational and organizational advancements and advised Blumberg to stop meeting separately with the "Jewish boys" when he came to Baltimore. Such practices, she warned, "created quite a bad feeling among the Gentile activity in general."[28]

Jewish members denied the charge that they enjoyed favorable treatment in the union. To explain their positions of leadership, they stressed their role in founding the union as well as their majority in the membership. Moreover, they also suggested that the Amalgamated's special brand of the new unionism drew distinctive strength from the political ideas of Jewish immigrants and that the ACW's Italian members had little experience in either unionism or socialism and often lacked "class consciousness." Years later, Jacob Edelman recalled that the ACW's local leadership held high expectations for Jewish members: they were expected to "improve themselves." It did not have similar expectations for Italian members, who, on the whole, were less likely to attend public lectures or evening classes. "Visit the evening classes at the Johns Hopkins University," advised a reporter for the *Baltimore Sun* who was quoted in the ACW's biennial proceedings, and there "will be found in the classes studying sociology, philosophy, or political economy no carpenters, no steel riveters, no printers, but nine chances out of ten there will be found two or three keen-faced Jews who work by day in the big clothing factories."[29]

"Bonds of love which . . . cannot be sundered": The Education of Amalgamated Members

From its inception, the ACW championed workers' education as a means to create and cement loyalty to the union and as a necessary component of workers' control over industry. Education, ACW leaders explained, "gives workers power" and "is the basis of permanent and responsible organization in the clothing industry." Education fostered unity, for only educated workers would abandon all divisions among themselves in favor of a class-based union: the "crystallization of class consciousness" among workers "is only possible" through education, alone responsible for equipping them, "individually and collectively, for a successful stand for what is theirs."[30] Education, and not higher wages or better working conditions, the ACW insisted, made workers "citizens" of industrial democracy:

> Nor can we stop and rest on our laurels when we succeed in securing better conditions for our members. If we content ourselves with that and make no effort at higher elevation we simply confirm the worker in the status of a biped beast of burden. To a worker of that character a reduction in the working hours means no more than it does to the dray horse or the galley slave—more physical rest in order to be in better working condition the next day. Better wages also have the identical value—more fodder for the beast of burden.[31]

Labeled a necessary part of "progressive economic organization," education took on special importance in the early years of the Amalgamated.

74   Only education could create a "unified, disciplined and enthusiastic" membership, and the ACW, along with the International Ladies' Garment Workers' Union, became a sophisticated and active proponent and practitioner of workers' education. A national education department was established in the ACW in 1920, although many cities had already formed their own education societies or organizations within the ACW. At the national level, the ACW sponsored a lecture series, drawing on such sympathetic speakers as Charles Beard, Scott Nearing, and Leo Wollman. In Baltimore, Jewish members faithfully attended the Workmen's Circle, listening to a variety of speakers from union leaders to "the liberals and intellectuals" from Johns Hopkins University and Goucher College. Union members started their own "workers' libraries" to begin explorations into "proletarian culture," more frequently dubbed "prolecult." At Circle meetings, they also read and discussed books of literature, history, and economics, spiritedly debating the consequences of incremental versus radical reform.[32]

The Amalgamated's industrial pedagogy served a variety of functions as it evolved over time. In addition to the immediate goal of instilling loyalty to the union and the larger goal of creating "enlightened citizens" for industrial democracy, the ACW also sought through its published literature, rallying speeches, educational programs, and evening classes to Americanize its members, create unity among its diverse membership, and recruit new leaders for the union. The union's arbitration system and its rulings served as "the primers for teaching the science of industrial citizenship." Many of these efforts coalesced into the ACW-sponsored Baltimore Labor College, which held weekly classes for workers but which never matched the success of its counterparts in cities like Boston. Between 1916 and 1920, as the ACW became more successful at beating back the opposition from the UGW and from local employers, it focused more on the "educational mission" of the union movement. Education, the ACW resolved, must be regarded as "an organic part of the union." Not only must it include all subjects, but it must excite and involve the workers themselves, as it prepared them to assume their responsibilities in the new industrial order. "There is as much natural intelligence in the average working man," the ACW affirmed, "as there is in the average university professor, the difference is only in the opportunity. When a workingman is accorded an opportunity to learn he is just as capable of receiving instruction and enlightenment as anyone of the so-called 'higher classes.' Nature has not endowed the workers with inferior faculties than it has the nonworkers. It is our duty to furnish this education to our members."[33]

The ACW's educational director was J. B. S. Hardman, a Russian immigrant deeply influenced by the turn-of-the-century revolutionary fervor, and he explicitly linked education with the worker's power at the workplace and in society. Although later he would become disillusioned with the prospects for workers' education, Hardman early on defended its necessity and conveyed his vision of it with clarity and passion. "Workers' education," he explained, "is the education workers get nowhere else." Not merely education for workers, the ACW brand of workers' education formed an integral part of union organization: "the union attains power in and control of industry by organization, and workers' education must be a part, or a variety, of the organization task of the union." Education, the ACW confirmed, "will make [workers'] lives worth living and will tie them to their organization with those sacred bonds of love which though invisible are most powerful and cannot be sundered."[34]

The Baltimore District Council officially launched its "Educational Campaign" in February 1918, but even before this many of the city's locals had begun to emphasize the "value of educational work" among their members. Women members took the lead, holding lectures, picnics, and Amalgamated dances to heighten awareness of the necessity for the union and promote harmony among its members. Local #170 of buttonhole makers organized a lecture series in 1917, inviting a number of women union leaders and educators to speak on such topics as "The Eight-Hour Day," "Man's Struggles for Freedom," and "Women's Contributions to the Labor Movement." After the remarkable success of the series—"at which prominent persons have discussed the labor movement and other subjects of interest to women workers"—Local #170 established an ACW Educational Society. The local explained that women members wanted more opportunities for enrichment and advancement in the union. Significantly, it did not overlook the role of educational work as a means of controlling the industry, and women members of the ACW also regarded such issues as market control and power on the shopfloor as essential to their success and that of the union. As the *Advance* reported of Local #170's educational activities, "The girls and women are active in the organization propaganda that is conducted constantly to keep up interest in the maintenance of the domination of the Baltimore market."[35]

Soon after its founding, Local #15 of cutters and trimmers combined with the Jewish local, #36, to sponsor a wide range of educational activities and to find ways to help members attend night classes. Jacob Edelman, who began work as a tailor in 1912 and advanced rapidly in the industry to the po-

76 sition of cutter, fondly remembered how his union brothers routinely announced that they had finished their own work and were now preparing to do "Jake's work," while he crouched under a cutting table to read his law books. This kind of informal support of educational activities received regular sanction among union members, and a commitment to enhancing opportunities for all workers drove many of the locals' programs and practices.[36]

Significantly, these efforts were not always about individual achievement. Indeed, even when the activities focused on the advancement of a single member, as in Edelman's case, the rewards were seen as communal. Edelman's success—or that of Hyman Blumberg, or Dorothy Jacobs, or Ulisse DeDominicis—meant union success. As Jacobs delighted in pointing out, her union sisters proudly called her "Our Dorothy." The initiation of new events heralding class consciousness further indicated the importance the union attached to educational activities. In 1917, the District Council organized its first May Day celebration, attracting that year five thousand members of the "Amalgamated family." August Bellanca spoke of the need for class unity against industry; Blumberg rallied the crowd in English, with occasional Yiddish references; and a Lithuanian organizer from Boston also spoke of the need to educate union members and to fight the inequities of capitalism. All of the speakers reminded workers of their special obligation to the international labor movement. The celebration of May Day not only was "the largest of its kind" ever held in Baltimore's garment industry, but also reaffirmed the union's role in tying workers to their larger place in history. Strouse and Sonneborn even closed their factories for the event at the insistence of the District Council. During the rest of the month, ACW locals sponsored lectures and meetings to "discuss the importance of the International Labor Movement at this time."[37]

The Educational Campaign that the District Council launched in 1918 signaled an even more vigorous effort to "make the membership understand fully the history and the evolution of society, especially in relation to the labor movement." Although the goal barely reflected the grand design outlined by Hardman and other members of the ACW's leadership, still it adhered to the notion of elevating workers through educating them. As its organizers explained, the Baltimore program was an attempt to reclaim the respect and dignity owed all working people and affirmed the importance of collective educational experiences. This last objective figured prominently in their plans, for they believed that when members of the rank-and-file shared uplifting experiences that acknowledged the triumphs of the labor

movement, they would behave more as one and would be both enriched and **77**
empowered. Particularly targeting the diffident Lithuanians, local organizer J. A. Bekampis explained, "We try to educate the people and we make
them [a] little more alive and active in [the] organization."[38]

The lecture series of the Educational Campaign ranked among the most
prestigious in the city. It consistently attracted large and diverse audiences,
including Baltimore's leading philanthropists and socialists, many of its major clothiers, particularly Siegmund Sonneborn and Eli Strouse, and Judge
Jacob Moses. Joseph Schlossberg, the ACW's general secretary at the national level, began the series with a talk on the "underlying principles of the
antagonisms between Capital and Labor," in which he argued that although
no successful union could ever forget those principles, cooperation with
owners could be achieved on a basis of mutual respect and authority. His lecture drew 800 people to the hall and delighted the District Council as "one
of the most successful gatherings in the history of the Baltimore labor movement." Schlossberg himself declared that "it is a maxim in Baltimore that
everything attempted by the Amalgamated is carried through to success."[39]

The lecture series probably did more for the reputation of the ACW than
for the workers themselves. An unanticipated benefit of the Educational
Campaign, despite the radical message of many of the lecturers, was that it
legitimized the Amalgamated in Baltimore: the union now appeared as an
institution strongly committed to education and to the value of public enlightenment. Its program was especially attractive to the city's "liberals and
intellectuals," who usually had to depend on the Socialist Party to sponsor
major lectures. Still, the ACW's rank-and-file also took pleasure in their
union's ability to draw such interest and to attract distinguished speakers and
guests. Many of them attended the lectures as well. The *Baltimore Jewish
Times,* which devoted considerable attention to the ACW, proudly reported that the meetings sponsored by the union's Educational Committee were
"attended for the most part by the Jewish members of the Amalgamated."
The District Council ensured that some of the lectures dealt directly with
the immediate interests of ACW members. For example, Maynard Shipley,
the editor of the socialist paper, *Public Ownership,* gave a talk entitled "Economic Evolution for Baltimore Members of the Amalgamated Clothing
Workers of America."[40]

The Amalgamated's educational efforts also invigorated interest at
Goucher College and Johns Hopkins University in the education of workers. Some professors openly challenged the protocols of academic profes-
sionalism and the traditions of academe by calling for adult education cours-

78   es as well as curricular changes that would reflect the importance of the growing labor movement. Broadus Mitchell of Hopkins and Naomi Riches of
Goucher emerged as among the favorite speakers of the garment workers.
Few in number and facing considerable opposition from academic administration, however, these professors usually confined their efforts to providing occasional lectures or delivering speeches during strike meetings. Moreover, programs for workers' education at the university rarely went beyond
offering evening classes. Still, Mitchell participated actively in the Baltimore
Labor College, formally organized in 1920. He was particularly enamored of
the Amalgamated and its brand of "new unionism," which, he declared, "has
broken away from craft demarcation" and "is frankly looking for a changed
social order." Impressed by the "sincere impulses" of the ACW's men and
women, Mitchell led classes every Saturday evening at the Progressive Labor
Lyceum to train "well-equipped thinkers," who will "gain in power" and will
"plan for the general good."[41]

Members of the Amalgamated played a prominent role in establishing
and guiding the Baltimore Labor College. Its purpose, said one member, was
to provide an education that would enable workers "to be better [union]
members." Both Mamie Santora and Sadie Dressner of Local #170 of buttonhole makers served on the Labor College's Board of Directors. Other
board members were predominantly from the Jewish locals, #15 and #36, but
J. Cherniauckas of the Lithuanian local, #218, also took an active part.[42]

Advocates of workers' education, even those committed to socialism, also
supported the sentiments of middle-class Progressive reformers, who regarded education as a means to uplift and Americanize the immigrant working-
class. The ACW shared those sentiments and especially encouraged members to attend classes in English-language instruction. Many union members
did enroll in such courses, and the issue of "the accent" became a serious one
among garment workers. ACW members such as Jacob Edelman worked
hard to eliminate the traces of the Old World from their voices. Carefully
scrutinizing the sounds and habits of the lecturers and professors they observed, they affected similar patterns and prided themselves on sounding
"American." Even while appealing to ethnic loyalties, then, the ACW facilitated the process of Americanization. National and local ACW leaders believed that to control the industry, it was necessary to have as union members Americanized workers who were familiar with the English language and
American customs. That goal took on special urgency during World War I,
when all immigrants became suspect. But the functional need to communicate with employers, especially in negotiating and arbitrating, continued,

and union members were often selected for key positions on the basis of their ability to communicate in English. Dealings with arbiters or management demanded English skills and, as both Edelman and Sara Barron later recalled, their success often hinged on the respect they won through their ability to communicate.[43]

Although local ACW members and leaders may have exaggerated the importance of command of the English language to success in persuading intransigent employers or winning concessions in the courts of arbitration, they perceptively understood the value of teaching members the history, purpose, and organizational structure of their union. Although later described as a part of the process of assimilation, a necessary companion to English-language instruction, the early efforts of the ACW to "initiate its members into the mysteries of self-government" reflected less a lesson in Americanization than a concerted effort to tie workers to their union in an environment of unions competing for members and employers who promised welfare capitalism.[44]

By giving workers a say in the union, the ACW attempted not only to broaden its appeal, but to cement the connections between members, their families, and the union. Organization meetings focused on the union's role in correcting injustices at the workplace, on the structure and function of the union, and on the responsibilities of its officers. Dorothy Jacobs lectured to women workers on the role of the Joint Board, the confederation of the city's locals. She explained that the shop chairwomen and chairmen, the locals' delegates to the Joint Board, and the business agents who dealt with management all constituted the "activity" of the union, and she delineated the processes of decision making from the grass-roots level to the General Executive Board. Jacobs urged women to use the power of making official resolutions—both locally and nationally—to raise their voice in the union. Explaining that the biennial national convention was, at least in theory, the union's supreme governing body and provided a forum for the discussion of policies and procedures, Jacobs instructed her Amalgamated sisters to ensure their issues received attention by introducing formal resolutions that the convention was bound to read and address. Many years after retiring from the Amalgamated, Barron could still recite its organizational structure, pointing proudly to what she termed the union's "true democracy."[45]

The real lesson of the union's organization, ACW organizers told their sisters and brothers, was the importance of interdependence and solidarity. The union's success depended on mutual support and cooperation; an effective union—one that could settle grievances, win better conditions and

80   higher wages, and promote the causes of the working class—demanded not only loyalty, but full knowledge of the workings of the union. The claims were grand and the rhetoric susceptible to criticism and cynicism, but the lessons took hold. Both Barron and Edelman attended ACW classes and lectures; they even shared some of the same instructors. Barron recalled that she "paid Dr. [Broadus] Mitchell a quarter a week to learn what the union movement was about." Edelman, too, singled out Mitchell for the quality of his lectures on political economy. They heard, by Mitchell's own account, a rather uncomplicated history of unionization, which emphasized the need for working-class solidarity, union loyalty, and socialist principles. They were taught the value of organization and unity.[46]

Many years later, both Barron and Edelman were able to recount nearly flawlessly the history of the city's ACW, giving the precise dates of major struggles, highlighting the "Battle of the Scissors," and celebrating their union's ultimate victory over the UGW. Never herself a victim of the UGW's discrimination against ethnics and women, Barron nonetheless gained firm ideas about the rival union, speaking passionately against it, savoring the ACW's triumph, and ultimately dismissing the UGW as completely unnecessary: it "never did nothing for you." She stayed with the ACW all her life, and, as she joyfully acknowledged, the union stayed with her: "I didn't have too much social life, outside the union social life. But I loved it. We accomplished a lot of exciting things." Although Edelman moved on from his position as ACW cutter to become a prominent labor lawyer and member of the Baltimore City Council, his firm grasp of ACW history in late life exemplified the effectiveness of the Amalgamated's early efforts at education. Their praise of the union as a source of opportunity and inspiration represented more than boosterism or ballyhoo. Their glowing portraits of union sisters and brothers, their still intimate knowledge of the ACW's history and organizational structure, and their expressions of gratitude for having been part of what they saw as a "great union movement" all went beyond standard union loyalties and instead provide a valuable gauge for determining the efficacy of the ACW's industrial pedagogy.[47]

Amalgamated leaders cultivated in members a strong attachment to their union. They relied on lectures, meetings, pamphlets, cartoons, and music to help them create "bonds of love." They spoke freely and passionately about the need for such strong emotional bonds, frequently referring to the union as a family and promising members support and respect. From the start, Baltimore's organizers requested from the national office advice and "educational materials" to use to win new recruits. They used all "types of entertainment" to "arouse interest" in the union and to maintain the excitement they themselves felt as organizers. At the close of organization meetings, they led participants in singalongs, distributing songbooks entitled "ACW Songs for the Workers" that encouraged members to "Sing with Spirit." The organizers faithfully recorded which songs worked best, which drew the loudest participation, or which helped most with organizing efforts. These activities encouraged in members a sense of belonging and a sense of purpose.[48]

Organizers also hoped to foster personal attachments and familiarity by attracting members to the union hall. Presenting it as a center of union activity, organizers encouraged members to regard the hall as the "workers' home"—a collective home where members got jobs, discussed grievances, and planned strike strategies. Workers would also find there opportunities for cultural enrichment, educational advancement, and social entertainment. The ACW hall, Edelman recalled, welcomed all the members, tying them to each other and to the union. Early on, the ACW expanded its headquarters on Redwood Street so that locals could meet there, rather than rely on separate meeting rooms scattered throughout Baltimore. The Amalgamated attempted to build a loyalty greater than the traditional pride in craft that was nurtured in small, specialized union halls. The union hall, the local ACW believed, should serve more than its traditional function of providing a place where members swapped stories about work and bosses and celebrated special holidays; the Amalgamated hall should be a home for all the workers of the industry and serve as a school for industrial democracy. Although the ACW did not get its long-desired new headquarters on Redwood Street until 1937, the local leadership ensured that the Amalgamated hall became a special place for its members.[49]

Some of the ACW's practices departed from its goals of industrial democracy and worker solidarity, however, and none more than its behavior toward its women members. Few groups were as isolated or demeaned by the union as they were. The women labored with remarkable constancy on behalf of the union, yet they received unequal treatment, little recognition, and considerable opposition on issues they regarded as crucial—issues that dealt with the Amalgamated's basic principles. Most leaders made little effort to attract women or keep them as members: the "bonds of love" they promoted were of a distinctly masculine nature, and the ACW, with its programs, policies, and propaganda, reinforced the image of maleness in its struggles and victories. Yet this was a union for an industry in which more than half the workers were women. The weight of these numbers, the sup-

82   port shown for women's equality by a few male leaders, and the force and dedication of the ACW women all challenged the exclusion and subordination of women in the union. All the women members wanted, Hyman Blumberg explained, was a place in the union. "The sentiment of the girls in this city [Baltimore] is that their question is being ignored entirely."[50]

DISCRIMINATE AGAINST

INFERIOR
UNCLEAN
SWEAT-SHOP
CLOTHING.

INSIST UPON
THIS LABEL

ISSUED BY AUTHORITY OF
9746113 UNITED GARMENT WORKERS V. AMERICA UNION MADE
REGISTERED

ENDORSED BY ALL TRADES UNIONS
AND LEADING REFORM SOCIETIES.
SEE OVER

Advertisement of the United Garment Workers of America, 1910s. An affiliate of the American Federation of Labor, the United Garment Workers (UGW) represented the skilled garment workers and focused on selling union labels to employers rather than organizing the newer immigrants who arrived at the turn of the century in Baltimore. By linking the union label to the battle against sweatshops, the UGW appealed to the public's fears of unclean clothes.

Gas-powered garment factory in Baltimore, 1890s. In the nineties, both large and mid-sized firms adopted gas power, which allowed more rapid cutting, sewing, and pressing. This crowded steam pressing room produced pants.

The Strouse brothers, 1880s. After the Civil War, they joined to create Strouse & Brothers, which became one of the top five men's clothiers in Baltimore. The company moved to the loft district with the other major manufacturers after the turn of the century. Unable to survive the post–World War I recession that hit the garment industry especially hard, it closed its doors in 1922.

The cutting room of Jacob Goldberg's factory on Fayette Street, Baltimore, 1910s. Even after the rise of the "sky-scraping" factories like Sonneborn's, smaller enterprises continued to flourish. Goldberg workers used old-fashioned shears and hand cutting on the multiple layers of cloth. Larger factories used cutting machines—unless it was cheaper to contract out to such small firms as Goldberg's.

Founders of the Amalgamated Clothing Workers of America, 1915. Rejected as radical foreigners by the United Garment Workers, this group of predominantly Jewish garment workers led the strike at Sonneborn's in 1914 and thus brought about formation of the Amalgamated Clothing Workers.

Several of the Baltimore founders (Chicago contributed the other originating local) earned national reputations as important leaders in the immigrant workers union, including Dorothy Jacobs (top row, fourth from left); Hyman Blumberg (second row, third from left); Jacob Edelman (second row, first from right); Samuel Skolnick (bottom left); and the fiery Sara Barron (top row, sixth from left).

Henry Sonneborn Company, 1910s. The skilled tailors at Baltimore's premier manufacturer were men and women of different ethnicities. Women still earned less pay for the same work, even when sewing alongside their fellow workers.

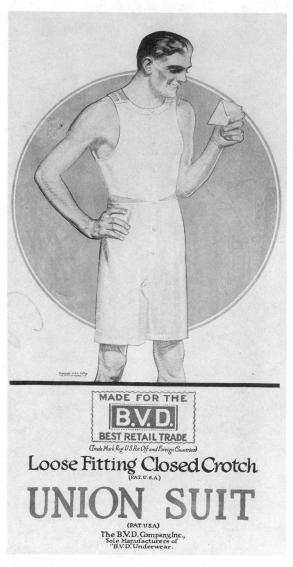

The B.V.D. union suit, 1920s. In the twenties and thirties, many Baltimore shops produced men's accessories and undergarments. These shops often eluded the grasp of the Amalgamated, but Sara Barron and Millie Jeffrey both worked to unionize B.V.D. and force it to conform to the New Deal hours-and-prices codes.

4

The "Forgotten" Workers

Sisters of the Amalgamated

Writing in 1940 about the American clothing industry, an author sympathetic to the Amalgamated Clothing Workers (ACW) described female workers as the "forgotten women" of the industry.[1] Women's role in the union and the workplace had not yet received the recognition it deserved. The ACW had been more receptive to women than the traditional craft unions, but there remained an ambivalence toward total equality in the union that resulted in a divided membership and a male-dominated leadership.

Women working in the men's garment industry in Baltimore attempted to puncture that ambivalence, demanding that the union live up to its claim as an organization for all workers. They asked for no special favors, and, despite the popular wisdom that viewed them as temporary workers uncommitted to either union solidarity or the sanctity of workers' control, they recognized and valued the importance of skill and the tradition of worker independence on the shopfloor. Still, they also insisted that the ACW, which had done so much to accommodate itself to the significance of ethnicity among its union men, should also grant proper recognition to the "women's issue"—an issue, they reminded their union brothers, that existed as a result

84   of inequality of opportunity. They also expanded their role in the public arena, endorsing suffrage as a right that women as well as men should have and
promoting the ballot as a means to address the problems of America's wage
earners. Drawing on issues of class and gender, they articulated a simple message of economic justice and political equality for working men and women.
Those goals also led them to unite with the city's middle-class women in the
fight for suffrage, an alliance that provided them with valuable lessons in the
power of organization. Ever growing numbers of women joined the Amalgamated, and they joined with high hopes, drawing strength from their activist predecessors.

Complex discussions about equality, representation, and discrimination filled the pages of the *Advance* from 1915 until the Great Depression.
Women of the ACW who wrote letters to the editor or lengthier commen-
taries in the *Advance* concurred that women faced discrimination on the
shopfloor and in the union. They noted inequalities in pay and advancement
and decried the union's policy of "looking after the men first." They particularly objected to the special and burdensome duties that women were expected to bear during strikes.

> One day the women were told that each one was to take a collec-
> tion box and stand at every corner of the busiest district as a collec-
> tion was to be made for the strike. [Only women were assigned to
> ask for money, and] I was one of them. It was very cold then . . . .
> Finally, at six o'clock with stiff hands and a numbed body, I went to
> Headquarters. When I came in, there I saw a man, with his feet on
> the table and smoking a cigar. This man counted my money, then,
> looking at me displeased, he said: "Is that all you got?" . . . The
> women do the work but men get the credit.

"We feel that if we take our places on the picket line," explained another
ACW woman, "we are entitled to 'our' places in the shops."[2]

Yet, not all women agreed on the solution to the problem of unequal
treatment. Two different, but related, solutions to the "women's question"
emerged among sisters of the Amalgamated. A significant minority believed
the union should simply enable women to organize and achieve recognition
and respect on the basis of shared identity—their gender. They compared
women locals in the union to "race-based" ones and called on the union to
grant women locals the same legitimacy afforded Italian or Lithuanian lo-

cals. If ethnic identities provided special opportunities and assured fair consideration in the union, why shouldn't gender? After all, women accounted for half the ACW's total membership.

Many union sisters acknowledged a shared identity based on gender but emphasized instead the principle of equality and the importance of a collective union identity that rested on universal truths and principles. Explained one ACW member,

> A democracy that is capable of successful operation is one in which usefulness and functional significance determine representation. . . . Sex is not a title to distinction outside of the province of sex proper. All women agree that it is wrong that men take advantage of the fact they are men, that they entrench themselves in their positions, that they utilize their strength, that they cling to power they happen to be holding. But may not men also think that women are silly who claim preference for no other good reason except that they are women?

According to this view, it was through education and organization that women would assume their equal place in the union: "they will have to match power with power and prove that they are stronger, before the others will 'yield' power to them." Arguing against a "representation of numbers and not of human beings," the women who advocated this approach to winning equality called for a collective educational effort and thorough mobilization of women members. True industrial democracy could not be achieved merely through recognition based on numbers or special interests, they believed. No one should be entitled to a privileged place in the union or on the shopfloor, but everyone should be entitled to an opportunity to win respect and recognition.[3]

Mixing idealism and power politics, the latter approach more closely conformed to the union's message and mission. Yet it was the more difficult one to follow, for even mobilized women could not always shift the balance of power and not all men conceded the principle of equality. Ultimately, even women who preferred a common union identity that transcended differences in skill, ethnicity, and gender found it necessary to demand reform and representation based on their numbers in the union and their shared identity as women. Separatism soon was seen as the first step toward unity with the men.

"GIRLS CAN'T EXPECT TO MAKE A LOT OF MONEY"

Since the rise of the sweatshops, Baltimore's reformers and labor leaders had complained about poor working conditions and inadequate wages. City boosters eager for new business often billed the city as a "low-wage town," and its men's garment industry certainly lent credibility to the claim. A federal investigation of the industry in 1908 found Baltimore workers earning significantly lower wages than their counterparts in other urban clothing centers. A group of male garment workers in Baltimore averaged but 70 percent of what a comparable group earned in Rochester, New York, for example. Baltimore's women fared even more poorly, averaging but 67 percent of the wages reported by Rochester's women garment workers and only 65 percent of that earned by women in Chicago's clothing shops. In a late-nineteenth-century survey of average wages paid to women, Baltimore ranked twentieth among twenty-two cities, and as late as the 1930s, women workers in Baltimore's men's garment industry earned about 40 percent less than their counterparts in Chicago. Thus, while national averages in the first decades of the twentieth century indicated that women earned just about half what men did in garment factories, the wage disparity between men and women in Baltimore was often even greater. Even disregarding the skilled, exclusively male occupations and comparing wage rates only for comparable work, women received often dramatically lower wages. Women who did sewing by hand on vests, for instance, earned but 40 percent of that earned by men who performed the same sewing. Such disparities persisted even after the union was created and World War I increased the demand for labor. The explanation was simple, one employer informed a factory inspector. Not only were female workers relatively unskilled but, after all, "they're only girls, and girls can't expect to make a lot of money."[4]

Baltimore's garment factories were filled with "working girls" who expected a good deal more than their employers anticipated. They had eagerly left the sweatshops, despite the closeness of the neighborhood and the familiarity of language and custom, to join the rank-and-file of the factories, where work rules and discipline were more pronounced. More than half the workers at Sonneborn's and Greif's were women, and their numbers continued to grow during the war years. Greif, in particular, specifically sought to recruit women, believing that he could deter unionization and reduce his payroll by hiring women, offering them some concessions that hinted at welfare capitalism, and allowing them to be trained for "men's jobs." Looking for employees for one of his new shops, he promised the "coolest workrooms in the city" to women workers; another of his advertisements declared, "Wanted—20 girls at once" to receive "good wages while learning piece-work."[5]

Work in the clothing factories offered an array of experiences for wage-earning women, even though it consumed most of their days and denied them economic independence. Sara Barron recalled the excitement of starting work at the Sonneborn factory, after having worked in the basement of the smaller Wohlmuth firm, where, at age twelve, she pulled threads for ten hours a day. At Wohlmuth's, she recalled, "it was hot, and there wasn't even no payroll. They used to give my [older] sister the money for me too." After the 1914 strike and the creation of the ACW, Barron left Wohlmuth's for Sonneborn's and was delighted by the change—the factory was bigger, cleaner, and more modern. Moreover, at Sonneborn's she no longer had to hide during the occasional visit of the child-labor inspector, which at Wohlmuth's had required her to jump into large bins of clothing scraps until the "danger" had passed. She was still violating the state's child-labor law at Sonneborn's, but she didn't worry about losing her job, since the already overworked inspectors were not likely to bother the city's leading clothier. At her new job she advanced quickly, acquiring other skills and earning additional money, although "it was never much." She moved from thread puller to sewing-machine operator, taking pleasure and pride in her new skills. She also joined the union. That decision brought her still greater and more diverse experiences both on and off the shopfloor.[6]

The shopfloor of the clothing factory presented women an amalgam of contradictions, mixed messages, new opportunities, and traditional limitations. Lower wages and limited jobs for women reinforced traditional notions of female subordination and dependence, yet these same features of women's wage-earning experience also created tiny fissures that afforded at least some measure of independence and provided the grounds for ultimately challenging those inequalities. Such was the experience for a number of women working in the clothing factories who, with the aid of the Amalgamated or, sometimes despite the Amalgamated, attempted to improve their working and living conditions.[7]

As historians have demonstrated, working women turned to leisure activities as an expression of individual independence and to compensate for the numbing drudgery of factory life. They also used the camaraderie on the shopfloor to mediate the worst effects of factory work. Like their counterparts in New York, women garment workers in Baltimore relied on weekend outings, picnics in neighborhood parks, and the occasional purchase of a special dress or hat to relieve the monotony of factory work. For Sara Barron, window-shopping along fashionable Howard Street was a special luxury, although, given her early socialist training, she balanced those outings with clear convictions about class and wealth. Moreover, the reality of persistently low wages also intervened: a 1918 U.S. Department of Labor survey of working women's buying habits found that almost half spent "the barest possible minimum for decent clothing."[8]

Women garment workers were able to construct an environment on the shopfloor that offered friendship and support and often served as a buffer against the intrusions of management, particularly the foreman or forelady. Most of the women working in the city's major factories were young, ranging in age from fourteen to the midtwenties. Before World War I, they were often immigrants; afterwards, according to the census, they were more likely native-born daughters of "foreign or mixed" parents. Often, neighbors or sisters worked in the same factory and spent time together after their long workdays. "If I was ever lonesome," Barron affirmed, "I'd call up some of the girls and we'd go out to dinner together."[9] Although most were young, the small differences in age were still significant. Younger women and teenage girls looked to the older workers for guidance and assistance. They were expected to have more expertise about the ways of the factory and of the world. As Barron remembered, the youngest women showed deference even to those only a few years older, rarely challenging their authority and always relying on them to deal with the foremen or foreladies.[10]

Cooperation with occasional conviviality generally characterized the workrooms where women stitched collars, sewed hems, or made buttonholes. Because they performed detailed tasks and were paid by the piece, however, speed and accuracy counted most in tallying their weekly earnings. The women who worked the fastest sometimes irritated others, and direct competitiveness could flare tempers. Other quarrels sometimes stemmed from ethnic differences, which at the minimum hindered communication. Most women adopted a cooperative, or at least detached, approach to their coworkers, however. They joined together in the face of harassment from bosses, bristled at foremen who used improper language, and often isolated the few workers who returned flirtatious advances from shopfloor bosses. They relished their brief respites from their noisy environment, and lunch breaks were a special time for chatting with friends, away from their workplaces. The tedium of sewing work made snatching a few minutes for playful conversation especially rewarding.[11]

"They were always reminding us that we were just girls," Barron later complained of her bosses. Indeed, the gender issue was pervasive: it helped define work rules and discipline, as well as wages and the division of labor. The evolution of the men's garment industry reflected the unevenness of industrial development: the reduction and redefinition of skills as a result of mechanization, the subdivision of labor, and the availability of women workers; and the seasonal rhythms of the production process. The industry's occupational structure also suggests the arbitrariness of assigning positions on the basis of gender. Even though women and men performed many of the same jobs in the production of men's clothes, it was always for different pay rates. Only the skilled positions at the top of the labor hierarchy—cutters, trimmers, and pressers—remained the nearly exclusive preserve of men. Although women and men shared the occupational terrain of the garment industry, each factory usually still divided jobs along lines of gender. This practice resulted in part from the traditional belief that women needed to be protected from the most arduous features of factory work. It stemmed from other compelling forces as well, including a persistent effort to deny women access to those jobs, which was also inextricably linked to the belief that the preservation of skilled work meant the preservation of male exclusivity.[12]

In the garment trades, the sexual division of labor often depended on tailoring traditions, the types of garments produced, the quality of fabric, and the subdivision of tasks. The use of fine fabrics and the manufacture of higher grade men's suits and the top-grade men's overcoats all usually signaled men's work. Efforts to define feminine versus masculine work on the shopfloor were not always consistent, though, and variations occurred from factory to factory even in the same city. Both men and women operated sewing machines in Rochester, Baltimore, and Chicago; in New York, however, that job belonged almost exclusively to men. In Baltimore, both men and women did edge basting, but in Chicago it was women's work and in New York it was men's work. To be sure, more men than women labored on the finest men's garments in Chicago under the label Hart, Schaffner & Marx or in Rochester at Hickey Freemen's. In contrast, in Baltimore, where the best men's garments were not quite at the level of those made at Hart, Schaffner & Marx but were nonetheless considered of fine quality, more women performed a wider variety of tasks. At Greif's, they even worked as cutters, trimmers, and sleeve setters—all positions occupied exclusively by men at Baltimore's other major clothiers. Thus the effort to define the stages of production along lines of gender defied industrywide generalization, and distinguishing "men's" from "women's" jobs at times required imagination or tortuous explanations.[13]

90   Those inconsistencies along with the periodic relaxation of gender barriers, particularly during the war years, instilled in women workers a respect for the different skills required for jobs and a firm belief that ability, and not gender, should determine who performed those jobs. Moreover, women in the men's garment industry prided themselves on acquiring new skills. Not only did Sara Barron later acknowledge her ambitions to "move up" in the industry, but others recorded at the time their desire to unfold the mysteries of the trade and their exhilaration at taking on new challenges and responsibilities. As employee Sadie Goodman wrote to Dorothy Jacobs in 1925, "Your letter came just at the right moment. I wanted so much to tell some one what a 'skilled operator' I was getting to be, and so now I can tell you. You know I have never worked on a machine before so it is a *great event in my life.*"[14]

Through their eagerness to learn and their successes with new jobs, women garment workers affirmed the importance of work and the primacy of merit. Or so they hoped. In fact, their male bosses, coworkers, and union brothers often resisted those lessons, marginalizing women's accomplishments and relegating them to a subordinate role in the factory and the union hall.

"The equality of the sex in industrial life": Allies among the Middle-Class "Ladies"

Beginning at the turn of the century and continuing through the 1920s, commentators in the press, pulpit, and politics presented new images of women to the American public, which responded with some support and much concern. "The New Woman," as she was called, stood for a variety of things, and the meanings changed over time. At the turn of the century, she was the social reformer cleaning up society's ills, particularly the problems of the cities, in the tradition of domestic feminism and "municipal housekeeping." She also led the fight for women's suffrage in the years before World War I. In the 1920s, she was the "flapper," fearless and flaunting. More than imagery was changing, however, and important trends were underway that permanently altered women's public and private roles in American society. Although excluded from the popular imagery, working-class women, too, held new expectations, as they carved out distinctive roles for themselves.[15] All of the "new women," whether they spent their afternoons toiling at Sonneborn's or sipping tea in Guilford, one of Baltimore's posh neighborhoods, had certain beliefs in common: they firmly supported the twin themes of activism and a larger public role for women and they shared a faith in and respect for the ability of women. These shared sentiments enabled women, on occasion, to transcend the barriers of class and ethnicity and to cooperate on the basis of gender.

Winning the right to vote was one such occasion, and garment workers stood in the forefront of the struggle for suffrage. They cooperated with middle-class women reformers, many of whom had earlier supported wage-earning women in their efforts to win wage increases, better working conditions, and union recognition. Such reformers had targeted the city's sweatshops in their own efforts at "social housekeeping," and they had proven themselves durable allies to women workers, holding mass meetings to publicize their problems, lobbying for legislative reform, and publicly repudiating city police for failing to treat women workers as "ladies." They were a diverse group, some from conservative Democratic families and others from more progressive backgrounds. They belonged to the National Consumers' League (NCL), the Baltimore Women's Suffrage League, and the Women's Trade Union League (WTUL). A few, such as Elisabeth Gilman, daughter of Johns Hopkins University's first president, Daniel Coit Gilman, were Socialists; listed in the city's Blue Book and a member of the "Red Party," she was often dubbed the "socialite and socialist." Others included Elizabeth King Ellicott, Maryland's leading clubwoman, whose commitment to women's reform activism was as firm as her standing in Baltimore's Social Register, and Edith Hooker, a suffragist and the president of the Just Government League, whose wealth and prestige enhanced press coverage of her activities in support of working women and suffrage.[16]

During the lengthy strike against Sonneborn and Schloss Brothers in 1909, "young women strikers," reported the *Baltimore American,* already "stirred up" in favor of woman suffrage, invited Ellicott, president of the Equal Suffrage League, to speak to them at the Labor Lyceum on East Baltimore Street. In her address, Ellicott championed the ballot for offering women garment workers "additional duties and responsibilities as well as improved conditions of protection and proper recognition . . . . Equal pay for equal work is the fair proposition." Eager for such expanded opportunities, the garment workers responded enthusiastically, some promptly joining the Equal Suffrage League, others the Just Government League, and many the newly organized Wage-Earners Suffrage League.[17]

After fifteen-year-old Dorothy Jacobs organized the United Garment Workers (UGW) local of buttonhole makers in 1909, Edith Hooker also sought to engage working women in the suffrage crusade. She invited fifty women from the Sonneborn factory to attend a suffrage lawn party at her country estate, and between entertainment and a luncheon, Hooker and other activists of the Just Government League delivered speeches "to inspire enthusiasm for equal suffrage among working girls of the city." Again, such efforts were scarcely necessary; that same month, one UGW national organizer visited a meeting of the buttonhole makers local and reported that "every girl" was "an earnest advocate" of woman suffrage.[18] After the lawn party, Hooker requested and received an opportunity to speak before the Baltimore Federation of Labor (BFL). Inspired by the immigrant girl's action, Hooker took to the BFL meeting other advocates of labor reform as well as suffragists. Jacobs did not hear her speech that night; the meeting was restricted to men. Still, the BFL under the progressive leadership of Edward Hirsch responded favorably to Hooker's message: "The working women are down because their education is deficient. Give the ballot to women, and working women and children will have the education that is their right." Promising "hearty support" from the "union men," Hirsch publicly linked the BFL to the suffrage movement, although not all its members would offer similar pledges.[19]

The cooperation between women clothing workers and middle-class reformers intensified in the years before World War I. Their joint commitment to public activism and social reform also made them allies in militant action, even cell mates in jail. In the great 1913 strike against Greif's, for example, women garment workers and their suffragist allies formed a picket line to block scabs, an action that landed nine women in jail for "parading without a permit." Included among those arrested, and scandalizing the city's female elite, were an official of the Federated Jewish Charities, a social worker also well known for founding the City Dance Hall, and a local leader of the suffrage movement. All of these women belonged to the Just Government League. Hooker immediately came to their aid and to that of the arrested women clothing workers—including a fourteen-year-old girl—by filing charges against a member of the police force for "conduct unbecoming an officer." The police officer, the complaint read, used rough language and behavior and slurred two young workers who, he said, "look like a couple of Italians and ought to be fed on soup." Visibly disturbed by the incident, Hooker insisted on a public hearing of the case.[20]

Press coverage of the event focused on the "indignation" felt by middle-class women carted off to jail, and indeed the genuinely offended women provided reporters with very good copy and quotations that shook the sensibilities of the readership. One sympathetic reporter from the *Baltimore*

American called the arrests sufficient to "ruffle the composure of any organization." At their court hearings the following day, dressed in attire that,
according to the *Baltimore Sun,* was "in decided contrast to [their] sur-
roundings," these "new women" could barely restrain their "outrage" at
their "rough treatment" by police. One of the arrested suffragists explained
that she had been at Greif's for only a few minutes when an officer grabbed
her arm and "hurried me across the street to the patrol wagon." The *Baltimore Sun* also published a letter to the editor from one of the arrested garment workers. Deriding the conditions at "Greif's 'model plant,'" this "new
woman" vowed that "I am in this fight for health, life and justice in behalf
of the workers, and I intend to stay in the fight until we win."[21]

Although the police officer was exonerated and the strikers failed to win
concessions from Greif, the experience tied women workers and women reformers together in ways obscured by the class-based coverage in the press
and served as a dress rehearsal for the alliance they would forge under the
banner of the Amalgamated after 1914. Their united voice reached new intensity when, only a month after the arrests, the two groups participated together in a massive national suffrage parade preceding President Woodrow
Wilson's inauguration in Washington, D.C. Marching from the Labor
Lyceum in East Baltimore to the city's train depot on Charles Street, about
150 women garment workers, some of them wearing sashes that read "Greif's
Strikers Support Women's Vote," joined a contingent of 350 middle-class suffragists to travel by rail to the nation's capital. In Washington, they walked
with the "Wage Earners" section of the giant parade, behind special working-class floats, one depicting a sweatshop and one "a man and a woman
working together, demonstrating the equality of the sex in industrial life."[22]

Tweaking class distinctions, perhaps, but also consciously attempting to
mute those divisions among women, the women garment workers dressed
fashionably for the march, in what the *Baltimore Sun* termed "nobby cos-
tumes." They were not just "putting on style," but, as one worker explained,
were expressing their support for their middle-class allies. In turn, a few
of the latter, who had earlier been arrested with the strikers, found themselves more comfortable marching with the "Women Wage-Earners for
Suffrage"—a decision that also drew attention from the press.[23] Of course,
divisions still existed, and women who organized to promote class solidarity would find that alliances with middle-class women could be strained and
fitful. Nevertheless, the possibility for joint efforts had been fully demonstrated, and the necessity for them also pointed up.

Persuaded of the value of that cooperation, a number of middle-class

94   women reformers, who had restricted most of their energy to suffrage and good-government causes, turned to developing an active chapter of the WTUL in Baltimore. In New York, the league played a vital role in reaching out and organizing working women. Although it foundered in the face of male-dominated unions and middle-class feminism, it made remarkable strides toward alleviating those divisive forces by identifying the issues that united women. Hoping to duplicate that record in Baltimore, Elizabeth King Ellicott invited Helen Marot, the secretary of New York's WTUL, to help organize a Baltimore league in 1911. The officials of the new organization were a mixture of middle-class reformers and union activists, and women garment workers constituted half of the executive board. Mamie Budwinick of the buttonhole makers local would prove to be especially important on the board. The Baltimore WTUL pledged "to promote the interests of the trade organization of women," but Marot, although impressed with the group's "spirit," worried about its prospects. Privately, she wrote to Margaret Dreier Robins, president of the national WTUL, "I think they are going to have a hard task, perhaps even harder than some of the rest of us have had. I realize from what I heard that the Central Body in Baltimore [the BFL] is not the best." Ellicott was more optimistic, though she too confided to Robins her concerns about "the Federation of Labor men" and "many of their arrogant and ignorant" positions. The fear of conflict with the BFL would soon be realized, but initially the WTUL prevailed on the Federation to provide free rooms in the Labor Lyceum and to offer "all the assistance we are willing to accept." League activists, both women workers and their middle-class "allies," met regularly to plan organizational and suffrage work and also to sponsor teas and other social events to bring their two constituencies together.[24]

Two meetings of the WTUL were particularly important for the city's garment workers. One, the first public meeting of the league, was held at the Labor Lyceum on February 16, 1912, and was addressed by local labor leaders and by Rose Schneiderman of New York, a member of the national executive board of the WTUL and an organizer of the International Ladies' Garment Workers' Union. As "a worker among workers as well as a worker for women workers," reported *Life and Labor,* Schneiderman proved especially effective. Her "call to action [rang] true" and "resulted in many applications for membership to the League."[25]

A second meeting, hosted by Edith Hooker at her home in the fashionable Mount Washington section of Baltimore, combined entertainment and education. About fifty women, most of them garment workers, gathered at

Hooker's estate to dance the tango, eat ice cream, and listen to Agnes Nestor, a labor official of the Glove Workers' Union and the president of Chicago's WTUL. Asked by Hooker to explain the necessity of the league, Nestor roused considerable enthusiasm among her listeners, and she left them with an invitation to act: "I feel confident that with the spirit now prevailing among the women workers of Baltimore[,] this city will soon have a league that will prove a credit to the city." Indeed, the secretary of Baltimore's WTUL rejoiced to national officials that the consequence of having "Miss Nestor as a drawing card" was that "a vast number of persons who were not members signified their intentions of joining the League."[26]

Another organization in which upper- and middle-class women reformers cooperated with Baltimore's garment workers was the NCL. Though initially established by members of the city's Social Register, Baltimore's chapter of the NCL attempted to bridge social classes in its goals and activities. Its first campaign aimed at the rather modest objective of encouraging early Christmas shopping, so that saleswomen would not be so exhausted they could not enjoy their own holidays. Soon, however, NCL members were pressuring local stores and factories to improve working conditions and campaigning for protective legislation for working women and children. Cooperating with local labor activists, the NCL took a leading role in the 1912 agitation for a ten-hour law for working women—a special concern of garment workers—by sponsoring rallies at social clubs, college campuses, and union halls.[27]

On the eve of the founding of the Amalgamated, then, the city's women garment workers had already demonstrated their commitment to the union movement, to a greater public role for women, and to cooperation on the basis of gender. They recognized the importance of the ballot, they fought for the right to strike, and they identified themselves as women workers who wanted recognition and respect at the workplace and in society. They constructed their world with a sharp awareness of class but they also understood their place in the world as women. Given their training as "new women," they identified fully with the rhetoric of the "new unionism."[28]

"THE SPIRIT OF THE BALTIMORE WOMEN RIVALS THAT OF THE MEN": DOROTHY JACOBS BECOMES THE FIRST WOMAN ORGANIZER

The early successes and failures of the Amalgamated convinced many of the union's leading activists of the urgent need for a woman organizer. Since its

96   establishment in 1914, the ACW had welcomed the buttonhole makers local from the UGW, but the other immigrant locals consisted almost entirely of men, and large numbers of female operatives remained untouched by
the union movement. They constituted the majority of the men's garment
workers in the city, and the ACW's plans to discipline the industry and control the market depended on the organization of women workers. Having
been essentially ignored by the UGW and often dismissed by their male
coworkers as young and unskilled, some of these women workers, especially those without either a familial attachment to socialism or a sibling or father in the union, viewed the ACW with caution. Getting them to convert
to the new unionism of the Amalgamated required organizational campaigns that reflected their own special concerns about ethnicity, gender, and
class and about family, independence, and social interaction. Just as the recruitment of immigrant men demanded special efforts, particularly the
preservation and promotion of separate languages and the accommodation
to work habits rooted in old ways, making women loyal members called for
organizational drives led by women. They responded enthusiastically to the
union message when it was delivered by and for women.[29]

Few women as much as Dorothy Jacobs accepted that challenge for the
Amalgamated, and still fewer held the support of the city's women members,
once they had signed their union cards. Her organizational activities in Baltimore illustrate the problems and the possibilities of the role of gender in
the Amalgamated. From organizational drives to educational activities, the
ACW constructed a form of new unionism that recognized and praised the
contributions of women even while it relegated them to a subordinate place
in the union. Naturally, women felt both empowered and frustrated; their
effort to construct a union that benefited all its members remained fitful,
stymied by male opposition and, sometimes, by their own alienation and
disillusionment.[30]

As discussed in Chapter 2, during the 1914 strike against Sonneborn,
when workers rejected scientific management and bolted the UGW in favor
of the Amalgamated, Jacobs took up the cause of the new union as an un-
paid organizer. She visited the homes of immigrant men and women, "talk-
ing union" and urging them to support the ACW. Presuming that conventional wisdom was correct and men more than women would respond to the
call for a new union, Jacobs instead found the men surprisingly "ignorant of
organization," fearful of "what their fellow workers would do and say," and,
even more important, skeptical of organization "because the work had been
commenced by women." Women workers also surprised her; they showed

genuine interest in and support for the union, though they expressed some
uncertainty about their ability to serve as full and effective members.[31]

Her success among women workers in the 1914 strike, along with the
collective achievements of Local #170 of buttonhole makers, provided a new
framework for advancing the cause of unionism. Totally committed to the
ACW's promise to liberate the working class and drawing from their own
campaign to win the vote, Baltimore's women garment workers early determined to have an equal voice in the union. In 1914, for instance, the women
workers of Local #170 drafted a resolution to be presented at the Amalgamated's national founding convention in New York. Two of the 5 women
among the 175 delegates at this first convention were from Baltimore—both
were very young buttonhole makers, who were thrilled to be at the convention and eager for the responsibility they believed it entailed. Introduced by
Jacobs, Local #170's resolution requested that the ACW hire "at least one
woman organizer" for the city, noting the dangers to unionization when "unorganized women" formed a majority of the workers. The resolution constituted an appeal to end degrading work conditions for women and a warning that the presence of an unorganized workforce of women threatened the
goal of industrial democracy. The women of Local #170 signed their resolution, "Yours in the struggle for the organization of the working class."[32]

Although the convention unanimously endorsed the resolution, the
ACW failed to appoint a woman organizer until 1916, and the consequences
of that delay were significant. The ACW's paid organizers who dominated
the early campaigns in Baltimore included Hyman Blumberg, David Wolf,
and Harry Madanick, and within months on the job, all three were clamor-
ing for a woman organizer. Only a woman, they believed, could persuade
"the girls" to join a union, attend meetings, and pay dues. Moreover, given
the number of women working in the Baltimore market, they saw organization as critical, for all the gains made for men would be lost without unionizing the women workers. All three also insisted that Jacobs was the only
woman for the job, praising her in their letters to Sidney Hillman and other union officials and noting her remarkable dedication and spirit. Although
still working as a buttonhole maker, she managed to assist the full-time organizers, continuing to visit homes of workers and holding special meetings
for women.[33]

The consensus among Baltimore's union activists on the need for a
woman organizer found little support among several locals or, at least initially, within the national leadership. Despite the adoption of resolutions
and the repeated appeals of Blumberg, the ACW's general secretary, Joseph

98 Schlossberg, resisted appointing a paid woman organizer. He preferred the union to be financially "more comfortably situated" before making such an appointment. Blumberg countered, "I do not think that the General Office will make any mistake in placing a woman in the field immediately, and even from a financial point of view, it would be a paying proposition in the near future."[34]

The appointment of a woman organizer was also stalled locally by men's resentment at union dues going to pay a "girl organizer." A number of men openly balked not only at having a woman in a position of leadership, but also at hiring a woman to appeal especially to women. At one of the weekly meetings of the local District Council, representatives from the Polish and Lithuanian locals voted against having a woman organizer; the Jewish local, #36, apparently divided on the issue, voted to table the motion, pending further study. When Mamie Santora, heading a committee from Local #170, "appeared" before the council and insisted on debating the proposal for a woman organizer, "the discussion was ruled out of order by the chair." Grumblings about the proposal solidified into strong opposition and filtered up through the ranks, prompting Blumberg to try to reassure Schlossberg that the "fair-minded boys . . . agree that a woman in this city is absolutely necessary." When the ACW strike against Greif in 1916 made the need for a woman organizer painfully clear, Blumberg rebuked the "less progressive element" in the union—the "professed radicals"—who "imagine that it is a terrible crime for a woman to legislate in an organization where 50% of the membership are women."[35]

Only after persistent requests and a sinking realization that the Amalgamated's defeat at Greif's seemed certain did the union appoint Jacobs to the position of temporary and part-time paid organizer for the special purpose of organizing women workers. This belated response to women workers stood in marked contrast to the ACW's prompt response to other organizational challenges. It had swiftly dispatched special organizers to Baltimore to attract Lithuanian, Italian, and Bohemian tailors and operatives, and it had committed additional resources for pamphlets and propaganda to be printed in these languages. Similarly, after steadfastly refusing to use any local funds to support the organization of women, the District Council in 1916 levied a special assessment on all Baltimore union members, twenty-five cents for men and fifteen cents for women, to fund the establishment of an exclusively male cutters' local.[36]

Operating within the confines of inequality and barely muted hostility certainly frustrated Jacobs and her Amalgamated sisters. Beyond colliding with the rhetoric of the union, the opposition from their union brothers contrasted sharply with the emphasis on equality and opportunity that accompanied the suffrage movement and the U.S. entry into World War I. Nevertheless, women garment workers, especially those in Local #170, pushed on tenaciously in the struggle for equality. Jacobs had attended the meeting at Edith Hooker's house to hear Agnes Nestor discuss the WTUL, and she had become an active member in Baltimore's emergent branch of the league. Amalgamated women had such influence in the WTUL, an affiliate of the BFL, that they were able to persuade the league to continue supporting their efforts even as the BFL denounced them as "seceders." They explained to the league's middle-class members that the Amalgamated not only endorsed women's suffrage but, unlike the UGW and the Federation, actively encouraged the unionization of women, offering them an equal voice in the union.[37] Although acutely aware of the symptoms and consequences of inequality, the Amalgamated women only occasionally despaired at the "less progressive element" and, more often, soldiered on to educate women on the value of the union and persuade men of the value of women.[38]

To a great extent, women sought separate organizers and gender-specific organizational efforts not as a means to distinguish themselves from union men, but as mechanisms to ensure that the sexes stood together on equal footing. They embraced the idea of a collective world and wanted a partnership with the men in the union and with other workers in society. Their call for worker solidarity recognized the importance of both male and female workers. They envisioned a union in which sisters and brothers were companions working toward common goals and standing together against common enemies. Unlike the ethnic members, who saw the union more as a loosely federated organization of separate and equal groups, the Amalgamated women saw separatism as a necessary first step toward attaining complete integration into the union. Consequently, early on and in every city that was a major clothing center, women in the ACW championed the appointment of women organizers, the establishment of a separate Women's Department at the national level, and the dedication of part of the *Advance* to a special treatment of issues facing women workers. In many cities ACW women also experimented with or actually established a separate women's local within their district councils.[39]

Separatism, then, included a variety of things, representing a continuum of gender-based activism. Women's organizational efforts at once acknowledged their enhanced independence as wage-earning women and their sharpened class identities as union members. Their course of action was

100 not always easy to follow, and women of the Amalgamated alternately advanced and retreated, sometimes challenging their subordination in the union and other times acceding to unequal treatment. Activism driven by a heightened awareness of gender-based distinctions in a union unwilling to sanction equality presented the possibility for both competition and cooperation.

Direct competition and petty rivalries between men and women occurred both in the union and at the workplace. Even such leaders as Jacobs, who consistently worked to harmonize those differences, had to acknowledge what she termed "the ever present tension between men and women."[40] Moreover, as she and other women leaders painfully learned, merely calling attention to the special needs or even the significant contributions of women risked alienating the union men who saw the workplace and the union as symbols of masculinity and who believed, as historian Alice Kessler-Harris has shown, that wage-earning women challenged men's privileged economic position and the sanctity of the working-class family. Still, the ACW's women leaders in city after city publicized the achievements of the union's women members, and they occasionally could not resist pointing out the differences in the record between union men and women. Writing for the Women's Page of the *Advance,* for example, Jacobs proclaimed that women in Baltimore had taken the lead in educational work and added triumphantly, "The spirit of the Baltimore women workers rivals that of the men."[41]

The most persistent competition occurred over jobs, and it served simultaneously to challenge successfully men's opposition to the organizing of women members and to ensure women's subordination at the workplace and in the union. Even before America's entry into World War I in 1917, worried Amalgamated organizers noted a trend among some employers to hire "girls for men's jobs." Some locals that had initially rejected hiring a woman organizer subsequently and grudgingly endorsed the "organization of the girls" in order to preserve men's higher wages and the distinction between "men's" and "women's" jobs. Reporting on Greif's, which remained beyond the reach of the ACW, Hyman Blumberg gave the General Executive Board "the startling information that women have at last invaded the ranks of the clothing cutters," and the union feared an expansion of that practice. Throughout the war years, the local ACW maintained steady vigilance against such "invasions," warning employers who, in responding to new government contracts, set up shops with "all girls" that men's jobs should be filled by men after the war ended. Employers shrewdly manipulated men's fears about competition from women. During the war years, for example, **101** manufacturers maintained that if male workers did not agree to postponing wage increases they would divert work to their shops that employed only women at lower wages.[42]

What one ACW member termed an "assault" on men's jobs during the war figured locally as one of the chief problems at the workplace. There were, of course, many other problems: the pressure of keeping up with inflation, the creation of "overnight shops" that all the major and medium-sized clothiers attempted to hide from the Amalgamated, and the persistence of ethnic and discipline problems among skilled and semiskilled workers on the shopfloor. Moreover, all employers, even Sonneborn, constantly encroached on contractual agreements with the ACW, and minor arguments and arbitration hearings with management seemed endless. In short, despite unionization, the workplace continued to be contested terrain. But from the perspective of many male union members, the sharp rise in the number of women working in the garment industry particularly signaled grave danger. Both union and nonunion companies in the city responded to the increased demand for military uniforms by hiring new women workers and paying them less than men.[43] Greif became even more outspoken against unionism, boasting of its putative welfare capitalism and advertising for women to work at jobs "once exclusively done by men." "War shops," as they were called, sprang up throughout the city and represented little more than the old-fashioned sweatshops at the turn of the century. According to the ACW, most of the war shops employed "only girls." Once the ACW detected such a war shop, it sent in a woman organizer to "organize the girls" and persuade the company to hire men for the more skilled jobs.[44]

The ACW's efforts to halt what it saw as the degradation of wages and skills produced dramatic increases in its female membership, but it reinforced the distinctions between "men's" and "women's" jobs and perpetuated gender-based wage inequities. That said, the union's arrival at these war shops also usually meant higher wages for their women workers. Union records document wage adjustments as high as 30 percent. New women members were grateful for the increases, and they joined the union eagerly. By 1920, about half of the ACW's membership in Baltimore consisted of women.[45]

The Amalgamated's campaign to organize women as a device to exert greater control over the industry and to maintain discipline on the shopfloor complemented fully the arguments for the unionization of women that the ACW's female leadership had already developed. "Unorganized women," Ja-

102   cobs declared as early as 1915 and many times thereafter, "are a menace to men." She and other women organizers often appealed directly to men's self-interest in order to woo detractors and convert the undecided—all of whom questioned both the propriety and necessity of organizing "girls." But for Jacobs and her union sisters, merely organizing women was not enough: women had to become "active members of the Union."[46] In pressing for greater acceptance of the ACW's new recruits, Jacobs again turned to men's self-interest, explaining, "I know for a fact that the women have been the competitors of men, that they have been breaking down the standards in the industry because they have not been active in the Organization and nothing is done for them." She warned, "The men are the losers by their neglect of the women members. Their wages are cut in half by women's competition."[47]

The two-pronged attack of appealing to men's self-interest and warning of competition did not always bring the desired results. Granting women the right to sign a union card was very different from affording them an equal place in the union. Many men resisted and resented women's effort to claim their rightful place. This contention within the union was more than a competition between the sexes. It was a struggle between two very different definitions of the new unionism and industrial democracy: one that embraced industrial democracy for union sisters and brothers alike and one that restricted the benefits of industrial democracy to union men. The changes wrought by Progressive reforms, the suffrage movement, and the war coalesced into a special historical moment when union women attempted to challenge their subordination and demand a role in the ACW's experiment in industrial democracy. Their effort lasted only a few years, but it left an enduring imprint on the Amalgamated in Baltimore.

"To learn the value of our organization": Educational Outreach by Jacobs and Local #170

In 1916, the same year she became the union's first paid woman organizer (albeit on a part-time basis), Dorothy Jacobs was elected to serve on the ACW's General Executive Board. Barely twenty-two years old, she joined the highest policymaking council in the union, one of seven members and the only woman. In 1917, she became the Amalgamated's first full-time woman organizer and extended her campaign to organize women from Baltimore to the other major clothing cities. Her activism was a model for all women in the ACW as well as critical to their efforts to share power with their union brothers. She offered them legitimacy and a voice at the highest level, and **103** her dedication to women, so visible in all her actions and words, not only drew women to her side but helped unite women with each other. She was, as Sara Barron and Jacob Edelman confirmed, reliable, caring, and extraordinarily effective in an arena traditionally reserved for men. Indeed, Barron fondly recalled her as "the second best speaker in America," saving top honors for Eleanor Roosevelt.[48]

In many ways, moreover, Jacobs's career mirrored the lives of many women who confronted the contradictions posed by the opportunities and limitations they regularly faced in the union and at the workplace. For Jacobs, the ACW's primary goal was to ensure the betterment of the working class. This she regarded as going beyond material improvement to include women as independent wage earners, even while she acknowledged the importance of the working-class family. Yet in 1918, when she married August Bellanca, also a member of the General Executive Board, she resigned her position. She cited health reasons, but her keen sense of her position as a woman in a nontraditional role influenced her decision. She worried that some ACW members would criticize her for accepting a paycheck while married to another member of the board. In addition, she had to reconcile her leadership role in the public sphere with her own views about marriage and the traditional responsibilities as a wife that she wanted to assume. Although she hardly adopted a traditional wifely role, continuing her work on behalf of women and returning in 1924 to head the ACW's Women's Department, her departure from the General Executive Board suggested to many women the kinds of decisions they faced as women and as workers.[49]

Women organizers of the ACW, and Jacobs in particular, also represented models of union loyalty. They sought to make their union sisters similarly committed, early targeting them for special educational activities. They wanted to show union men what they genuinely believed—that women could make equally effective union members—but they also believed that women *should* be a part of the new union movement and that their contributions would strengthen the union for all members. The ACW's brand of unionism was, for them, an almost natural convergence of class and gender, and they expected that, ultimately, members of the Amalgamated would see each other as workers and citizens of industrial democracy, without regard to ethnicity, gender, or skill.[50]

That idealism, often portrayed in romanticized imagery, scarcely conformed to the daily practices and policies of the union, but it energized women of the Amalgamated, who were already imbued with the rhetoric of

104   equality and women's suffrage. Regarded by both men and women leaders as "difficult" to organize and "maintain" as members, rank-and-file women received special attention from women leaders in an effort to create durable bonds to the union, inculcate class consciousness, and ensure their allegiance to the ACW's goal of industrial democracy. Special lectures and courses focused on creating "positive attitudes" toward work and the union. The syllabus for a course titled "Women in the Workshop of the World" explained that the course was designed to "help girls see the place of work in the life of a woman; to help them to recognize the dignity of all labor; and to develop in them a sense of fellowship with all those who work."[51]

Led by members of Local #170, women dominated the ACW's educational activity in Baltimore. They helped arrange successful lecture series (as discussed in Chapter 3) and attended ACW-sponsored classes and addresses. Sara Barron said of her evening classes that "they made me feel more a part of the union" and that she "had big responsibilities" to help advance all working people. Women also extended their educational work to the shopfloor, setting aside weekly meetings for union sisters to talk with their shop chairwomen. Frequent shop meetings were held to ensure union discipline among women members and to offer "lessons" in the "government" of the shop. All this activity, Jacobs affirmed, promoted union loyalty and class consciousness: "in this way, I expect the girls to learn the value of our organization." She was delighted to find, moreover, that "the girls are very enthusiastic about this."[52]

To a greater extent than men, Amalgamated women also combined education and entertainment, continuing the pattern previously established among garment workers and women reformers in the WTUL and the suffrage movement. They held lawn parties, dances, and weekend excursions to make "newcomers [feel] more at home in the organization" and to instruct them in its meaning. Through their social activities, they expressed their commitment to the union and to each other. As one woman organizer acknowledged, "Entertainments are used to arouse interest in the organization" and, as a consequence, "many girls and women have become good workers for the union." Separate women's activities enabled women members to "be more comfortable" when discussing union matters; meeting together as women made them feel "more at home." Women organizers reached out to all members, and not just the women, sponsoring activities that promoted unity throughout the union. They rarely sponsored social events not open to all union members, though the same could not be said of some of the male-dominated or exclusively male locals. They encouraged fre-

quent and open interaction among the locals, believing that participation in **105**
social activities would also help mediate ethnic tensions. Dances were a way
to highlight those ethnic differences and give members a chance to educate
each other about new foods, habits of dress, and folk customs and music.
Women from the buttonhole makers local took the lead in all these activities and earned their local the reputation for having the "most successful
dances," which regularly attracted more members from the other locals than
most other events, even those sponsored by the District Council. "Through
the social organizations of women workers," Jacobs wrote in the *Advance,*
"they have been able to excel the men in educational work."[53]

Women organizers also gently chided their union sisters for not "fight-
[ing] for themselves" in the union and urged them to speak out in their own
interests. The Women's Page of the *Advance* weekly carried such challenges,
which often simultaneously criticized men for devaluing their sisters and
women for allowing it to happen. "There are thousands of women workers
in the clothing industry and in the Amalgamated Clothing Workers of
America," observed Jacobs in 1917, "but we never see them, and never hear
of them. The women remain in the background and the result is that their
interests suffer. When persons do not fight for themselves their interests are
not taken up." Comparing men with women, she declared, "the women put
life into any organization when they become active. They have the fighting
spirit that is often lacking in some of the men." By affirming women's "special character" while also encouraging them to demand their say in the
union, Jacobs presented the difficulty women faced in conforming to both
the traditional image of womanhood, which placed a premium on selfless-
ness and generosity, and the new model of womanhood, which demanded
equality and opportunity.[54]

"A SEPARATE ORGANIZATION OF OUR OWN": EFFORTS AT THE UNION'S NATIONAL AND LOCAL LEVELS

Women continued to operate in the union from that peculiar amalgam of
tradition and aspiration, pushing against some limits while reaffirming others. Their major goal centered on redefining class and the union movement
to include women as workers, cooperating with their union brothers. Although they faced intensive local opposition to their efforts, they obtained
at least verbal support from the national level. Sidney Hillman and the other male members of the General Executive Board agreed with such women
leaders as Dorothy Jacobs and Mamie Santora that young women workers,

106 untaught in the world of work and unaccustomed to the responsibilities of union membership, required special assistance. They were sympathetic to what they saw as the "plight" of the woman worker and believed that the ACW could improve her lot as well as preserve the wage structure for men and women. Their approach was paternalistic, though, and they never fully subscribed to the notion that women members could also do much for the union.[55]

Arguing for a Women's Local during the War

In 1917, most of the women in Baltimore's ACW began agitating for a separate women's local, one that would complement the gender-based activism of Local #170, which consisted almost exclusively of female buttonhole makers (a few of the machine buttonhole makers in the local were men), and would also enable women of diverse skills to join together in a local of their own. Women who belonged to the separate ethnic locals complained that they were marginalized at union meetings, which were held at "inconvenient times"; were never selected to serve on committees; and were unable to persuade their union brothers to assist them in the union. They explained that just as they were ready to cast a ballot for the cause of the working class, they were eager to exercise a greater role in the affairs of the union. Empowered by their participation in the suffrage movement, the WTUL, and the ACW's own educational programs, they argued for a separate voice, pointing to the organization of locals along ethnic lines and to the successful operation of women's locals in other cities. They also reminded their union brothers of their loyalty to the Amalgamated, as demonstrated by their frontline picketing and their nights in jail. Finally, they noted that although they paid less in dues than their male counterparts, they also earned less, and they held primary responsibility for fending off the employers' "attack on wage standards" during the war. The organization of women helped "preserve union standards in the industry." Women, they concluded, were vital to the success of the union and the strength of the industry.[56]

Separate institutions, ACW women affirmed, would enable them to be better union members. Drawing heavily on the class-based teachings of the union, they argued for the opportunity to demonstrate their commitment to working women and men. Jacobs assisted them in their effort to win support for a women's local; she used her positions on the General Executive Board and as the ACW's woman organizer in 1917 to publicize in the *Advance* the Baltimore women's accomplishments. After the first discussion of creating a separate women's local took place in July 1917, Jacobs wrote a lengthy article headlined "Baltimore Women Workers Were Leaders in Building Up Strong Organization There." She asserted, "Baltimore has been very fortunate in having this splendid cooperation of its women in the industry, and for that reason has been able to build a very strong organization." Months later, after women had complained to her that a number of men intended to block their creation of a local, Jacobs introduced the subject into an article otherwise discussing the organization of women in New York. Praising the "active women in the Organization in Baltimore," she declared that the "men [now] realize that they are a great help." Dismissing the opposition she had been warned about, she claimed that the "women's organization in Baltimore is constantly growing and the men realize that they can't do without the women." By November, her support had become more explicit: union women "are anxious to have a Local of their own, and they shall have it," she wrote. She had recently visited Baltimore, she explained, and the ACW women had expressed "enthusiasm" at having "a separate organization of our own." Women workers, she continued, "are in need of a separate organization of their own through which they can conduct campaigns for [the] betterment of their condition," and she vowed to help them create a "permanent organization for women in Baltimore."[57]

In addition to lobbying for a separate organization within the union, Baltimore's ACW women joined with the city's women reformers to call for "equal pay for equal work." As "patriotic union women," they proclaimed, they refused to countenance employers' assaults on wage standards; they also denounced wage inequities between men and women and informed their union brothers and employers alike that the best method for preserving men's wages was to pay women the same amount. Women, they noted, "are competitors of the men as long as they are compelled to work for smaller wages than their brothers." Pointing to their hard-won skills and union cards, they called for a worker solidarity that did not discriminate against women. Preparing to use the ballot as a "weapon" against the "capitalist class," Amalgamated women placed their attempt to create a women's local and their demand for equal pay for equal work in the context of larger reforms for women, explicitly linking their role in the union to women's expanding role in society.[58]

Scarcely deterred by the opposition they encountered, ACW women began in earnest to transform at least part of the union into a place where they could "feel at home." Optimism and idealism guided their efforts. They constructed a separate identity in the union, but one that was animated by the spirit of cooperation and companionship and that only occasionally showed

108 a trace of competitiveness. For example, they altered union pamphlets detailing how a shop chairman ought to operate, marking through the word "man" and replacing it with "lady." They displayed suffrage banners at the meeting room of Local #170. They continued to cooperate with the city's WTUL, attending a series of discussions titled "Suffrage and Its Relation to the Working Woman" at the league's headquarters in the Munsey Building on Calvert Street, strawberry festivals at Edith Hooker's residence, and WTUL rallies and dances. As Sara Barron recalled, Santora and Jacobs were terribly excited about the possibility for Baltimore's ACW women to take the lead in advancing women in the entire union. In 1918, when Jacobs resigned from the General Executive Board after her marriage to August Bellanca, she recommended and the board agreed that Santora, from Local #170, should replace her on the board. Continuing a tradition among Baltimore women of ACW leadership, Santora would also lobby for greater recognition and respect for union sisters.[59]

Momentum for the Women's Local Slows but Activism Grows

Despite Santora's consistent efforts, Dorothy Jacobs Bellanca's resignation in 1918 slowed the momentum for a separate women's local in Baltimore. Although opposition to the local was limited to a few union men, they were vocal and persistent.

Still more important in undermining the Amalgamated women's campaign for their own local was the abrupt change in the economic climate that accompanied the end of World War I in late 1918. The sharp decline in demand for uniforms and other clothing production left many of the city's manufacturers, who had expanded to satisfy government contracts, with too many shops and too many workers. Nearly overnight, thousands of workers, the overwhelming majority of them women, were laid off, and the ACW suffered significant losses in membership. The workforce in Baltimore's clothing industry had reached a peak of twenty-seven thousand workers, but by 1920 fully ten thousand of them had lost their jobs. Nationally, the postwar depression hit the garment industry especially hard, and many of Baltimore's "sky-scraping" factories were unable to survive. Strouse & Brothers, one of the city's five major manufacturers, limped along for a few more years before permanently shutting down its factory in 1922. Not only had clothiers overextended themselves, they had also contributed to the dramatic inflation of the war years, raising prices for clothes in the region by more than 100 percent in two years. By 1920 they were saddled with unsold inventories and overhead costs from their many shops. Even Sonneborn was bulging with unbought goods, and its future seemed questionable. The Maryland State Board of Labor and Statistics attributed the postwar depression in the clothing industry to the public's refusal to "buy at the present prices."[60] Unemployment and persistent inflation, along with major shifts in the city's industrial terrain, now faced the ACW.

Indeed, the postwar economic changes threatened to destroy the industry and the union altogether. Employers scrambled to maintain profits, holding unprecedented sales of clothes from the factory floor, closing most of their contract shops, and reducing sharply the wages of the workers who still held jobs. Violating contractual agreements with the Amalgamated, they engaged in lockouts and sought to erode the union's power significantly. Some employers, moreover, manipulated the public's fears about radicals and immigrants during the postwar "red scare" and helped portray the ACW as a union of "reds." Conservative trade unionists in the BFL also continued their battle against the Amalgamated by denouncing it as an organization of Bolsheviks and socialists. German Americans had already come under attack during the war, and nativist hysteria fueled by the *Baltimore Sun* had resulted in the renaming of German Street, in the loft district where many clothiers were located, to Redwood, after the first Marylander killed in the war.[61] A union associated with immigrants and socialism, as was the ACW, had to defend itself against the scrutiny of the public and the encroachments of city employers. The environment was hardly conducive to creating a new women's local, and the Baltimore women were forced to postpone that objective and head for the front line on picket duty, as the ACW struck frequently between 1919 and 1922, attempting to hold on to its gains.[62]

Although now on the defensive, like their union brothers, Baltimore's ACW women continued to take an active role in the union. Indeed, their activism in the 1920s became renowned in union circles in other cities and often served as a model for women elsewhere. As the *Advance* reported, "The Baltimore women are on the firing line, and enjoy it." In the industry's open-shop campaign of 1921, for example, Local #170 of buttonhole makers, "the famous 'Women's Local,'" spearheaded a plan to help New York garment workers' families survive a lockout. Its members, like those of other locals, had agreed to a voluntary assessment of 10 percent of their wages for the ACW's "Million Dollar Lockout Relief Fund," but they added a second weekly "sacrifice tax" of twenty-five cents per member, donating money that "would otherwise go for candy or movies." Moreover, they canvassed the shops and streets of Baltimore to collect additional funds and began making layettes for "new arrivals in the families of locked-out workers." Finally, they

110   attracted national attention by holding a "Tea and Package Party," with games, raffles, music, and dancing, to benefit what they called the "New Babies Fund." Women who worked, declared the members of Local #170, encountered "special" problems, and "new babies arriving in strike time are a pretty difficult problem" for their union mothers. All these steps furthered the local's "long and honorable record in the history of the Amalgamated."[63]

In the union's national organizing campaign in the following year, Baltimore's ACW women played a similarly prominent role, adopting as their slogan "You can always depend on Baltimore." A Women's Organization Committee chaired by Barron worked steadily to unionize unorganized women garment workers, occasionally, in "bands of two or three," bursting into meetings of American Federation of Labor locals to publicize union plans and appeal for cooperation. When the machinists and other trade unions responded positively to the women's pleas for solidarity, the astonished reporting secretary of Baltimore's Joint Board, David Kohn, exclaimed, "Too much praise cannot be given to the work being done in this city by the Women's Organization Committee."[64]

Baltimore's women activists also spread the gospel of new unionism outside the city. Of course, Jacobs, as the ACW's first woman member of the General Executive Board, and Santora, as her successor, played major national roles. Santora led in agitating for a separate Women's Department in the national body and traveled widely to help organize and encourage separate women's locals and other women's associations, called "activities." Less well known figures also had an impact beyond the city. Sadie Dressner, president of Local #170 and the women's representative at Schloss Brothers, was invited to address the Philadelphia Joint Board on "various women's problems in the organization and activities of women" in Baltimore. Dressner expressed her astonishment that "there was no women's activity in Philadelphia and that there were no women represented at the Joint Board." (Eventually, under Santora's tutelage, Philadelphia's ACW women organized a "women's activity club" and undertook organizational work, educational programs, and social functions.) Dressner also attended the first Bryn Mawr Summer School for Women Workers, an experiment in labor education endorsed by the American Federation of Labor but viewed with some suspicion by ACW radicals. There, amidst ninety women gathered from across the United States, she earned "a reputation for unending discussions of unionism" and left a reporter convinced that her militancy would result in a proliferation of ACW locals in other cities when the other women returned to their homes. The "hotly rebellious" Dressner, the reporter predicted,

would return to her own work in Baltimore promoting "proletarian eman- **111**
cipation."[65]

Another reporter also testified to the reputation of Baltimore's ACW
women. The famous labor journalist and activist Mary Heaton Vorse wrote
that wherever she traveled in labor circles across the country, "someone
would rise up and proclaim: 'Oh, but you ought to know the Baltimore
girls!'" Intrigued, Vorse visited Baltimore and came away impressed not only
by the ACW women's organizational activism, but by the effectiveness of
their inclusive social activities. Through them, she wrote, "the industry was
getting acquainted over again. People from different shops, and girls and
men from different trades, were getting to know one another. And there were
a few people from the outside—girls from the International which is not
strong in Baltimore, girls from the Stenographers, some rare A.F. of L.
men"—in short, "forerunners" of true labor solidarity. The "spirit" of Baltimore's ACW women inspired Vorse, who observed, "They had, as someone
has put it, 'Got unionism under their skins,' and there was 'No Surrender!'
written in their hearts."[66]

One other incident drew attention to Baltimore's ACW women and further illustrated their continuing struggle to achieve equality amid serious obstacles and competing visions of activist reform. In 1922, Amalgamated
women joined Edith Hooker of the Just Government League and the Baltimore chapter of the WTUL to endorse pending state legislation that would
establish equal rights for women. Testifying before a House committee in
Annapolis to dispel the claim that organized labor opposed the measure, they
declared their support for "the bill which proposes to place women on an absolute equality with men."[67] The national WTUL, then working closely
with the NCL, the American Federation of Labor, and other groups to defeat such measures in order to preserve protective legislation for women
workers, was furious and sent Agnes Nestor to Baltimore to investigate.

"I might as well have talked to a wall," Nestor reported of her conversation with Hooker, who insisted that Baltimore's ACW women, "of course,"
favored the equal rights bill, as did most other women workers in the city.
Only "upper class women of means and leisure" opposed the measure,
Hooker declared. At the same time, Rose Schneiderman visited the ACW
headquarters in New York and persuaded Joseph Schlossberg to write the
Baltimore Amalgamated, denouncing the legislation as "dangerous to the
working woman" and insisting that "our organization in Maryland should
oppose it." Regarding the "Baltimore situation" as "hopeless," Nestor urged
the national WTUL to withdraw the charter of its Baltimore affiliate. Re-

1 1 2 fusing to drop their support for the equal rights legislation, the members of the city's WTUL promptly voted to disband, and its former officers then returned to Annapolis as individual citizens to champion the bill before a Senate committee. Joining them, in defiance of Schlossberg's admonition, was a delegation of Baltimore's ACW women headed by Santora.[68] If elsewhere women reformers rejected equal rights measures in favor of protective legislation, out of a decreasing belief that "women could be integrated into the labor movement on an equal basis with men," the Amalgamated women in Baltimore still held to a notion of equal treatment for men and women, because they believed their union brothers had the capacity for social change.[69] Bolstered by the respect and recognition they had won, these ACW women were convinced that their fearlessness on the picket line, their regular displays of loyalty and reliability, and their leadership in educational activities would prompt men to welcome them as their equals.

Creation of a Women's Department at the National Level—and the Price Paid Locally

Pointing to their victory in the suffrage struggle, their patriotism in the war, and their many contributions to the union, women from locals throughout the nation pressed for the creation of a separate Women's Department in the ACW. As Baltimore's Mamie Santora, the lone woman member of the General Executive Board, explained at the ACW's national convention in 1924, such an office would help organize the unorganized women and would allow women "to complain and to ask for things which will benefit not only the women but which will be of benefit to the Organization and to all the workers at large." The convention adopted the resolution, and the General Executive Board asked Dorothy Jacobs Bellanca to serve as director of the department. She accepted the appointment, but only after refusing a salary, again deferring to her husband's paid position in the union and explaining that this was her "contribution" to the ACW.[70]

Much had changed since 1917, when Jacobs Bellanca had last worked for the union; even the women's advocacy for separatism had a different tone now. Although they acknowledged the positive national changes that had occurred for women, in making a case for a national-level Women's Department in the union, they emphasized more the dangers of neglecting women workers. They spoke less of their recent political victory in achieving suffrage than of the need to remedy the problem of unorganized women. Rather than celebrating women's accomplishments, they stressed that even unionized women "have not assumed their share of responsibility, forcing the recognition of the particular problems—economic and psychological—of the women in the trade." A decided shift in emphasis had occurred. Their argument for a Women's Department was no longer only an appeal to men's self-interest but more closely resembled a plaintive plea for help and sympathy. Gone, too, was the trace of competitive spirit with which earlier the women had favorably compared their determination and courage during strikes with men's—a common feature in Jacobs Bellanca's earlier articles and speeches. These changes, of course, reflected larger, social trends, but they were also grounded in the defensiveness of the union movement and the difficulties of the Amalgamated in the 1920s.[71]

One thing that had not changed was the women's belief that separate institutions were the first step toward their fuller integration into the union, and for some men, the prospect was alarming, rather than reassuring, just as it had been in 1917. They reacted harshly to the creation of a separate Women's Department, rejecting its necessity and repudiating its mission. Harry Crystal, a member of Baltimore's Joint Board from Local #36, denounced the department and all women who supported it and called for all locals to boycott its activities. Led by Santora, a number of women members reminded him that it was "our Dorothy" who was heading the department and urged him to adopt a more conciliatory stand. Again they argued that women would be more effective union sisters as a result of the department's work.[72]

Resistance to the department hardened, however, and the gulf widened between the men and women of the Amalgamated. A number of women even refused to participate in an organization campaign in 1924 until they were granted more recognition and respect. Denouncing the men who devalued them, they declined to perform their assigned tasks in an organizing campaign at a clothing factory, explaining that they refused to work with men who regarded them as unequal. Santora confided to Jacobs Bellanca that a "group of men that we have here never think of the good that is done for the organization by the women but for their own selfish interests fight the women to the nail, and I don't know how much the women will do in the organization campaign, as they are very disgusted with the treatment and the doings of the boys."[73] The dispute spilled over to the shopfloor, where shop chairmen ignored the complaints of women members or publicly ridiculed them, demeaning their work and questioning their competence.[74]

Dramatic evidence of the hostility of many male ACW members toward the aspirations of their union sisters appeared in the voting for members of the General Executive Board in 1924. Whereas the women of Local #170 con-

114   tinued their custom of supporting all members of the semiofficial slate with near unanimity, many of Baltimore's other locals refused to vote for the city's own Mamie Santora, then actively pushing for the establishment of a Women's Department. In 1922 she had captured 88 percent of the Baltimore vote, but in 1924 her support plummeted to less than half that, and she owed her reelection to votes from locals in other cities. In Baltimore, only the Italian, Bohemian, and Lithuanian locals (#51, #230, and #218) joined Local #170 in voting for Santora with the same show of strength they displayed for Hyman Blumberg, Baltimore's first ACW leader and favorite son, who had early on joined the General Executive Board. Predominantly Jewish locals often voted strongly against Santora. Local #36, represented by Harry Crystal on Baltimore's Joint Board, gave Santora only 36 of its 489 votes, and Local #15, the cutters' local where men were entrenched as well-paid, skilled workers, gave Santora an even smaller proportion (6 percent) of its votes. Both locals voted unanimously for Blumberg, however. Local #247 failed to cast a single ballot for Santora, although it cast 152 votes for every other member of the winning slate of board members. The opposition to Santora did not reflect ethnic issues, for the locals most hostile to Santora supported the Italian leader August Bellanca by rates ranging from 88 to 100 percent. In fact, it might be more accurate to say that ethnicity may have encouraged some men to vote for Santora despite her gender. Overall, the 1924 union election was another indication of serious opposition to an active organizational role for Baltimore's ACW women.[75]

Resuming the Argument for a Women's Local in 1924: Things Are Different
    As mentioned, in Baltimore and other cities, the decline of the clothing industry during the postwar depression put the ACW on the defensive and, moreover, threatened to bring back the sweatshops run by petty contractors, many of whom had lost their jobs in 1920 and 1921. Baltimore's Joint Board responded to this industrial trend away from large manufacturers to contract shops by focusing its organizational efforts on the latter. The city's clothing economy was changing significantly. It increasingly resembled the industry as it had been at the turn of the century, but now, in the early 1920s it was mostly women who worked in the small shops, while men predominated in all of the large factories, with the exception of Greif's. This structural change helped diminish the role of women in the ACW, for the union increasingly saw the small shops and the women who labored in them as only irritants to the industry. Local #170 attempted to compensate for these changes by promoting the role of women in the other locals as well as its own. It took the

lead in organizing the newly formed sweatshops and worked to counter the problem of runaway shops (shops relocated in rural, nonunion areas), which increasingly affected the city's industry.[76]

In addition, although the city's ACW women were frustrated by their local opponents, they were inspired by the establishment of the Women's Department at the union's national level, and they renewed their campaign for a separate women's local in 1924. The male opposition was stronger and more vocal than in 1917, and the position of women in the union more vulnerable. Nonetheless, a number of union men cheered them on, and members of the Italian local in particular supported their efforts, swearing their allegiance to Mamie Santora. Although aware that the fight for their own local would not be easy, the women determined to push ahead. As Bessie Malac explained, "It is poor policy to fear a group of men who at all times seem to push the women in the corner and bar their way from their rights."[77]

Initially, Dorothy Jacobs Bellanca supported the Baltimore women's initiative, convinced that it complemented the kind of work promoted by the Women's Department. Sensing the level of opposition, however, she also advised caution. Further complicating her position was the resentment she herself encountered when she visited union halls in New York and other cities. Amalgamated men decried the "special attention" given to women workers, rebuked the General Executive Board for wasting their money on activities for women, and denounced what they regarded as displays of favoritism to women members. Jacobs Bellanca continued her work for the Women's Department, but, given her primary commitment to the union and her belief that separate institutions should facilitate unity, she grew more uncertain about gender-divided activities.[78]

Advancing rapidly beyond this cautious policy, Baltimore's ACW women began meeting and canvassing other workers about the need for a women's local. They invited Jacobs Bellanca to speak to their new recruits, and when she counseled against dividing the union, for the first time a few women challenged her advice. *They* were not dividing the union, they maintained, the men were. The women recited the taunts and insults they endured at the workplace, the peremptory refusals of shop chairmen to air their grievances, and the repeated sarcastic references made to the "so-called" women's local. Jacobs Bellanca and Santora applauded their persistent efforts on behalf of women but, as national union officials, still expressed concern about the possible consequences.[79]

Undeterred by the men's hostility and firmly committed to the creation of a local as "absolutely necessary," the ACW women formed a "Women's

116 Activity" in 1925 to demonstrate the contributions a women's local would make to the union and to prepare for a formal adoption of such a local. The opposition intensified, and men shouted down women at union meetings and called them "conspirators" against men and the union. The members most visible in the Women's Activity, including Bessie Malac and Sara Barron, received the harshest criticism. Both were shop chairwomen and found particularly objectionable shop chairmen who refused to carry out their responsibilities for sister members. As Malac complained in a letter to Jacobs Bellanca:

> The "Women's Activity" has been slurred and sneered at, and very very bad remarks, absolutely insulting, have been said to us and about us. But, when a chairman of a department acts contrary to his assigned duties then it is time to act. One of the girls employed by Benesh's firm had some difficulty with her boss, she turned to her chairman for advice and guidance, and he in return told her to go to the "Women's Activity" for advice and leave him alone, besides other remarks that he made to her which are not decent to express even on paper. This girl almost lost her job, she was defenseless and disappointed in the man who was supposed to be her advisor and helper.[80]

Through Santora, Jacobs Bellanca urged women to rise above the snide mockery, to "ignore rumors and accusations," and to "seek cooperation of everybody in the [Baltimore] office." Members of the Women's Activity, Jacobs Bellanca maintained, "can gain more by making a joke of their slurs than by paying attention to them." This advice was difficult for women to follow, for they found fewer and fewer opportunities to be a partner in the union, even a junior partner.[81]

Determined and desperate, the Women's Activity decided in March 1925 to sponsor a union event in the tradition of Local #170. Combining education and entertainment, the scheduled party would, they hoped, assuage tensions and instill "good feelings" about the activity. They would, moreover, donate the money they raised to the Joint Board. Their numbers had been growing—more than five hundred women had attended one of their meetings—and the proposed party would also enable them to show their strength. They found the Joint Board uncooperative, however, and Local #36 objected even to advertising the party, maintaining that the women represented "no official group" and could not sponsor union events. Despite pleas from members of Local #170, other locals refused to sell tickets and Local #36 promised to boycott the event. Yet, the Women's Activity overcame the obstacles, appealing to their union brothers and their own family members to support the event. Proudly displaying banners "beautifully" stitched with the words "Women's Activity of the A.C.W.A.," they attracted a large turnout and had a "happy time." As one member of the Activity exclaimed, "I don't think that there was ever a group of women with so much hope, determination, and anxiety, and strong will power to succeed in this undertaking as we were, and the result is, BRAVO, we have won, we succeeded, we triumphed over our affair."[82]

That enthusiasm was shortlived and marked the high point of the second and last campaign to establish a separate women's local. Mirroring and reinforcing the disintegration of the effort at the local level was the abandonment at the national level of the Women's Department. Believing that the department served to divide men and women, Jacobs Bellanca herself proposed dissolving it, noting that "very often one has to do things against one's self for the benefit of the organization. What I see always is the organization first and the individual second."[83]

Locally, the members of the Women's Activity were less sanguine when told that the Joint Board would never grant them a charter for a separate local. They voted to keep the money from the party for the activity, prompting Jacobs Bellanca to object to their efforts to establish what she regarded as a separate labor organization. Santora, too, opposed continuing separatist activities and agreed that the local Women's Activity and the national-level Women's Department had been too divisive. Both Jacobs Bellanca and Santora urged Baltimore women to bury their differences with union men for the sake of "class solidarity." Some did; others did not. Even Jacobs Bellanca, who had departed from her own principles in hopes of promoting the greater good, never fully recovered from the ACW leadership's abandonment of the department and the vicious criticism she endured from ACW men. Sara Barron, a participant in the Women's Activity, "stayed active with the union," but years later she vividly recalled her disillusionment with her union brothers. Indeed, at the time, Jacobs Bellanca found it necessary to have a "heart-to-heart talk with Sara," whom she regarded as "the strongest exponent of the women's question." Advising her to be a "good soldier" for the union, she declared to Barron that it was "very unbecoming" for her to claim that "she is being persecuted" for supporting women in the union. Other members of the Baltimore activity, no longer optimistic about having a place in the union, also questioned a workers' solidarity that excluded

118 women. "I know it will be sometime," Santora solemnly predicted, "before you can enlist the Women's Activity to take an interest in the organization again."[84]

The rejection of the Women's Department and the Women's Activity signaled a stark repudiation of an equal and fully active role for women in the union. As women attempted collective efforts within the framework of the new unionism and confronted boycotts of their activities, they painfully learned of the absence of working-class unity and witnessed the rejection of their initiatives at self-help and mutual assistance. This was, in part, a new development in the union—one, of course, long in coming but foreshadowed in a number of earlier defeats of women's plans.

Still, the events in 1925 were measurably different from the successes and failures in 1917, when idealism more than realism had ignited the campaign for separate institutions. When, for example, the first women's local of the ACW was founded in 1917 in Rochester, New York, it represented a major victory over welfare capitalism in a city resistant to unionization. Few complaints about separatism were heard. When the women in New York discussed forming their own local, "the boys" wished them well, acknowledging that their meetings were at "inconvenient times" for "the girls." Yet, in 1920, the situation was different. Women continued to speak their mind, pointing out inequalities on the shopfloor and within the union with considerable frequency and with the awareness that gender-based organization can encourage. At the ACW's 1920 biennial convention, for example, women representatives from Chicago demanded equal treatment, one even asking "why rank and file men were appointed General Organizers and women were not. Were women's foreign accents more objectionable than men's?" Such boldness constituted an episode of "rampant feminism," as Ann Blankenhorn, who also attended the conference, later wrote. But, increasingly, male ACW members resisted women's efforts at expanding their role within the union. When Amalgamated women in Chicago attempted to launch their own local in 1920, they met serious opposition—the kind that their sisters in Baltimore would understand fully in 1925. As Sarah Rozner of Chicago declared about her 1920 experience, "Up to that time I was mainly class conscious, but when I saw that [the men] were so ruthless, so indifferent to . . . the women, I thought how can we stand by and ignore it?" In Baltimore, too, as Jacob Edelman recalled, a growing assertiveness among women before and during the war years, when "they got a lot of power in the union," was matched by a growing reluctance among some men to accept

significant changes in the public influence of women. Thus political, eco- **119**
nomic, and social changes in the postwar environment, along with the concerns among union men about women's visibility in the ACW, figured
prominently in making separate institutions more suspect and susceptible
to rejection.[85]

Some scholars have suggested that separatism failed not primarily because of these changes—the decline in the industry, the challenges to the
union, and persistent male opposition—but because ethnic working-class
women, especially Jewish women workers, rejected it. Uncomfortable with
the separate gender-based cultures that characterized middle-class women's
reform, the argument goes, ethnic women tied their activism to the family
and the community and were therefore more "content to follow men's leadership in the unions rather than insist upon female organizations freer from
male control."[86]

Little in the Baltimore experience corresponds to that argument. Jewish women led the separatist movement in the years before the war, worked
closely with the city's leading reformers and educators, and never defined
separatism as a challenge to men or male authority, but only as a vehicle for
women to serve as companions in the union movement. This is not to say
they didn't think companionship rested on equality. Though their activism
in the union was rooted in their families and communities, they were affected by important changes in their social, political, and economic status.
They also took seriously the lessons they learned from the ACW about industrial democracy and industrial citizenship. The ACW's rhetoric of equality and class solidarity along with its educational activities made many of the
union's women highly sensitive to inequity and inequality, providing them
with the basis for challenging their subordination at the workplace and in
the union. As labor's "new women," they held high expectations for the new
unionism.

At the Amalgamated's biennial conventions in 1926 and 1928, women
members from Baltimore as well as Chicago and Rochester continued to
push for another national women's bureau. At the 1928 convention Sidney
Hillman decided to put the issue to rest: "if we were to establish the Women's
Bureau, it would tend to separate our organization into two national offices,
one for women and one for men, one for this group and one for the other
group." The union, he concluded, would make "greater progress if we forget about group divisions."[87]

The role of the women in the ACW would thus remain ambiguous: at

120 best, they could be junior partners; at worst, ignored dues-paying members. Women like Sara Barron reluctantly adopted the former model and stood by their union, carrying out responsible, if subordinate, roles and continuing to organize women in garment factories throughout the city and state. They wanted equal roles; they settled for less. They believed the cause of the union was worth the sacrifice.

5

Recession and Reaction in the 1920s

The Amalgamated and the
Garment Industry in Baltimore

In recognition of Baltimore's expanding place in the industry and the Amalgamated Clothing Workers' (ACW's) triumphs in that city over the United Garment Workers (UGW), the Industrial Workers of the World (IWW), and recalcitrant employers, the ACW held its third biennial national convention there in 1918. A strike was in progress at Schloss Brothers, where divided union loyalties among the cutters still precluded the ACW from achieving a complete victory, but it failed to detract from the celebratory atmosphere that accompanied the convention; the hardest battles, some speculated, had already been won. In his introductory remarks, Hyman Blumberg, himself brutally beaten by UGW members during the violent struggles of 1916, even managed to crack a joke about the disease of "Fergusonitis" that plagued the city, a reference to the antipathy of Baltimore Federation of Labor (BFL) president John Ferguson toward the union. His discussion of the BFL sounded more like banter, free from the alarming phrases he had earlier used to describe the situation in 1916.[1]

Having achieved so much progress in three years, Baltimore's new union could barely contain its enthusiasm. Emboldened by the recent victories and almost cocky about the future, its leaders even invited all "scab agents" to the

122 city and dared opponents to "again attempt an attack on our organization!" "Organizations that have been in existence for twenty-five, thirty, and forty years," exclaimed another Baltimore member, "have not dared to undertake the tasks the Amalgamated has in Baltimore. And we have succeeded." He added triumphantly, "even the spirit of the Amalgamated was first born in Baltimore. The Tailors' Council, you will remember, had its origins in Baltimore."[2]

Granted, as the union entered the second decade of the twentieth century, the "Fergusons" no longer threatened its success—the BFL itself expelled Ferguson for strikebreaking activities in 1920. However, other, more ominous forces loomed. These forces in no time would reconfigure the city's industrial terrain and permanently diminish the Amalgamated's size and effectiveness. In fact, in the 1920s, the ACW barely managed to stay afloat, and the few members who stood with the union looked more to their past glory than toward realizing new promise.

"TO PRESERVE THE INDUSTRY"

At the ACW's next national convention, held in Boston in 1920, enthusiasm remained high, although tempered by a few disconcerting signs for the coming year. The optimism reflected the ACW's continuing successes in Baltimore since the 1918 convention. In 1919, both employment and unionization in Baltimore's clothing industry reached historic peaks. The ACW, moreover, secured a new contract, won even without the customary strike, which gave garment workers a forty-four-hour workweek, a dramatic reduction of ten hours per week since the union's first struggle with the Sonneborn company in 1914. The ACW seemed so successful, in fact, that in December 1919 the *Baltimore Sun* published a lengthy series on the city's labor movement and, in expressing more than a little concern about the bargaining position of the Amalgamated, described the union as a "closely-knit power" in the city's economy. Soon after the formation of the ACW, according to reporter John Owens, its members "began to get what they wanted and to get it quickly." Not only had they won shorter hours and higher wages—"only an incident in the social significance of what the Amalgamated has accomplished"—but they had scored a more important victory: "in shops in which Amalgamated workers are employed the control of the workers is divided between the employers and their agents, and the workers and their agents." The arbitration system, he added, "is really the heart and starting point of a system of joint control between employers and workers."

The union's record in Baltimore, he concluded, was so extraordinary that the "next step" might be the dismantling of "private ownership, as it exists now," for the ACW had already "taken away from the owners all the usual powers of ownership except determination of general policy and profits."[3]

The ACW, of course, viewed its success differently—as introducing "civilized rule in Baltimore." In celebrating that triumph and in expressing their gratitude for the union's leadership, the Baltimore ACW members presented Hyman Blumberg with the complete works of Leo Tolstoy at the 1920 convention.[4] However, a number of ACW members, although publicly rejoicing at their gains, privately voiced concern about the problems involved in moving from a wartime to peacetime economy. Layoffs, inflation, and the potential for open-shop campaigns and "profiteering" among the clothiers all signaled new problems for the union.

Their apprehension proved prescient, for in the next two years national membership in the ACW dropped from 175,000 to 127,000, and in Baltimore membership plummeted from 10,000 to a mere 2,000. Moreover, many of the workers who remained in the union were unable to pay dues regularly. The postwar depression, although short in duration, ravaged the garment industry nationally and permanently transformed Baltimore's clothing economy in Baltimore, reducing its size and altering its structure. In 1920 Baltimore slipped from its prewar ranking of third in the nation in the production of men's clothes to fifth, where it remained throughout the 1920s and 1930s. By 1929, the value of men's clothing production in the city was still about 27 percent less than it had been in 1919. Even more significant, from the perspective of the ACW, the market was no longer dominated by large factories producing medium- and high-priced men's clothes. The postwar collapse forced a major readjustment, and a number of large and midsized companies closed their factories.[5]

The Strouse company was the first important firm to fail. In 1920 it advertised its liquidation sale, opening its factory to the public for bargains in men's suits and overcoats and attracting many customers until the doors finally closed in December. Morale among the fifteen hundred ACW members who lost their jobs at Strouse was low, and the prospects for getting new work slim. With insufficient funds in the Joint Board treasury to provide unemployment assistance, local leaders offered little more than consolation, watching fearfully as other major companies either faltered or attempted to roll back union gains. Sonneborn even closed down for a few weeks during the busy season, already overstocked with unsold inventories, and when it reopened, workers were lucky to get two or three days of work each week.[6]

124   At the national level, Sidney Hillman had attempted to stave off the economic chaos that resulted from the loss of wartime government contracts and the exorbitant price hikes of clothing manufacturers. He organized a conference in Washington, D.C., where the clothiers from the "Big Four" markets—New York, Chicago, Rochester, and Baltimore—and from Boston met to discuss labor and industrial issues with the ACW. Although the conference pointed up the virtues of rationalized industrial and labor policies, as well as the necessity of comanagement between labor and employer, it settled little and the industry remained vulnerable.[7]

Locally, once the bubble burst, companies began to slash wages and hours. The union resisted at a number of shops, resulting in a series of strikes and lockouts in the early 1920s. At Sonneborn's, however, the ACW, with the assistance of Judge Jacob Moses, struck a deal that allowed a speedup on the shopfloor in exchange for maintaining wage levels. Commenting on the union's commitment to an industrially responsible role in the manufacture of men's clothing, Moses praised the ACW for jointly conducting with employers "time studies" of workers to help eliminate inefficiency and standardize operations and productivity. This approach reflected the Amalgamated's determination to exert control in the industry, but it also alienated some workers, who believed it clashed with their own efforts at control of the workplace and who could still recall the 1914 strike against Sonneborn's attempt to apply the same principles of scientific management to the shopfloor.[8]

As industrial conditions continued to decline, Sonneborn soon reopened the wage issue. Scarcely five months after the 1920 agreement, the company requested a flat 25 percent wage reduction. Negotiations under the ACW's contract with Sonneborn resulted in another compromise. Dr. William Leiserson, serving as the impartial chair by the consent of both parties, allowed reductions of 5 to 10 percent for most garment workers, exempting only the cutters, whose wages remained unchanged at $45 a week. Other savings in operating costs would have to come from management, not labor, Leiserson stipulated. A year later, a new agreement reduced wages by another 10 percent. Again, the ACW emphasized its own responsibility for the industry. "The future of the Amalgamated in Baltimore is inseparably bound up with the future of the industry," declared Blumberg. Thus the union aimed to "preserve the industry" by cooperating equitably with employers to achieve the best conditions for all concerned. And on the subject of wages, the union, "cognizant of conditions, has agreed with the employer on wage readjustments that were mutually satisfactory."[9]

Most of Baltimore's clothing companies, however, were not willing to negotiate with their workers or accept such compromises. They preferred to improve their competitive position against the influx of petty entrepreneurs by unilaterally slashing wages without having to worry about union "interference." What they sought, said Blumberg, was "the old order of things wherein the industry during every depression would attempt to cure all their evils by deflating labor."[10]

Other employers also used the fears generated by the war and the red scare to challenge the ACW's legitimacy. Not content to cast doubt on its loyalty to American ways, they charged that it had no role in a system of free enterprise and warned employees that union affiliation would mean unemployment. Newspaper attacks on the ACW confirmed their belief that co-management spelled economic ruin. Indeed, the purpose of the *Baltimore Sun's* series of articles on the city's labor movement was to sound a warning against the ACW as the "most dangerous foe" to the city's tradition of conservative labor unionism.

The series acknowledged the ACW's introduction of the "rule of law" into the workplace, but it suggested that such a development resulted not so much from a desire to cooperate with capital as from a desire to subvert it. The reason, according to *Baltimore Sun* reporter Owens, was simple: the ACW's members were mostly Russian Jews, "not bred in the old American spirit" but in the "class spirit, the 'underdog' class spirit of Eastern Europe," who "talk of 'workers' solidarity'" and who threatened the city's longstanding asset of "loyal American labor." Members of the ACW, Owens continued, were dangerous precisely because "they do not fight merely for this or that advantage; they have a theory, a program, a philosophy. And they have plenty of brains in their leadership . . . because they believe in a proletariat [and] their tendency is to keep their brains within their own ranks, while the tendency in most of the balance of labor is to graduate brains into other stations of life." Fired with zeal to achieve workers' solidarity, the ACW represented the "contagion of radicalism" slowly spreading into the labor movement. Moreover, they were determined to succeed: "it is impossible to gather together that number of Jews without finding a number having strong minds and intense emotions."

Leveling his final charge against the Amalgamated, Owens pointed to the supreme danger: "they are proseltyzers [sic]; they are evangelists of their own brand of labor 'gospel'." They would not be content to limit their union to the clothing industry, for "it is inevitable that members of this organization will widen their field of operation. It is in the nature of the men and they

126   can no more repress it than a musician can repress his love of music, or the born preacher repress his impulse to tell other men how to order their lives." Only constant vigilance could prevent the triumph of labor radicalism.[11]

Doing its part to watch for possible sources of radicalism, the *Baltimore Sun* kept up a steady flow of criticism of the ACW. Union activities once praised now became the focus of scrutiny, and the newspaper even dropped its earlier complaints against John Ferguson, now attributing his ouster from the BFL to "radical" agents in the union movement. The ACW no longer even found support for its educational activities in the pages of the local press. When the union sponsored a lecture series in 1920, the *Baltimore Sun* referred to the "radical" ACW and claimed that the speakers "presented an industrial program fully as radical as ever propounded in Baltimore."[12]

A number of employers also stoked the flames of anti-Semitism and raised the specter of radicalism in efforts to turn back the ACW's gains. Several manufacturers proved especially adept at reviving the ethnic hostilities in the union, even prompting some groups of Bohemian and Lithuanian tailors to bolt the ACW in 1920 and to reject affiliation with any major union in favor of setting up their own ethnically based worker groups to deal with management. Conservative employers also attempted to distinguish between recognizing "respectable" unionism and the ACW's brand, claiming they could not submit to radicals controlling the workplace. Accordingly, workers at many of the city's garment factories heard a familiar refrain throughout the decade of the 1920s: join a union, and the business will either move out of the city or shut down.[13]

The ACW still had a number of allies who refuted such charges and objected to the thinly veiled attacks on East European Jews. Among clothiers, both Siegmund Sonneborn and Eli Strouse stood by the union as an instrument of industrial responsibility and economic stability. Even after shutting down his factory, Strouse continued to speak out against the ACW's critics, dismissing charges that the agreement with the union had forced him to close and adding that without the union, his firm "could not have navigated" during the war. Productivity, he affirmed, had increased as a result of his association with the ACW. Members of the faculty at Johns Hopkins University and Goucher College also supported the Amalgamated, accusing the *Baltimore Sun* of collaborating with employers in an open-shop drive. Broadus Mitchell, a professor of political economy at Hopkins, paid special tribute to the ACW's policy of comanagement, insisting that "the employer has been given the chance to prove the efficiency of his absolute control and he has shown that in time of business depression he is unable to keep the wheels of industry turning." Members of the philanthropic community, too, pointed out the union's significant role in a variety of progressive reforms.[14]

This open support did not persuade other firms, and employers continued the assault on the union, waging open-shop campaigns throughout the city. The proliferation of contract, or what were also called "corporation," shops in the 1920s further complicated the union's effort to control the industry. In 1920, lockouts occurred at a number of shops, and the ACW responded by calling a citywide strike, exempting Sonneborn, Schloss, and a smaller firm. At the outset of the strike, Blumberg explained that it was intended to restore the discipline of the union to the city's garment industry: "The small contract shops are attempting both to bring down wages and establish open shops by making individual propositions to their workers, ignoring the existence of the union. We shall insist that all negotiations be made through the union." Moreover, he continued, the manufacturers were reviving practices familiar to garment workers and their unions and "playing one shop against another in an effort to bring down wages and at the same time force the union out." The strike resulted in clashes between strikers and strikebreakers, landing four ACW members in jail. It also brought new union agreements with a few medium-sized firms, but the struggle was hardly over, and lockouts and strikes continued until the middle of the decade.[15]

"Cut-throat competition"

The persistence of hard times in the Baltimore market along with the general open-shop campaigns in the city and nation imposed special hardships on loyal union members. When strikes occurred in other cities, employers often diverted production to their Baltimore shops or to contractors in Baltimore, thereby offering local workers much-needed employment. Such was the case in a major lockout in New York in 1920, but Baltimore's ACW members remained firm and refused to do "scab work" for New York firms. Resistance, however, occasionally softened after workers experienced months and sometimes years of insufficient work or inadequate wages. Union leaders found it difficult to keep members active and loyal and nearly impossible to detect encroachments against union standards in a city of multiplying small shops, some run by petty contractors, others set up by larger factories attempting to escape union wages or produce inferior goods under different

128 labels. More and more manufacturers were also attempting to survive the downturn by expanding into different, and usually cheaper, lines of clothes, or starting altogether new kinds of businesses such as men's furnishings.[16]

Organization drives in such a chaotic industrial environment meant weeks of work, frequent shop meetings, and repeated visits to homes—an enormous effort sometimes undertaken merely to sign up fifteen or thirty workers in a shop. Small victories were too easily undone, and the durability of the shops themselves hardly inspired confidence. Even medium-sized firms proved vulnerable. Philip Kahn, for example, signed with the union in 1921 but sold his company in 1924. Isaac Hamburger locked out seven hundred workers in 1921 rather than sign an agreement with the ACW, and in March 1922 he liquidated his manufacturing interests to focus on retail sales of men's clothes. As the city's clothing industry steadily eluded the grasp of the union, Blumberg and other ACW leaders intensified their efforts not only to hold on to Baltimore, but to ensure that it did not injure union control in the other cities in the region. So serious was the threat that Sidney Hillman himself led a rally at the city's Folly Theatre in late June 1922 in preparation for a major strike that was to begin in July.[17]

Some twenty-five hundred garment workers turned out for the rally, and Hillman drew cheers and extended applause when he vowed that the ACW would take back its control of the industry in Baltimore. Promising a "fight to the finish" with the city's contract shops and a return to "decent wages and a civilized standard of living," Hillman declared that the postwar depression would not break the will of the national union: "the spirit of the Amalgamated knows no submission. After two bitter years it has lost here and there on the fringes, but it is stronger in numbers and spirit than before."[18]

Samuel Rudow, manager of Baltimore's Joint Board, was equally enthusiastic. Attacking corporation shops that undercut unionized establishments by paying lower wages and working "unlimited hours," Rudow promised an organizational campaign to curb "the evil effects of these shops on the rest of the industry." The immediate goal was to organize the shops and secure a 20 percent wage increase for their workers, bringing their wages more into line with those paid by ACW-affiliated manufacturers. The long-term result would be to "stabilize the industry." Optimistically, Rudow declared that "everything points to a vigorous and successful campaign to put the A.C.W. of A. back in the position of power and influence it has enjoyed in the past." The crowd roared its endorsement of the campaign.[19]

July came, and the ACW called out its members in a major strike. The initial response was heartening for the union, for more than four thousand garment workers joined the picket lines throughout Baltimore, closing down two hundred factories and shops. Manufacturers fought back, aided by the city's police force and the judicial system: strikers were arrested, and judges issued injunctions against the strike.[20] With women workers predominating in the contract shops, Mildred Rankin played an especially active role in planning the strike and mobilizing pickets. Formerly an organizer for the Women's Trade Union League, she was now one of the ACW's general organizers in Baltimore. Joined by Sara Barron, leading "a committee of girls," Rankin worked furiously, appealing to women workers, organizing picket lines, and maintaining morale. Ulisse DeDominicis and J. A. Bekampis, also general organizers, played similar roles for Italian and Lithuanian workers, the latter of whom were particularly bunched in the city's sweatshops. Strikers held daily rallies at Brith Sholom Hall, Dom Polski, and the Lithuanian Hall, where Hyman Blumberg and Mamie Santora of the General Executive Board and Joseph Schlossberg, the national union's general secretary for the national ACW, delivered spirited addresses. "Baltimore," declared Schlossberg, "is being watched by the other cities in the present crisis, and must show them that it can well take care of itself."[21]

Within a few days, the ACW efforts seemed to bring success. Rudow and Rankin signed agreements with a number of shops, calling for increased wages and stabilized rates on piecework, and workers began to return to their jobs. The Baltimore Joint Board, which had also been encouraging the owners of contract shops to meet and organize themselves, scored another victory when one hundred shop owners gathered at the Brith Sholom Hall to express their sympathy for the union's efforts to rid the industry of "cut-throat competition." As one shop owner explained, "The object of the contractors' organization is to standardize prices for the various grades of work. The contractors are tired of cut-throat competition that has made the business unprofitable. Everyone will benefit, the workers as well as the contractors."[22]

Although a number of small and midsized firms signed on with the union, pledging to observe standardized wage scales throughout the city, other shops resisted. This lack of unanimity resulted in an almost immediate erosion of the labor agreement and of union gains. As unionized contractors watched nonunion ones win new production contracts by sweating their workers, the voluntary commitment to rational economic policy faded before the realities of profit and competition. Within a short time, local ACW leaders complained repeatedly about contractors' violating the new agreements. Still more bitterly they noted that even union members, "afraid

130   of being out of work," were guilty of "disloyalty to union standards and conditions" by accepting below-scale wage rates. Given the industry's depressed conditions, moreover, even many of the nonunion shops could not succeed. "In their cut-throat competition," noted one Baltimore reporter, "they have forced prices down so low that many of them are being driven to the wall."[23] The ACW gains for both workers and industrial stability proved largely evanescent.

The strike of 1922 was not without consequence, however. It demonstrated the importance of national-level support, even if nothing more than speech-making visits by the Amalgamated's national officers, including the president. It also suggested that the contract shops, although posing an enormous administrative problem for the union, could be reckoned with. Finally, it pointed up the necessity for the union to do precisely that: to revise its policy of focusing primarily on larger manufacturers and make serious organizational efforts at unionizing the smaller shops. After all, the industrial situation in Baltimore differed from conditions elsewhere only in degree, and every major clothing center suffered from the volatility of contract shops and the reality of sweatshop conditions. More important, every manufacturer had begun to set up "runaway shops" in rural areas to escape the union, and the ACW, while preferring to deal with modern inside shops more characterized by industrially responsible behavior, had to come to terms with the changing industrial environment.[24]

Still, Baltimore's ACW continued to decline, as did wages and conditions in the industry. By early 1923, the deterioration of work conditions forced Judge Jacob Moses, the official arbiter for the industry, to speak out against the return of sweatshops. Demanding an end to the "sweating system [which] is flourishing in Baltimore," Moses called on "state and city officials to enforce the anti-sweatshop laws so that this inhuman and oppressive method of grinding and sweating workers in the clothing industry shall be forever abolished from our midst." The city's clothing industry, he warned, would never regain its economic stature or national market, for it would be permanently blemished by acquiring the "reputation of producing sweat-shop clothing."[25]

The *Advance* reported the Baltimore meeting addressed by Judge Moses, Broadus Mitchell, and others attacking the spread of sweatshops in the city in the same issue in which it ran a story that quoted general secretary Schlossberg as declaring, "One of the great achievements of the Amalgamated is the elimination of the sweatshop from the clothing industry." Baltimore ACW leaders were further anguished when their own careful study of the city's sweatshops revealed that "practically all of the sub-contractors" had at one time been members of the union. "This means," reported an indignant De-Dominicis, "that union members undertake to exploit their fellow workers and to undermine the organization through which there has been secured for them an American standard of life and work and those conditions in the industry which enable them to prevent exploitation."[26]

Further evidence of the unmaking of the union could be found everywhere. References to the Baltimore ACW in the national organization's biennial proceedings took on a nostalgic glow, and members were urged to remember the past glories and struggles of the union. The 1924 proceedings, describing Baltimore as "one of our Great Battlefields," explained that "to those who are acquainted with the history of our Organization, Baltimore always brings memories of heroic battles fought and won by labor's hosts under the banner of the Amalgamated Clothing Workers of America." In 1926, the ACW again celebrated Baltimore by looking backward: "The chapter written in the history of our organization by the Baltimore membership is one of valor and fighting spirit among the members." Its struggles "will always remain vivid in the memory of the membership." Famous for its past— but silent about its future—the ACW in Baltimore became a symbol to the union of its utter dependence on an industry's vitality and the cooperation of its employers.[27]

By 1925, the average dues-paying membership in Baltimore had slipped to just under two thousand. The Joint Board had been unable to balance its books since 1922, going from a surplus in the treasury of $28,836 in 1921 to a deficit the very next year. The Amalgamated's General Office in New York intervened to extend credit to the Joint Board from 1922 through 1925, but thereafter it declined to provide assistance. "There is one burden the General Office is not ready to assume," it explained, "and that is to pay the rent for a local organization and to meet its payroll. Those are matters that the local organizations must themselves meet." The inability of Baltimore's Joint Board to fulfill such minimal functions served as a harsh reminder of its undoing. And as the union neared collapse, it passively accepted the advice of the General Office to meet its expenses by raising union dues—a bitter pill for workers still struggling in a low-wage town. The national office also advised eliminating the "difference in rate of payment between men and women," without acknowledging the substantial wage disparities between union sisters and brothers. Hard work and sacrifice, the national office insisted with unconscious irony, would bring success to Baltimore's ACW.[28]

DIVERGENT PATHS: BALTIMORE AND THE NATIONAL OFFICE
IN THE "PERIOD OF REACTION"

Despite its financial troubles, the Baltimore ACW continued to mount organizational campaigns with each new production season. However, it did so with diminishing effectiveness, only partially obscured by its occasional bursts of activism. Always promising to "insure that the standards in the market are kept up," the local Amalgamated launched campaigns in 1924 and 1925 to "end the evils" practiced by the "smaller houses in the city" and to unionize the mail-order houses, which had increased dramatically in number. By 1925, Baltimore, with about eight thousand garment workers, had more than two hundred shops producing men's clothes, and the smaller shops had eclipsed the large clothiers in the amount of clothing produced. The city's clothing economy had come full circle, with petty entrepreneurs dotting the landscape and denunciations of sweatshops again heard in the press and the pulpit. This condition contrasted sharply with other urban clothing centers which had been similarly dominated by major manufacturers in the prewar period. With twenty-one thousand workers in 1925, Chicago had three hundred shops, and Rochester had more than ten thousand workers with only seventy-seven places of production. Further testimony to the changing shape of Baltimore's clothing industry came in 1925 when Sonneborn announced that its level of indebtedness jeopardized its future, although it vowed to devise new ways to continue production.[29]

Dissension in the union reflected and reinforced the embattled state of the Joint Board. Yet the sense of being under siege could also impose a necessity for unity that transcended many divisions. Union dynamics in the 1920s, then, had a seesaw quality: stormy confrontations with recalcitrant employers produced displays of union solidarity, while conflicts among the union's members often left deep rifts within the ACW.

One major internal conflict was the continuing dispute over women's position in the union. Women tried unsuccessfully for a sharing of power, but Amalgamated men steadfastly refused to sanction an equal role for their union sisters. As discussed in Chapter Four, a few ACW women rejected subordinate roles in the union, even refusing to participate in the organizational campaigns of 1924 and 1925. Other women, like Sara Barron, who (as she later noted) chose to "remain faithful" to the union, accepted their place and participated in the union's activities, understanding the necessity of the sizable hike in their dues and continuing to try to make the union a "home" as well as a house for all workers. Despite being defeated in their attempt to secure their own local, they stood at the front of the picket line in all the major organizational drives. The press and the union minimized their role, usually portraying striking and militant unionism as masculine activities of union men, but the arrest records of the major organizational campaigns demonstrate otherwise—invariably, they show more women than men going to jail for the union. Even though the "spunk" of ACW women did not receive the same respect as the "militance" of union men, the women proved instrumental in keeping the union alive in the 1920s. Although they did not confuse workers' solidarity with workers' equality, they consistently promoted unity among the membership, with less reason than most.[30]

Divisions based on skill and ethnicity also continued to trouble the union. Skilled workers occasionally positioned themselves as the union's aristocrats. The cutters local, for example, despite its status as a relative newcomer to the ACW, distanced itself from the other locals, cooperating, if at all, only with the local of Jewish tailors. Ethnic divisions among the ACW's male members remained paramount, as well. Denouncing the Jewish leadership of the union and its collaboration with employers, a large group of Lithuanian tailors left the union, ending an especially acrimonious struggle but leaving deep scars and an awkward form of cooperation between the remaining Lithuanians and the Jewish members. Many Lithuanians had only reluctantly sided with the ACW in the first place, and the Baltimore Joint Board's inability to maintain union standards in the shops, in combination with its financial problems, inspired little confidence among these tailors. They were further offended when the national organization withdrew the Lithuanian and Bohemian organizers from Baltimore to divert resources to cities that it regarded as having more promise for union success. Without the direct contact to the General Executive Board that the Italian locals had through Mamie Santora and the Jewish locals held through Hyman Blumberg, moreover, these groups felt more isolated and marginal. They made known their resentment, and their loyalty was regularly questioned.[31]

Forces were also at work, however, to help repair these divisions and foster greater cooperation. The emergence, for example, of a number of dedicated Italian and Polish members, enthusiastically willing to work with the loyal Jewish members, served to mediate some of the ethnic conflict. Such local leaders as Ulisse DeDominicis, renowned for his "class-conscious militance," refused to yield to ethnic tensions and rebuked those who did. The social forces of Americanization, immigration restriction, and the Amalgamated's educational programs intended to promote class unity among American workers all also helped to blunt, if not eliminate, the sharp edge

134 of competing ethnic identities. Though bickering continued, and complaints that the Joint Board and the General Executive Board favored Jewish locals persisted, the discontent was at a much reduced level. In the 1922 strike against contract shops, even the Lithuanian tailors who had left the Amalgamated participated, supporting the ACW's efforts to organize the shops though making no commitment to the union. In addition to strikes, social events often drew members together, regardless of their divisions. They all joined in the annual May Day celebrations, supported each other's political and social causes, and attended evening classes together. Emblematic of this unity and mutual assistance was a union celebration to honor the "martyred Matteotti" in 1924. "One of the largest meetings ever held" by the ACW, it was cosponsored by the Italian Local #51 and the Jewish Local #36 and held at the Brith Sholom Hall. Amalgamated women decorated the hall with flowers, receiving much praise for their efforts and pointing up the nature of class unity in the ACW. This festival at once represented cooperation among members and reinforced the subordinate place of women. The Baltimore ACW, Hyman Blumberg said proudly, is "100 percent" committed to the union.[32]

Waging war against a multiplying enemy, and waging it without sufficient funds, nearly exhausted even the loyal cadre of ACW members. Every new clothing season meant a new round of skirmishes, uncovering the location of new corporation shops, targeting others for organization drives, and resisting encroachments among employers renegotiating their labor contracts. The Joint Board's contractual negotiations with Sonneborn, the union's corporate mainstay, reflected the seesaw dynamics that characterized the ACW in the 1920s. Negotiations were always "carried on in a spirit of cooperation and good will," but they were always long and difficult. Still recovering from the postwar recession, Sonneborn fought tenaciously against any new concession, even as the company introduced new clothing styles—and work requirements—to stay competitive. The introduction of a new design offered both sides the opportunity to win new concessions, and both sides always negotiated tenaciously. Extending the length of collars might result, for example, in higher piece rates, but no employer, not even Sonneborn or Schloss, acquiesced easily on those matters. In 1925, Sonneborn introduced a new style of sports coat, with "lots of vents to stitch," prompting negotiations for three weeks and ultimately requiring the intervention of Judge Moses. Joint Board members complained of the time involved in such lengthy negotiations, and frequently called on Blumberg to help them out.[33]

Several local ACW leaders openly despaired of their general predicament in Baltimore. The victories were too small and too hard won and the setbacks all too frequent. The union's role in guiding the industry was barely perceptible. They suffered, they believed, from having too few union activists and felt hard-pressed even to balance the books. They drew strength from their own past achievements, but they frequently lamented the "current state of the union," expressing bewilderment at how to establish control of the industry. Organizers complained that they were unable to locate many of the small shops and, when they did, were uncertain how to negotiate with employers who were producing a variety of products—many of which they knew nothing about. They queried the national office about the appropriate rates for cotton suits and found particularly perplexing those shops that produced men's accessories as well as trousers, depending on the season. Working hard to preserve union gains, but uncertain and stymied, they remained helpless to halt the changes in the industry.[34]

Inevitably, as the ACW lost influence in Baltimore, the beleaguered and impoverished Joint Board gradually cut back its activities. Fewer organizers were employed, and fewer campaigns were launched. In 1927 the board went so far as to eliminate a business agent, a crucial local official. Anton Pasek, of the Bohemian Local #230 and a founding member of the ACW, "volunteered to withdraw from office in order to help the Organization," and his duties were divided among the remaining staff. The position of manager of the Joint Board saw rapid turnover, leading to further disorganization. When the *Advance* ran a story summarizing the activities of the ACW for the "relatively non-spectacular year" of 1926, it found nothing to report from Baltimore. The newspaper printed accounts of the union in nine cities and then listed by name "smaller cities" such as Indianapolis and Louisville, for which space did not permit coverage. Baltimore, one of the great founders of the ACW, went unmentioned.[35]

When Harry Crystal became manager of the Joint Board and promised Schlossberg that in 1927 the Baltimore organization would be "again up and doing," the *Advance* regarded the announcement as "one of the most welcome reports in many a day." And, indeed, a brief flurry of union activity followed. The Baltimore Joint Board launched a successful strike to prevent one manufacturer from reducing wages; blocked another clothier from establishing a runaway shop; and, working with Jacob Edelman of Local #15 of cutters, achieved some success in still another attempt to organize the small mail-order shops. These limited gains proved no more permanent than those produced by the decade's earlier campaigns, however, and ACW ef-

136 forts in Baltimore soon subsided again. Dissension within the board required the firm intervening hand of Blumberg, and Philip Rudich replaced Crystal as manager in a special election.[36]

It made little difference. The *Advance* could report virtually nothing from the city for the second half of the year, and the dismal pattern continued. In 1928, despite considerable police intimidation, Edelman led a strike against S. Ginsberg & Sons and successfully unionized the company's cutters. This one small triumph was accompanied only by a haphazard and ineffectual organizing drive among the city's Lithuanian garment workers and thus gave neither the Baltimore Joint Board nor the *Advance* cause for optimism.[37]

Ineffective and vulnerable, the ACW in Baltimore needed help from the national union to regain control of the city's clothing industry. At every ACW national convention in the 1920s, delegates from Baltimore locals introduced resolutions requesting aid from the national union. Pointing out that "the Baltimore market was more severely hit by the industrial depression following 1921 than other union markets," local delegates asked the national organization to relieve the "deplorable" conditions by sending "to Baltimore organizers to try and organize our market one hundred percent." Beginning in 1922 and continuing throughout the decade, the Baltimore ACW made its appeals for a major, nationally led organization campaign for the city. By 1928, the request was stark and candid, publicly acknowledging the weakness of the Baltimore union and asking for assistance "financially, morally and otherwise." At the same convention, Baltimore's ACW also urged the General Office to "appoint more Lithuanians [to] the organization," explaining that the "Lithuanian district in Baltimore is neglected because there is not a permanent business agent to take care of our members there." Such pleas, accompanied by passionate reminders that the city was the location of the union's founding struggles, regularly resulted in the unanimous passage of the Baltimore ACW's resolutions. Despite such support, the promised aid was rarely forthcoming. Baltimore seemed so unpromising and the General Executive Board had its own concerns.[38]

Nationally, too, the union experienced dislocations in the 1920s. To be sure, the ethnic and ideological wars in the ACW were not as severe as in other unions, but still the pages of the *Advance* were filled with charges and countercharges, as more radical members openly questioned the directions of the new unionism. Just as the Baltimore ACW's cooperation with Sonneborn to speed up the work pace, standardize production, and increase efficiency had alienated a number of workers, similar agreements in other cities produced fiery displays of opposition. The grievances seemed endless, from **137** the distribution mechanism for unemployment funds to cooperation with employers to new forms of discipline on the shopfloor. These issues were also accompanied by laments from some that the union had replaced its old socialist leanings with new principles of labor-management cooperation. Critics from New York and Chicago were especially vocal in the *Advance*. Helen Kaplan of Local #39 in Chicago, for example, decried the ACW's policies of "class collaboration." Its efforts at economic "readjustment," she declared, amounted to surrender to employers. Such charges against the union echoed throughout the membership.[39]

In large part, the battle was waged along ideological lines, with socialists and communists fighting each other for the loyalty of the rank-and-file. Sidney Hillman had earlier bridged that divide by welcoming the support of the communists; now he called on the socialists for assistance. Responding to the "factionalism" within the union, Hillman warned that splinter groups enabled employers to erode the power of the union. In January 1925, under the headline "Hold Our Banner High!" Hillman urged all members to "jealously guard our great and only weapon, solidarity."

> The only danger that confronts our organization is the danger from within. Dissension is to the life of an economic labor organization what cancer is to the individual. It saps the very life; it weakens and ultimately kills . . . . The Amalgamated must remain a united army of men and women ready to maintain and hold what we have and to march forward on the road to greater achievements.[40]

By the end of the 1920s, much of the unrest had subsided, the union having purged what it saw as the most intransigent sources of discontent.[41] Challenged from within and without, the Amalgamated emerged from the decade stronger in certain markets; much weaker in others; and slightly reconfigured, having been tested by its own rank-and-file. When ideological factions in other unions in the needle trades battled destructively in the 1920s, Sidney Hillman refused to make socialism and communism "irreconcilable enemies," and the Amalgamated remained, as one historian has noted, "essentially unscathed."[42]

Baltimore's ACW had not been part of the internal turmoil at the national level, although a few of its members also questioned the "managerial style" of the union. In the Baltimore ACW, the ideological lines were less distinct and the role of communist activists never significant. The union, strug-

138   gling simply to survive, felt removed from these ideological battles. Its now
anemic Joint Board barely limped along, hardly prepared for the coming tri-
als of the Great Depression.

Likewise, many of the policies and programs of the national office appeared remote to the Baltimore Joint Board. Baltimore members could only
read about the accomplishments of industrial democracy in action. They
didn't even have agreements with two of the three major companies in the
city, much less union banks, unemployment insurance funds, or experiments in housing. Indeed, an editorial in the *Advance* that urged members
to use the Amalgamated's banks in Chicago and New York invoked the situation of Baltimore's members as justification: "The great need for labor
banks was brought home to thousands of Baltimore workers, many of them
members of the Amalgamated Clothing Workers of America, several days
ago, when the old and well established banking house operating under the
name of Bernstein, Cohen, & Co., closed its doors, and it became known
that it is insolvent."[43]

Had Baltimore not been among the "Big Four" garment centers before
and during World War I, had it not experienced a golden era in the ACW,
the Amalgamated's decline there in the 1920s might not have seemed so dramatic and the policies of the national office so alien. The more Hillman and
others talked about union control in the industry, the more Baltimore's industry resisted—indeed defied—that control. As far back as 1923, Hillman
had declared, "We help the employers for one excellent reason. The clothing workers must make their living out of the clothing industry—just as
their employers. Until now labor has fought mainly from a sense of outrage
against exploitation. Henceforth, it will fight more and more from a sense
of industrial and social responsibility."[44] That was the same year that Baltimore's ACW launched an indignant campaign, aided by Judge Moses, aimed
at eliminating sweatshops and restoring minimal standards of decency in the
industry. The 1928 report of the General Executive Board further underscored the divergent paths of the local and national organizations:

> Vague terms, like union control, have under our arrangements, with
> many manufacturers, been translated into stern reality. Already
> many of the functions of supervision and management have, in
> spots, been taken over by the union. The savings that have been ef-
> fected by this procedure have gone to raise the standards and in-
> come of our members and to increase the business of unionized
> firms. At the same time, to a large extent as a result of these meth-

ods, the union has become more indispensable to the industry than **139** it has ever been.[45]

"Stern reality" was far different for Baltimore, where the ACW was marginal both to the industry and to the large majority of clothing workers. The garment industry itself no longer held the place it once had in the city's economy, and an ever greater proportion of its production came from small contract shops beyond the effective reach of the union. Before what local ACW leaders called "the period of reaction" set in after 1921, nearly three-fourths of men's clothes produced in the city had been manufactured in large factories, often under ACW control; now in an extraordinary reversal, most were made in small shops. Moreover, many of the surviving large firms were nonunionized and some, such as the Greif company and J. Schoeneman, Inc., were extremely hostile to any union activity.[46]

The fate of the Sonneborn company best illustrated the apparent failure of the ACW's experiment in comanagement and shared control of the industry in Baltimore. Hard-pressed by the changing conditions in the economy and the industry and plagued by internal familial leadership problems, Sonneborn tottered on the edge of failure throughout the second half of the 1920s. At Hyman Blumberg's insistence, the Amalgamated itself came to the company's rescue, first providing a union loan of $125,000 in 1927 and then extending another loan in 1930 as the Great Depression began to worsen Sonneborn's prospects still further. In 1930, the union also brought in a veteran manager from Hart, Schaffner & Marx in Chicago to run the Baltimore firm. Local union leaders predicted that "we are going to make it," but the company closed for good in 1931, and five hundred workers—all ACW members—lost their jobs. In its commitment to comanagement, the Amalgamated had once again transcended traditional labor union roles, but it had fallen short of success.[47]

The ACW in Baltimore was close to collapse. With almost palpable resignation, the Joint Board manager reported to the General Executive Board in 1930 that "we are not doing much organization work at present because of the depression." By 1932 the Joint Board did not have even one thousand dues-paying members. After a decade of hard times for the union in the city, the Great Depression threatened to be the fatal blow to the organization. Less than 10 percent of the industry was organized. Having attempted to defy the city's reputation as a "non-union town," the ACW now fell in line with Baltimore's other unions, beleaguered in spirit and microscopic in size.[48]

6

Remaking the Union

Workers and Clothiers in the Great Depression

News of the Great Crash in 1929 barely disturbed the clothing industry, already in decline in Baltimore and facing a "structural crisis" nation-wide.[1] The search for quick profits in an unstable industry propelled by fashion cycles and sensitive consumer demand, had brought the return of contract shops and sweatshop conditions. The Baltimore Amalgamated Clothing Workers' (ACW's) plans to rationalize the men's garment trade had foundered in a sea of economic contradictions and contractions. At the start of the Great Depression, the union was at rock bottom. The electricity at union headquarters had been turned off, and Jacob Edelman donated the money to pay the ACW's rent. Once a center of education and a vision of industrial democracy, the union hall now housed the local ACW leadership and a few loyal members who gathered together by candlelight for their monthly meetings. With the coming of the Great Depression, then, neither the industry nor the union possessed its earlier vitality—but both were preparing new plans to reclaim their past success and reverse a decade of decline.[2]

"Baltimore is a potential danger and the danger
must be checked"

Baltimore's industrial sector initially escaped the worst effects of the Great Depression. Unlike the depression that followed World War I, which had delivered quick devastation to the garment business, the Great Depression did not make its presence felt in Baltimore's industry until 1932. Although production nonetheless declined, unemployment rose, and already meager wages dropped still further, Baltimore at first fared somewhat better than other major urban clothing centers. The primary reason for Baltimore's comparative resistance was its "low cost of the product" and consequent ability to attract business from other cities. Although the total value of manufacturing did not plummet, the number of employed workers dropped sizably, which meant that fewer workers labored longer hours for less pay. Almost 45 percent of the city's garment workers earned less—sometimes much less— than twenty-five cents per hour, and the small shops resembled little more than primitive workrooms run by increasingly desperate contractors. Of the nation's ten leading cities in the production of men's clothes, Baltimore, which still ranked fifth in volume, had the lowest average capital investment and paid the lowest wages. Workers in the larger factories worked more regularly and at higher wages than those in the contract shops, enjoying a 26 percent differential in weekly wages and, on average, an additional four-and-a-half weeks of work each year. Still, those factories—the Greif company and J. Schoeneman, Inc.—were unorganized and, given the antiunion sentiments of the owners, likely to remain so. All in all, overloaded with the most unstable features, Baltimore's garment industry offered little hope for the union.[3]

Indeed, from the perspective of the national ACW, the Baltimore clothing market had become an irritant to the industry and a threat to the union itself. Baltimore's many small and unorganized shops began to undermine union control in other cities, finally prompting the ACW to pay the city the attention that the Baltimore Joint Board had so long sought. At the 1930 national convention, an ACW organizer emphasized the possible dangers an unorganized market posed for the unionized centers and called on the Amalgamated to begin organization work at once, "so that Baltimore will be put back into the position of strength it occupied from 1916 to 1920." In the private meetings of the General Executive Board, Hyman Blumberg also predicted that Baltimore could become "a real danger point," threatening especially the union's agreements with shops in New York. "Baltimore,"

142   Blumberg solemnly concluded, "is a potential danger and the danger must be checked."[4]

As other major clothing centers collapsed under the weight of economic depression, Baltimore's relative ability to withstand the decline merely emphasized its menacing role. In 1934, for example, the total value of men's clothes produced in Rochester, New York, reached but 28 percent of its 1929 level, and in Chicago it reached only 30 percent, compared to 53 percent in Baltimore. The concern about Baltimore took on urgency as New York firms began in 1931 to divert piecework to Baltimore's contract shops. Greif, J. Schoeneman, Sportswear, Inc., and other companies had factories in both cities and also began to shift more production to Baltimore. It cost firms about five cents per garment to ship roundtrip to Baltimore, and the low wages there made it profitable. Industry estimates placed labor costs at about one-third of the cost of the garment, and with the lowest wages of any clothing center, Baltimore promised a higher return. These arrangements threatened to undermine the Amalgamated's already sporadic hold on New York—known also as a "hotbed of anti-unionism"—and the situation demanded immediate attention.[5]

Sidney Hillman, alert as always to the intricacies and interdependencies of the clothing industry, recognized the danger. National membership in the ACW had fallen sharply to only 109,000 in 1931, and as early as 1930 he had privately conceded that the union was "not on a sound basis financially." Action was necessary. "The Baltimore market," he determined, "should be given real attention."[6]

Calling Baltimore a "menace" to the clothing market, Blumberg proposed "two ways" to "remedy" the problem: "one is to call a general strike, the other is to work on the contractors." The second proposal hardly seemed attractive, for it ran counter to the union's preference for dealing with larger firms and meant taking on all the administrative problems associated with dealing with small contract shops. The first proposal also had drawbacks, however. "There is," Blumberg recognized, "a great deal of bitterness among the members. They have all lost their jobs. The 500 Sonneborn people blame the union [and others also] are against us." Still, he preferred a general strike, for he saw a few hopeful signs—members "who are willing to work with the organization" —and he singled out the ACW women for special praise. Sara Barron, he affirmed, "organized 50 women who are doing a great deal of work and hardly get carfare for it." Predicting a good response in the larger contract shops, Blumberg advised exempting from the strike the union's arch enemy, J. Schoeneman, Inc., but still warned that "there is no telling what **143** we are stepping into. I will need a lot of help. I would like our people from various markets to be present."[7]

The proposed 1932 strike represented the Amalgamated's return to the city, and it gave the few remaining members in Baltimore fresh hope that the union would be rebuilt. The situation had changed considerably, however, since the ACW's founding strike in Baltimore in 1914. Now the ACW was on the defensive, repudiated by former members, who were jobless and without unemployment assistance. Many members, Barron later recalled, believed that the union had "neglected them" and remained suspicious of the new signs of interest.[8] Not only had Baltimore lost its place among the "Big Four" garment centers, but the local union had witnessed a decline in its position within the Amalgamated. A major strike was to be called not because the city represented an important opportunity for the union, but because it constituted an irritant to the organized industry. But compassion and pity for the predicament of Baltimore's workers also motivated some ACW leaders: "Sonneborn went out of business and the entire [union] activity in Baltimore is out of work. They are starving and want help. We ought to take care of our members in Baltimore the best way we can. They have been loyal to the organization and deserve help. The [General Executive] Board ought to find a way to organize the unorganized."[9]

In midsummer, Blumberg quietly moved into Baltimore to undertake preparations for the strike. With Ulisse DeDominicis to appeal to Italians and Frank Bartoss for the Polish workers, Blumberg met daily with groups of garment makers in the city's many shops to counter the "defeatist spirit" he found. Because of the predominance of women workers, however, Blumberg depended even more on the efforts of Mamie Santora and the "Activity Group" of fifty women that Barron had organized. Jacob Potofsky, the business manager of the *Advance,* left New York to aid in "the rebirth of the Baltimore organization" and now met Barron for the first time. She was, he said, "a bold, daring, and untiring worker whose spirit is contagious, who is virtually a dynamo." Led by Barron, Marie Catalana, and Catherine Moylan, the women's committee met regularly during the summer of 1932 to lay plans and contact workers. The strike was not the sudden flareup it appeared to be, Charles Ervin, an ACW official in Washington, D.C., later reported: "it was the result of patient, tireless work on the part of the members of this large committee of women clothing workers."[10]

"THE STORM CENTER OF THE STRIKE"

After eight weeks of preparation, Blumberg called a rally at the Fourth Regiment Armory on September 12 and invited Sidney Hillman, Dorothy Jacobs Bellanca, and other national leaders as well. Four thousand workers packed the building; hundreds more gathered outside. The crowd endorsed their beloved Hyman Blumberg's call for a general strike, and Hillman pledged national support. The following day, five thousand workers walked off their jobs at more than two hundred shops and factories, protesting their low wages and long hours and demanding recognition of the union. The strike was at once a bold and desperate move on the part of the Amalgamated, and the size of the turnout surprised even veteran union organizers. Workers from Greif's and Schoeneman's joined the ranks of the strikers, even though they had not been among those targeted for organizational work. The strike brought clearly into public view the plight of workers, most of them young women, in the "rag trade," which now in the 1930s recalled the sweatshop conditions that had outraged turn-of-the-century reformers. Three decades of social progress and economic modernization, lamented professor Jacob Hollander of Johns Hopkins University, had been unable to reach those most in need or to eliminate the sweatshop.[11]

The outside assistance Hillman had promised proved valuable. The Chicago ACW, eager to organize "Baltimore, so long a great sore spot," sent funds and union negotiators; ACW workers in New Jersey assessed themselves to support the strike, convinced that their "own economic conditions cannot be improved and safeguarded as long as there remain wide areas of open shop activity." Amalgamated cutters in New York City threatened to strike Cohen, Goldman & Company unless the firm accepted a union contract at its Baltimore subsidiary, Consolidated Tailors, Inc., whose huge plant was picketed by one thousand strikers.[12]

The major force in the strike was Baltimore's own workers, though, especially the "sister comrades" organized by Barron and now spurred on by Jacobs Bellanca's remarkable oratorical powers. "Going from hall to hall on the morning of the general strike," reported Ervin, "Dorothy Bellanca aroused the women strikers as probably a man could not have done." Some groups, led by Catalana and by Concetta Esposito, spread out in the ethnic neighborhoods of East Baltimore to contact workers at home and, if necessary, "argue with the entire family" to gain support for the strike. Barron took the lead in the more direct approach, throwing up picket lines around the

shops and factories, and soon focusing attention on the Industrial Building   **145**
on East Preston Street.[13]

Here, in what the *Advance* called "the storm center of the strike," were
located the "most notorious" workrooms in the city, the coat and vest shops
of J. Schoeneman, Inc. The striking women formed huge picket lines around
the building, clashing frequently with police attempting to restrict picketing. They taunted police as "cowards" and accused them of being "in the pay"
of the employer. Barron later proudly recalled, "We [women] were really the
ones who had something to do with mass picketing" in Baltimore. Charged
with "disorderly conduct," they were hauled off to jail, where they invoked
the legal assistance of Jacob Edelman, no longer a cutter at Sonneborn but a
labor lawyer. "I was locked up thirteen times," Barron remembered, and
Edelman, who had often been summoned in the middle of the night to secure her release, confirmed the number. Other women joined her, most not
as intrepid as she in the face of police, jail, and courtrooms and some of them
barely in their teens. Hundreds of women were taken away to jail; others simply moved into the line to fill their places. The *Baltimore Sun* took notice of
the "army" of women strikers bringing "terror to the people of Baltimore
City" and was able to reconcile traditional notions of domesticity with the
jarring spectacle of openly militant women only by questioning whether "we
have all unawares brought forth a race of Amazons in Baltimore." By making the women strikers more masculine, the newspaper was able to acknowledge their role in union activism.[14]

A Citizens' Committee organized under the leadership of Rabbi Edward
Israel, however, saw in the strike signs of desperation and struggle. Even
while calling the strike a "civic nuisance," they blasted the state government
for not enforcing sanitation and labor laws and demanded that the strikers
receive a fair hearing from the mayor. Schoeneman himself attempted to reduce the dimensions of the "spectacle" by securing a court injunction limiting the number of pickets. The action backfired when the strikers increased
their ranks, and arrests soared. Eventually, the state commissioner of labor
and statistics reluctantly investigated the garment industry and reported
such bleak conditions that the *Baltimore Post* headlined its account "Working and Starving." Still more shocking revelations emerged after the mayor
appointed a committee chaired by professor Hollander to investigate the
strike. An erstwhile Progressive who counted Judge Jacob Moses among his
close friends, Hollander was very familiar with earlier campaigns against
sweatshops and a strong advocate of "enlightened labor-management rela-

146   tions." Schoeneman and Greif, absolutely opposed to outside "interference," refused to allow Hollander's committee to examine their shops. Still,
the testimony of the workers during the committee hearings proved so dam-
aging that Schoeneman hurriedly made improvements in one of his worst
shops.[15]

Schoeneman's women workers complained of dangerous, unsanitary,
and often humiliating conditions: inadequate light and ventilation; rodent
and pest infestation so severe that they were unable to store their lunches
safely; and intimidation by male foremen, who forced them to work over-
time or lose their jobs, refused to allow them leave for personal or family sick-
ness, and regularly harassed those whom they found attractive. Professor Eli-
nor Pancoast of Goucher College surveyed wages for the committee and
found that almost half of the women workers "were either the chief or only
breadwinners of their families" but averaged only $7.67 for a sixty-hour
week. Pancoast calculated that an absolute minimum weekly wage for a
woman without dependents would be $9.59. Most workers were therefore
living at a level "below the decent minimum." Victims of hard times and the
scarcity of jobs in the Great Depression, they had generally accepted the dictates of their employers. When the fastest, most efficient workers questioned
the wage rates, they were informed that their meager earnings were a "decent
salary for any girl to make"—a statement reminiscent of the Progressive-Era
employer who had justified women's low wages by saying that, after all,
"they're only girls." Women also complained that although foremen fully realized that many of them had families to support, during slack times they
laid off women with children before they laid off women who had unemployed husbands at home. As one worker explained, "I took my two babies
over [to the foreman], and said 'For God's sake, Mr. Raab, don't take my job
away from me.' He said he couldn't help it. 'I have to let you off, there are
women who have to keep their husbands.'"[16]

Conditions for the few men working at Schoeneman's were only slightly better, but the investigation showed that foremen were less likely to shout
insults at, or make provocative comments to, the male workers. Moreover,
the men were not expected to perform janitorial duties at day's end, whereas the women were required to sweep and "pick up" on their own time before going home.[17]

The revelations about conditions in the garment industry shocked
members of the reform and philanthropic communities, and extensive press
coverage served to increase sympathy for the garment workers among larger sections of the public. The *Baltimore Post* described its "feeling of shame

and horror" when it printed the Hollander report of "an industry working on starvation wages, under unsanitary conditions, with little regard for health, hours, or anything but expenses." The newspaper demanded improvements in the garment industry "in the interest of civic decency." Sensitive to the *Baltimore Sun*'s earlier depiction of the ACW as a union of "un-American proletarians," Hollander facilitated the public's endorsement by stressing that the workers were no longer a "body of illiterate immigrants," but "Americans to the core." It was significant, he added pointedly, that the "young women who have been arrested for violating police regulations as to picketing and who were carted off to the station house should have sung during their period of detention, not the 'Red Flag' or the 'Marseillaise,' but the 'Star-Spangled Banner.'"[18]

The ACW's organizational activity in combination with spreading public support soon persuaded a number of manufacturers to sign contracts accepting union shops, improving working conditions, and granting wage increases of up to 30 percent. By the end of September, the ACW had unionized 133 contract shops and 61 inside shops, and it celebrated with a Victory Mass Meeting, addressed by Blumberg, Hillman, and congressman Fiorello LaGuardia from New York. Strike leader Catherine Moylan ("Our Mickey") presented flowers to Hillman, saying, "These roses will die, but our spirit will live forever." Receiving the greatest applause among the platform party were twenty Schoeneman workers, "dressed in white with red sashes," who represented their sisters still on strike.[19]

The 1932 organizational campaign, the union boasted, resulted in organization of about 70 percent of the market. Although this claim was probably an exaggeration, the drive had still transformed the union membership, added many new recruits, gathered much public support, and delivered a surprising blow to the many contractors long accustomed to sweating their workers without fear of unionization. Of the major firms, only Greif and Schoeneman resisted union inroads. Schoeneman, rather than deal with the union or substantially alter the conditions that had generated so much negative publicity, in 1932 simply moved his business to the safe, nonunion environs of rural Pennsylvania, leaving only a distribution center near the city. Moving vans loaded with factory equipment discreetly stole away in the middle of the night. When news of Schoeneman's "running away" reached union headquarters, Sara Barron led a group of workers in forming a human blockade to stop the move, but most of the equipment had already been delivered to its new home in Chambersburg, Pennsylvania, under the cover of darkness.[20]

148   The Amalgamated's failure to unionize either Greif or Schoeneman in
1932 foreshadowed the problems it would face during the remainder of the
Great Depression. The union's inability to prevent companies from simply
leaving the city also suggested more ominous trends. But the rejuvenated
union overlooked those warnings about the future. The ACW had spent
$12,000 on the 1932 strike, and the cost seemed well worth it. At least a sem-
blance of union control had returned to the industry, and workers in a number of shops enjoyed wage increases. The union drive in 1932 tended to eliminate many of the smallest contract shops, which employed as few as five
workers. It also tended to stabilize hours of employment at fifty to sixty hours
per week. Describing the turn of events, Blumberg exclaimed, "I think that
the most revolutionary change in our organization recently took place in Baltimore City. The general sentiment . . . is excellent, the morale has never
been better."[21]

Rebuilding the Organization

The launching of the New Deal with the inauguration of President Franklin
D. Roosevelt in March 1933 critically bolstered the ACW's plans to remake
the union in Baltimore and strengthen it nationally. Yet, the effects of hard
times worked at cross-purposes with the promises of the new president. The
1932 strike was a significant catalyst to mobilizing garment workers, but by
1933 the Depression made those gains shortlived. Indeed, by the middle of
that year Baltimore's garment industry was suffering an unemployment rate
of about 30 percent. Although still active in many of the contract shops, the
ACW now had to deal with the return of the homeworking system, with the
proliferation of tiny "Depression shops," and, most dangerous of all, with
the movement of a number of shops out of the city. Moreover, as persistent
dire economic conditions ensured that fewer and fewer men bought new
suits or overcoats, manufacturers shifted production to cheaper grades or began producing cotton shirts and other items of apparel. The complexities of
the men's clothing industry, which had proved daunting in the 1920s, now
overwhelmed the Baltimore ACW. Amalgamated organizer Newman Jeffrey
complained of having to "start from scratch" in the city's pants-making and
cotton garment trade, because the Joint Board did not even have a list of the
shops: "up to now [it] had very few contacts or names or addresses."[22] As
Sara Barron explained, the union had to undertake considerable "detective
work" to locate contractors and subcontractors and to trace the shipment of
clothes from shop to shop and to final distribution centers—all the while at-

tempting to organize the workers laboring in those many and diverse shops.   **149**
The Joint Board even had to spend some of its precious resources to purchase
men's suits from different shops, so that they could compare styles and the
degree of work involved and ensure proper piece rates.[23]

Industrial order was needed for the union to regain its strength in the
city, and the best hope seemed to be the New Deal, particularly the National Industrial Recovery Act (NIRA). Designed to promote economic recovery by bringing all employers under codes regulating hours, wages, and
working conditions, NIRA suggested the kind of governmental activism
that the Amalgamated believed was necessary for enlightened labor-
management relations and industrial stability. Hyman Blumberg waited
anxiously for its passage, fearing that "if the bill is not passed, Baltimore will
again be a nonunion market." Not only was it necessary to discipline the industry, but the preservation of union morale was also at stake: "the danger is
the state of mind of our people."[24] Although labor leaders, especially Sidney
Hillman, regarded the act that ultimately passed as favoring bankers and
business, they still gave it strong endorsements. Locally, both business and
labor also endorsed the regulatory possibilities offered by the National Recovery Administration (NRA), and the ACW's Joint Board took the lead in
using the new legislation to facilitate labor-management cooperation.

Not all observers joined this chorus of support, and some pointed with
alarm to the philosophical direction the program represented. The *Baltimore
Sun* forcefully denounced the NRA as a dangerous departure from American tradition and a "far-reaching step in the direction of a controlled national
economy." Many state and local political leaders sided with that position,
openly questioning the propriety of such an interventionist government.
The ACW moved ahead nevertheless, holding local meetings and affirming
that it had finally received the assistance necessary to rebuild the union in
the city.[25]

Cooperating with Blumberg, the Joint Board, now headed by Ulisse De-
Dominicis, arranged Baltimore's first "NRA conference" of workers and employers to begin deliberations to establish price and wage codes. Blumberg
returned to Baltimore for the conference, convinced that the NRA would
help maintain the "excellent morale" among members and raise the wages
of workers, especially women. It would ensure that women earned at least
$12.00 per week, which he conceded "is not much, but it would mean a lot
[to them]" and would represent in many cases about a "60 percent increase."
Calling for the standardization of prices, garments, and wages, Blumberg
told employers that "competition at the expense of labor alone will be ter-

150 minated." No longer, he declared, would Baltimore compete with eastern Pennsylvania for the "title of lowest wage center in the industry." The Clothing Manufacturers' Association, the organization representing large and medium-sized shops, disliked such comments, but it agreed publicly to abide by the NRA wage and price codes. Benjamin Le Bow, who chaired the association and who had earlier participated in wartime and postwar meetings of labor and management, later declared of his fellow employers that "they are not a damned bit pleased with this, but they know they've got to go along with it." As an admonitory measure, the ACW called a twenty-four-hour strike in the men's garment shops, saying workers would return to their jobs only for the "New Deal" wage of forty cents an hour.[26]

The imposition of wage and price codes on city manufacturers proved more challenging than the ACW initially expected. The promise of regulatory control often became buried in the myriad codes developed for the clothing industry. Moreover, the wage and price codes frequently reflected—rather than reformed—the chaos of the industry. Enforcement became a nightmare, as companies operated under several different codes and the city's clothing firms consistently attempted to use the lowest-paying code for all their workers. The task of determining compliance in such shops as H. Borenstein and Sons, which turned out one-third of its production under the men's clothing code and two-thirds under the cotton pants code, challenged even the most efficient administrator. Workers themselves needed, but did not always receive, detailed information about the codes and enforcement procedures and were left often confused about pay rates and forever suspicious of their employers.[27]

Monitoring code violations became another duty for the union's members, and shop chairwomen and chairmen regularly received instructions about ensuring compliance with the agreements of the "Blue Eagle," the symbol of the NRA. They kept careful records of the infractions they observed and discussed them at meetings of their locals and of the Joint Board. Enforcing the codes, Blumberg warned, "will be a tremendous job." When union representatives had what they deemed sufficient evidence of "employer chiseling," they presented their findings to the state's NRA compliance office or the Baltimore District of the NRA Grievance Committee. Those offices would then conduct their own investigations; if they found a violation, they would negotiate with the employer before beginning a public hearing or issuing a final verdict. "We had to dig up the facts," DeDominicis reported of one clothing manufacturer, "which we did. We collect-

ed 2 weeks back pay and intend to hold him in line regardless of what will **151**
happen."[28]

But city and state NRA officials supported labor only reluctantly and counseled patience among aggrieved workers. Compliance director Arthur Hungerford was convinced, as he said, that it was never necessary for unions to strike or engage in work stoppages in order to gain their rights under the NRA, and Colonel W. D. A. Anderson, the chair of the Grievance Committee, showed little sympathy for the ACW's efforts to enforce management compliance with NRA codes. At times he resented the union's vigiliance and its open criticisms of his own "lax" enforcement. Some code violations also ended up before another mechanism for possible redress, the Baltimore Labor Relations Panel. Headed by professor Jacob Hollander, this panel often relied on the legal advice of Jacob Edelman and was generally very sympathetic to the clothing workers. By 1935 it supervised labor disputes for all of District V, encompassing Maryland, Virginia, and Delaware. Still, the enforcement and compliance processes, even when labor had allies, were lengthy and cumbersome. Committed to the rule of law in the workplace, the ACW, more than other labor organizations in the city, persisted in using both means of redress.[29]

The investigations uncovered a variety of violations, most involving the "underpayment of wages" or the "failure to use the NRA label." They also revealed the primitive methods of record keeping used by even medium-sized firms, with some employers relying on workers to keep track of the hours they worked but then refuting the figures reported. Many contract shops attempted to use the lowest-paying cotton codes to set wage rates, when workers were producing men's woolen suits or overcoats. Nearly all of the workers who experienced these wage code violations were women, for the city's clothing manufacturers had responded to the Great Depression not only by worsening sweatshop conditions, but by hiring young women whom they believed they could pay the least. A few shops that produced what one NRA investigator described as "a very cheap-grade of men's clothing," suitable only for the "negro and poorer white population of the South," sought to suppress wage rates by hiring black workers for the first time, paying them miserably low wages and segregating them in separate workrooms. H. Borenstein and Sons committed such a violation, according to one investigation that, ironically, had been triggered by Borenstein's own request for a "blanket exemption [from the wage codes] for his shops, in view of the fact that negro labor on the whole is less efficient than white." When the NRA

152 denied his request and informed him that only President Roosevelt could extend such an exemption, Borenstein defied the code anyway. An examination of Borenstein's workers' pay envelopes found sizable discrepancies between code and actual wages: Frances Hill, for example, received $4.07 instead of $12.80 for a thirty-two-hour week, and Hattie Burston worked four hours longer than allowed and still received only $9.38, instead of the $14.40 required under the code.[30]

As manager of the ACW Joint Board, DeDominicis regularly reported "plenty of trouble" in attempting to enforce the wage and hour codes. Between 1933 and 1935, when the Supreme Court ruled the NRA legislation unconstitutional, the local ACW devoted much of its effort to upholding the Blue Eagle arrangements. As the minutes of the Joint Board and occasional press accounts graphically illustrate, the union conducted frequent work stoppages at uncooperative shops, set up special investigative committees to inspect shop conditions and pay envelopes, and gathered considerable information on employers who attempted to defy the standards. "The workers have learned," reported one Baltimore newspaper, "that the NRA will not help them unless they help themselves." As much as the effort to enforce the NRA strained the resources of the local union, it also gave the members new hope. By early 1934, the local ACW had come to rely on the New Deal agency to assist it in controlling the local industry, and contractors and manufacturers also recognized—and usually resented—the power of the codes.[31]

The most publicized NRA case in Baltimore involved the Greif company, which had expanded to become the nation's second-largest clothing company, with shops in Virginia and Pennsylvania as well as Baltimore. The dispute provided poignant testimony of the continuing difficulties faced by the city's unorganized garment workers, despite New Deal legislation. Indeed, Greif initially informed its workers, about three-fourths of whom were women, that under the NRA employers and government officials would establish labor policies that would eliminate the need for unions.[32] Hostile to worker organization and government regulation, Greif then announced plans to challenge the constitutionality of the NRA while it deliberately ignored the wage codes. The company not only refused to pay the NRA minimum wage established by the clothing code, but changed its payment plan from a piecework basis to a combined hourly wage and quota system, with the daily quotas set so high that workers complained they had to begin work before the official starting time and skip lunch simply to meet the required production schedule.

In April 1934, federal investigators visited eight Greif plants in three

states, only to find that the company had destroyed its 1933 pay records. **153**
Moreover, Greif officials refused to cooperate with NRA authorities, who ultimately found the company guilty of depriving its employees of more than
$35,000 by not paying the code's minimum wage. In turn, Greif filed suit
against the NRA, charging that the recovery program was illegal and that the
men's clothing code had been framed in violation of the law and represented an attempt to force "all manufacturers into [the ACW] or out of business." Greif also pledged never to recognize the Amalgamated or subscribe
to its philosophy of comanagement. While legal proceedings continued, the
NRA ordered Blue Eagle labels withheld from the Greif company for its violation of the wage code. Greif appealed to allies in the city, and the Baltimore Association of Commerce harshly denounced the federal government's
move against the company.[33]

Because consumers refused to purchase clothes without Blue Eagle labels, retailers began to cancel their orders with Greif. Under mounting financial pressure, Greif announced in August 1934 its willingness to abide by
the decision of an impartial mediator selected by the Department of Justice,
still refusing to acknowledge the legitimacy of the NRA in its regulatory role.
The arbiter found in favor of the NRA, ruling that Greif had violated the
wage provision of the code and suggesting that the company eliminate its
quota system and raise wages to a level more commensurate with those paid
by other companies in the industry. In order to gain the higher wages for the
workers, the NRA agreed not to "press for [full] restitution of the fair wages"
owed to employees, and Greif repaid only a fraction of the money due.[34]

By 1934, other Baltimore clothiers had joined Greif in objecting to the
NRA and its "intrusions." To avoid paying the mandated minimum wages,
some manufacturers abandoned their inside shops in favor of contract shops.
Some firms simply moved out of the city, believing that job-starved rural areas would not insist on enforcing wage codes and would remain free from
government standards and "union dictation." Because the future of the NRA
seemed uncertain, moreover, employers increasingly encroached on its provisions, and the ACW Joint Board prepared for a total assault. The Joint
Board also appealed to Baltimore's representatives in the House and Senate
for new legislation that would extend NRA arrangements, and DeDominicis joined Hillman and Blumberg in Washington, D.C., to urge continued
governmental support of economic planning. In May 1935, DeDominicis
called a special meeting to "acquaint the Joint Board with the crucial period
which we are going through with the N.R.A. and to discuss our agreements
for the coming season." Union leaders, he explained, "have flooded Wash-

154 ington with telegrams urging them to extend this act for a period of two more years. The manufacturers, on the other hand, are doing all in their power to break down this law so they can go back to the old methods." Predicting the appearance of even more sweatshops than before in the city, DeDominicis warned, "We must be ready for a fight to uphold the 36 hours [work week] and the minimum wage at any cost." Grimly he concluded, "If there was ever a time for labor to fight, it is now, because we have too much at stake."[35]

"SOMETIMES WE ARE COMPELLED TO DEAL WITH A PROBLEM IN ONE MARKET IN A WAY WHICH MAY CAUSE DIFFICULTIES IN ANOTHER"

Clothing manufacturers not only resented the NRA codes, but bristled at the Amalgamated's use of them. Indeed, the economic planning and coordination that the establishment of codes entailed represented many employers' first encounter with long-term planning, and their inexperience contrasted sharply with that of the ACW leadership. Fully informed about regional market differences and frequently much more knowledgeable about the legislation and the code requirements, ACW leaders overwhelmed clothiers and forced them to seek additional expertise, especially that of lawyers. For the ACW, the codes represented an opportunity to extend union control over production and distribution, an objective that particularly rankled owners strongly opposed to "co-management." Equally important to introducing rational planning into a volatile industry, according to the ACW, was the opportunity to eliminate permanently competition based solely on labor costs. That competition, according to the union leadership, would lead only to the ultimate ruin of the industry, through the constant relocation of shops in search of cheaper pools of labor. Finally, the ACW, convinced that businesses were too shortsighted to honor any proposed long-term arrangements for labor costs, also used the Baltimore clothing market to uphold the production and wage scales in other cities, a strategy that imposed hardship on both local workers and employers.

As a "low cost" town, Baltimore constituted an obstacle to the union's efforts to coordinate production in the eastern region. To minimize the "danger" that Baltimore represented to the unionized large factories in New York and Philadelphia, the ACW insisted in its agreements that manufacturers in Baltimore not produce certain grades of men's coats. With the support of outside manufacturers who hoped to escape possible competition from Baltimore firms, the ACW restricted the production of cheaper-grade coats in

Baltimore, completely prohibiting the manufacture of No. 1 and No. 2 coats, which were the least expensive coats and the best sellers during the Depression. The union hoped to preclude the sending of garments to Baltimore for finishing and to strengthen the position of its major unionized firms in Rochester, New York, and Philadelphia. The ACW claimed, with little justification, that Baltimore's workers were "not trained" to produce the coats and that its shops were not mechanized sufficiently to turn them out. The Baltimore market was left to produce the No. 3 coat, a full-basted, open coat, on which "virtually all the work is done by hand" and which retailed for at least twenty dollars, depending on the quality of the fabric, or more than double the price of cheaper grade coats.[36]

Baltimore's medium-sized firms and smaller contractors repeatedly protested to the federal government and to the Clothing Manufacturers' Association, charging that the ACW was attempting to drive them out of business in favor of larger factories under union control in other cities. The charges were not altogether unfounded, for Baltimore's industry was characterized by a number of features that militated against strong union control, at least according to the ACW's definition of control. First, in the union's view, the city's clothing industry was overburdened with contract shops, and the production of machine-manufactured coats made of many pieces, priced according to the piecework system, and carried on in hundreds of contract shops posed a "tremendous administrative task" for the union. As Hillman insisted during a meeting of the General Executive Board, "we must retain the larger houses, no matter at what cost." Another Board member further explained, "sometimes we are compelled to deal with a problem in one market in a way which may cause difficulties in another."

Second, more women than men worked in Baltimore's clothing industry, a gender distribution that did not hold for Philadelphia, New York, Chicago, or Rochester and ran counter to the national trend. Between 1920 and 1940, women made up about 50 percent of the national men's garment workforce, and the percentage decreased slightly over time. In Baltimore, however, women constituted 64 percent of the garment workers by 1939, up from 42 percent in 1919. Most of them continued to be young women, with little skill or union experience, and they did not count among the Amalgamated's preferred organizational recruits. Indeed, despite the union's public posturing toward "equal pay for equal work," the discussion among the ACW's leadership during the establishment of NRA wage codes suggested something very different from a philosophy of equality.[37]

The ACW wished to exert union control over an industry characterized

156 by modern manufacturers, or inside shops, guided by rational economic principles and dominated by male employees. The fear that women would displace men from their jobs figured prominently in the General Executive Board's discussions during the Great Depression. Responding to the proposal to set up different wage standards for men and women, one board member cautioned, "If we put a higher minimum for men, men will be barred from the industry," but the majority sentiment favored a lower wage scale for women. Only one member warned against establishing a "double standard" based on gender, and even he argued that a single standard would not harm men, for they would "not content" themselves with a minimum. Hillman, who also supported unequal wage scales, believed that men could be protected against competition from women because "the union can make its rules" on such matters as production and piecework. Organization drives among women were, from the start, often predicated on the union's desire to retain skilled positions for men and to prevent women from competing with men in a variety of jobs. Employers, of course, had exploited the fear of female employment in numerous union campaigns before and during World War I, and many union men supported the organization of women only in order to regulate and subordinate their presence in the workforce. Baltimore's clothing industry, then, diverged almost completely from the model preferred by the union. Indeed, as the city's Joint Board manager complained, in Baltimore, unlike other cities, the major companies—Greif and Schoeneman—"will not employ men cutters. They employ women workers instead." The rest of the employers in the city were "small frys."[38]

Reestablishing union control in Baltimore represented a calculated response to the new shape of the garment industry and an attempt to minimize the regional economic damage of the trend toward contract shop production in the city. It also resulted in a decline in production and the departure of additional clothing firms. By restricting the production of coats to No. 3 coats, the ACW made piece rates identical throughout the city and the task of supervising rates less complicated. But Depression conditions made the market for such coats marginal, and after significant pressure from the Clothing Manufacturers' Association, the ACW finally relented, allowing city producers to make the No. grade 2 coats beginning in 1935. Within a year, No. 2 coats accounted for 25 percent of all garments made in unionized shops in Baltimore, revealing the disingenuousness of the union's claim that Baltimore had inadequate workers and insufficient machinery to make these coats. The Amalgamated still held the line against the production of the cheapest coats throughout the Great Depression, fearing that the low cost of labor in Baltimore would attract new business and jeopardize the markets elsewhere. Such a development would cost union men their jobs and make the "large houses" vulnerable.[39]

The Amalgamated was able to enforce its standards of production largely because of the loyalty and dedication of its Baltimore membership. Yet, in 1936, the ACW, harking back to the past practices of the United Garment Workers, merely required employers to purchase union labels, rather than fully meet the Amalgamated's demands for higher wages or better working conditions. In Baltimore, the ACW simply sold union labels to "union" firms; wages for women workers remained extremely low, and the Amalgamated was able to prohibit the production of the more competitive No. 1 grade coats. Union supervision of the coat shops became easier, because they decreased in number; no longer competitive, small entrepreneurs either left the city or set up contract shops specializing in shirts, pants, and men's furnishings. These shops, too, threatened to duplicate the trend in men's coats and suits, drawing contract business from manufacturers in New York and Philadelphia. Accordingly, throughout the 1930s, the city's Amalgamated members attempted to unionize pants- and shirt-making factories, again responding to the changing nature of the city's clothing industry. One member of the General Executive Board instructed Ulisse DeDominicis, "Do everything you can to stimulate organization work among the pants makers in your city."[40]

Sara Barron and her "sister comrades" of the Activity Group were especially important in this organizational effort, and they were reinforced by national ACW officials who sent such additional women organizers as Mildred McWilliams Jeffrey, Beth Cunningham, and Hilda Cobb to Baltimore to help maintain union control in a changing industry. Overnight, shirt makers became pants shops, and the organizers were forced to keep track of the changes. Dorothy Jacobs Bellanca warned, "Most of the shirt houses are beginning to make slacks . . . and for that reason it is important that the pants shops be looked after so that we may have some control over the price rates."[41]

"OUR WOMEN WERE REALLY WONDERFUL"

Baltimore's loyal membership in the 1930s consisted mostly of women who worked in contract shops. Despite their two-thirds majority, women did not increase their numbers in local leadership positions. Usually only one woman sat on the Joint Board, and none ever served as its manager. As the

158 leading activist among the Baltimore women, Sara Barron played a major role in the Amalgamated's efforts to reclaim its position in the city, but she never received the appropriate reward for her labors. She later said that she learned the lesson of union activism from Dorothy Jacobs Bellanca, who had recruited her to the union during the early strikes at Sonneborn's. Although she did not possess Jacobs's intellectual abilities, she said, she knew the industry from top to bottom and could organize reliable and enthusiastic new members.

Persistent and dedicated, she never wavered in her commitment to the ACW, despite wishing that some of its individual members would adopt a more egalitarian model of unionism. Her organizational skills won her the respect and admiration of her union sisters and also led the ACW men to call on her often for advice and assistance. Unlike Jacobs Bellanca, who spoke of women's special character, praising women as mothers and nurturers, as well as fighters on front-line battles, Barron used the language of militancy, adopting the union messages of virility and strength; "marrying" the union; and remaining ever ready to take on new responsibilities, even dangerous ones, while gently chiding her union brothers when they expressed apprehension. "Take Sara [with you]," Hyman Blumberg once instructed a male organizer, "she's got a lot of nerve." Barron was more sympathetic to her closest women friends when they, too, hesitated before the dangers of picketing and the prospects of jail, but she still distanced herself from them. Mamie Santora, according to Barron, was "afraid to go out [on the picket line]. She didn't like to get arrested." Although Barron herself stood under five feet tall, she explained Santora's reluctance by describing her as "too little a girl." Barron's strength in action and voice defied her size, and her straightforward approach—Jacob Potofsky said "she takes no back talk from anybody"—led some men to call her "spunky" and others to wince and call her organizing techniques "crude."[42]

Together and separately, Jacobs Bellanca and Barron represented the possibilities and limitations of women's leadership in the union. Less threatening to conventional notions of female propriety and more traditional in her language and appearance, Jacobs Bellanca resigned from the General Executive Board when she married and thereafter always refused to accept a salary, even when she held the position of director of the Women's Department. She cared about women deeply and promoted them constantly, but her efforts remained carefully within the boundaries of acceptability; she usually refused to push beyond those limits, even when she was convinced of her cause. She was not confrontational and her voice in the union held no small influence. Her very style, which reinforced certain traditional notions about gender and undermined others, helped ensure her legitimacy and acceptability, just as Barron's outspoken and energetic displays of power prevented her from rising too far.[43]

Thanks to her role in the 1932 strike, Barron was elected to the presidency of the Joint Board, an office that had previously led to the position of Joint Board manager, but did not in her case. After serving for three years in the presidency, she was not asked to stay on and instead was replaced by a man, a cutter from Local #15. After that, her influence in the union was largely limited to organizational work. Militancy, which propelled young men like Blumberg and Ulisse DeDominicis to positions of leadership in the union, did not offer the same route for women. Still, Barron's reputation for toughness in the face of strikebreakers and armed police gave her personal pleasure at the same time that it legitimized her role as an activist woman in the ACW. "I always wanted to go picket," she recalled. "It was a lot of fun, a lot of excitement." In the Depression, she continued, women workers "helped to make the union stronger . . . . The women in the shops, the executive board, our women were really wonderful." Taking pride as well in her loyalty and dedication, she affirmed, "we picketed plenty, they could always count on us." "Spunky" women belonged on the battle lines, and Barron, at least in the 1930s, agreed, for she was "too busy" advancing the union, she later recalled, to think much about "discrimination" in the ACW.[44]

In addition to reviving the union, the organization drive of 1932 resulted in the formation of a new local, initially made up entirely of women. Although only seven years had passed since the struggle for a separate women's local and many of the same women were involved, the new local (#70) called itself the "American local" in an effort to emphasize unity within the union. At one level, the refusal to renew the debate on a women's local corresponded to a defensiveness felt among wage-earning women in general in the Great Depression. "It is amazing to see the vindictive spleen that is vented against the poor married women," reported the *Baltimore Sun,* but "to make scapegoats out of married women will never solve the [economic] problems." Even within the ACW, a Rochester local proposed that married women with employable husbands be denied membership in the Amalgamated. Women members, including those from Baltimore, vociferously denounced the proposal as "reactionary" and the General Executive Board declined to support it, but that such an initiative even came forth in a union with a membership nearly half female underscores the hostile sentiments of the time. At another level, however, the formation of the American local represented a genuine

160   desire to extend the membership to all, regardless of ethnicity, skill, gender, or race, for Local #70 was among the earliest ACW locals in the city to welcome African American members.[45]

Finally, the formation of Local #70 also resulted as a consequence of Jacobs Bellanca's advice. "Instead of having a women's local after the general strike of 1932," Barron later explained, "we talked to Dorothy and Dorothy said, 'Sara, don't get a women's local because Rochester isn't doing too much with a women's local. Let's get Local #70 and it's going to be a majority of women and then you'll be able to elect women to participate and be active.' Well, I thought it was the right thing to do. So, we got this Local #70, which became the largest local under the Joint Board and the officers were women." With a laugh, she added, "We gave a little bit to the men, too." By not emphasizing skill or ethnicity and by focusing on a shared American identity, Local #70 looked to the future and signaled a departure from the organizational basis of the other locals. It enjoyed strong support from not only Jacobs Bellanca but also Blumberg and Sidney Hillman. DeDominicis affirmed its establishment at a meeting of the Joint Board: "This is an English speaking local composed mostly of the younger element and the general office is interested to see a strong activity developed. As Brother Blumberg stated sometime ago, some good might come from a local of this kind."[46]

Local #70 emerged as the centerpiece of the expanded union activism of the 1930s, promoting educational, organizational, and social activities and inspiring other locals to renew their union spirit and vitality. This new local of women members took the lead in remaking the union, first organizing and then educating the new recruits.

Signs of "serious labor unrest"

The New Deal offered new political opportunities as well as organizational ones to the Amalgamated. In 1933, in response to NIRA Section 7(a), which asserted labor's right to organize and bargain collectively, the ACW conducted a national organization drive in the shirt-making industry, which had expanded in nonunionized contract shops in major cities and small towns throughout the East. In Baltimore, the union achieved only marginal victories but set the stage for a more protracted struggle at the end of the decade. Enforcing the NRA codes in the shirt-making industry led the Joint Board in 1934 to attempt to unionize the shops proliferating outside the city, particularly the shops of its most persistent foes—Greif and Schoeneman. Its most seasoned union leaders, including Sara Barron, who went on the payroll as an organizer, moved into the countryside of Maryland, Virginia, New Jersey, and Pennsylvania to unionize the Greif and Schoeneman factories there. Although it was a wise organizational strategy, the campaigns were too poorly funded and understaffed to make much headway. The work was also dangerous. Two organizers were arrested in New Jersey, and Jacob Edelman had to travel there to provide legal assistance. In Maryland, Barron was "nearly locked up and chased out of Westminster," the ACW complained, "under the pretension of a city ordinance which prohibited [the] distribution of circulars or approaching the people so that they will join the union." Outsiders agitating in small communities even encountered resistance from the workers they sought to help. At the Greif factory in Fredericksburg, Virginia, an organizer found that "women cutters who receive one dollar per day" were "satisfied." At Soudertown, Pennsylvania, another organizer reported the situation at Schoeneman's "hopeless," because "most of the workers are Mennonites" and "their church has told them that they must not work in a union shop." Despite such obstacles, the Baltimore organizers persevered. After meeting again in the city to discuss their plans of action, they returned to several outlying locations for "quiet educational campaign[s]." Barron, undeterred by her abrupt departure from Westminster, Maryland, volunteered to return to organize eighty pressers at a Greif pants-making shop.[47]

With only limited success at organizing "run-away" shops in rural areas, the ACW kept most of its organizational activity focused on the city. Recognizing that Baltimore's largest clothiers were staunchly antiunion, the Joint Board endeavored to maintain its presence in the contract shops and the medium-sized firms. In that effort, Local #70 again proved critical. Following Barron's lead, the women of that local fully understood the importance of the Amalgamated's retaining control of the city's remaining shops. They took part in organizational and educational activities, deriving support from the community of women they represented on the shopfloor. Ulisse DeDominicis also worked tirelessly as manager of the Joint Board, expanding the union's reach into new shops and production areas. Progress was fitful, for victories barely lasted from season to season. For example, the ACW had no sooner won a major contract with the Baltimore Clothes Company than the firm closed down, leaving five hundred workers and union members unemployed in 1938. The threat of companies' closing or leaving the city made some garment workers increasingly wary of unions and less willing to demand better wages or working conditions.[48]

Both the Great Depression and the New Deal intensified the drive for

162 collective action among the city's other workers, and union activity and membership expanded dramatically. At the same time, the signs of "serious labor unrest," as Maryland's commissioner of labor and statistics described conditions in 1936, hardened the sentiments of those who opposed unions. The *Baltimore Sun* accelerated its assault on organized labor, continuing to publish critical editorials and creating "pressroom committees" intended to forestall unionization on its own premises. The arrival in the city of the Committee for Industrial Organization (CIO) energized the trade union movement, but it also alienated those who favored more conservative unions and warned against the "communism" of the CIO.[49]

The general expansion of the labor movement in the 1930s brought to the fore many obstacles faced by organizing workers in general and the ACW in particular. Workers in all industries were never confident of having "the right to strike," and union activism often foundered in the face of hostile police actions and court injunctions. By 1937, Baltimore could claim a dubious national distinction for the behavior of its police during strikes. On March 9, 1937, a subcommittee of the U.S. Senate Committee on Education and Labor (the LaFollette Civil Liberties Committee) disclosed a letter from Baltimore's manager of the William J. Burns International Detective Agency complaining of the poor market for his services in the city. "The way strikes are handled here in Baltimore by various manufacturing interests," he wrote, "is, of course, to import skilled labor to take the place of the strikers, then enlist the service of the Baltimore Police Department GRATIS to guard the plant and protect the strikebreakers, and the strike is over in a very short while."[50]

For the ACW, then, the expansion of the union movement along with the activism of the New Deal promised the fulfillment of many of its long-standing goals. Attempting to rebuild its union in such a climate proved frustrating as well as exhilarating, however. In the ACW's 1932 strike, judicial limitations on the number of picketers had resulted in mass arrests. When it mounted another major organizational campaign in 1935 to uphold the provisions of the NRA, judicial restrictions were even more severe and the police more numerous. The ACW joined with members of the city's Socialist Party to condemn the behavior of the police: "In any other city, not more than one or two police would be assigned to a shop of this size," but "in front of this shop we see at times 16 or 17 policemen with a patrol wagon." This show of force, the ACW complained publicly and through Edelman's legal services, was not to prevent violence, but "for the purpose of intimidating the strikers, to discourage them, and to encourage the strikebreakers . . . . In

some cases, the policemen at the door even open the door for strikebreak- **163**
ers."[51]

"An old established union"

As the ACW continued its efforts to rebuild its organization in the latter part
of the Great Depression, both new and old problems emerged. Except at a
few companies, the city's garment workers had initially responded positively to the union. Its reputation was good, and conditions were so bad in the
clothing industry that promises of wage increases could usually attract even
the most equivocal worker. As the Depression years wore on, however, and
more companies moved out of the city, workers increasingly feared that signing a union card would eliminate their jobs or even the company. The ACW
thus had to try new organizational and educational techniques. Furthermore, remaking the local union did not always match the national Amalgamated's goal of limiting the influence of the Baltimore market, and issues of
workplace discipline resurfaced, as workers challenged the directives of the
General Office. Finally, changes in political practices and policies also
marked a new direction for the union. With the ACW's reestablishment in
1932, it had developed mutually supportive ties with the city's tiny Socialist
Party. By 1936, however, the Amalgamated had joined forces under the Democratic banner, actively campaigning for FDR and the New Deal. Some
Socialists felt betrayed; others understood. As the city's leading Socialist,
Broadus Mitchell, later observed, "The New Deal took the wind out of the
sails of the Socialist party."[52]

From the mid-1930s until the outbreak of World War II, the local ACW
followed a precarious course that attempted to maintain minimal standards
in the contract shops, win agreements with the larger firms without "chas-
ing" them out of the city, and observe the dictates of national union policy
that limited the growth of the men's garment industry in Baltimore. Buoyed
by the passage of the Wagner Act in 1935, the local ACW immediately devised plans to test its efficacy through the National Labor Relations Board
(NLRB). Designed to curb unfair labor practices, the NLRB signaled official approval of unionization and promised unions and their workers a
greater say in labor-management decisions. Baltimore workers responded
forcefully to the Wagner Act, asserting their rights to organize and bargain
collectively through an upsurge of labor activism. Indeed, the number of
worker-days lost through striking jumped 91 percent and Baltimore ranked
third among the ten largest cities in the number of strikes recorded. For its

164 part, the ACW conducted numerous "stoppages" at Baltimore's contract shops and prepared for a bigger showdown in the 1936 manufacturing season. It also filed the nation's first case under the Wagner Act in the garment industry, charging the Friedman-Marks Clothing Company with discharging seven employees for union activities.[53]

If the NLRB legitimized unionism among Baltimore's workers, it had no such effect on many employers. Attorneys for Friedman-Marks even refused to participate in the NLRB hearing of the ACW complaint, alleging the unconstitutionality of the Wagner Act, and six other Baltimore clothing firms vigorously opposed an ACW organizational drive launched in 1936. Having cut wages and violated union agreements, they now sought to eliminate the Amalgamated from their shops altogether. A few firms supplemented their customary use of police by hiring what the ACW called "labor goons" to intimidate striking unionists on the picket line. More violence occurred at the infamous sweatshop of A. Abrams and Sons in the loft district, where strikebreakers even hurled bottles from the factory windows. After a few weeks, most of the companies restored the wage cuts and signed union agreements. One firm, however, shut down its Baltimore operations and shifted production elsewhere, rather than accept the union. Workers lost their jobs, the Joint Board manager lamented, for the "crime [of] join[ing] the union."[54]

The ACW tried once more to unionize the Greif company, sending the intrepid Sara Barron back to Westminster, Maryland, in 1936 to corral the support of the pressers as a first step toward unionizing the plant. Greif conducted an effective campaign against the Amalgamated, warning workers that the ACW was linked to communism and threatening to declare bankruptcy rather than recognize the union, the precedent for which had already been established by other clothing firms. Moreover, Greif tried to outflank the Wagner Act by setting up what Barron called a "fictitious company union" among its workers. Having previously made sporadic efforts at welfare capitalism, it now attempted to use "employee committees" to stave off the Amalgamated challenge. As in 1916, the company counted on the support of a few "loyal" workers to spread its message. The ACW called in the NLRB to determine whether the manufacturer had engaged in unfair labor practices to block unionization by organizing and funding the Carroll Workers Association of Westminster. "Our only hope," Ulisse DeDominicis declared, "is that the workers tell the truth. We have a few signed up but Greif is carrying on a terrific propaganda in Westminster."[55]

Although defeated at Greif's, the ACW, in keeping with its preference for institutionalized arbitration mechanisms, still relied heavily on the NLRB to win recognition and challenge employer infractions at the workplace. The union's efforts were not without success, and the ACW soon earned the reputation of being simultaneously one of the city's most militant unions as well as the one most committed to arbitration.

Steadily accelerating its pace, the ACW widened its organizational campaigns to include the severely underpaid workers in the laundry business and those in cotton-goods production, targeting especially the shirt and pajama industry. These new efforts responded to the decrease in the production of men's garments but also caused occasional jurisdictional disputes with the Baltimore Federation of Labor (BFL) and the small, but periodically active, International Ladies' Garment Workers' Union in the city. The ACW, moreover, was not as well prepared in these industries as in the men's garment industry. Amalgamated officials were unfamiliar with the owners and the products in the shirt and pajama shops, and success required learning new piece rates for shirts and pajamas as well as understanding the regional market and Baltimore's place in it.[56]

The issue of race raised another barrier to unionization. In this issue, not all rank-and-file workers fell in line behind the union leadership. In a city divided by race and often openly hostile to African Americans, employers were able to exploit racist sentiments, thereby pointing up the fragility of workers' solidarity. Under DeDominicis's leadership, however, the ACW made special efforts to organize blacks. Convinced that "colored workers in Baltimore are eager to organize," the Joint Board worked closely with the Baltimore Negro Labor Committee. The union made its greatest gains in industries dominated by blacks, for white workers often balked at joining integrated locals or unions. Still, even in the city's rag-picking industry, where the ACW signed up a number of black workers, DeDominicis found that the "bosses [were] especially concerned with promoting race hatreds to preclude organization." Outside organizers brought in for the major campaigns against the Marlboro and Aetna shirt factories found racism a serious obstacle in unionizing laundry workers, who washed cotton shirts in the shops. Occasionally resented by both black and white workers, organizer Newman Jeffrey found himself in the position of outside agitator. More often, he was unable to persuade white workers to organize together with blacks. Frustrated by his lack of success at the Marlboro factory, for example, Jeffrey complained that racial divisions made it "quite impossible to work here with any

166 degree of effectiveness." He then proposed that "local Baltimore people," and not outside organizers, should "assume full responsibility for the cotton garment work."[57]

The rise in labor activism in the latter part of the Great Depression provoked serious opposition in the city and at once enhanced and limited the ACW's organizational efforts. The introduction of the CIO in Baltimore significantly advanced the city's labor movement, but the division at the national level between the industrial-based organization and the American Federation of Labor was matched by an especially bitter division at the local level that also served to hinder the cause of unionism. Disagreements between the BFL and the Baltimore Industrial Council—the CIO's counterpart in the city—filled the pages of the city's newspapers and alienated workers from both organizations.[58]

Long an advocate of industrial organization, the ACW welcomed the Baltimore Industrial Council to the ranks of labor in the city. Indeed, it took the lead in organizing the council and provided copies of its own educational pamphlets for the council's organizers to use among steelworkers and autoworkers. Sara Barron took special pride in helping the CIO "get active here," and other ACW members also aided the Baltimore Industrial Council in its struggles against employers and the BFL. DeDominicis served as vice president of the Maryland CIO State Council as well as manager of the ACW's Joint Board. However, the CIO, like the ACW after World War I, represented a departure from conservative trade unionism and therefore became vulnerable to charges of communism. To be sure, a few active communist organizers undertook successful campaigns among Baltimore's autoworkers and maritime workers, but their influence was not widespread. Still, the specter of "communist infiltration" engineered by the CIO filled the rhetoric of the leaders of the BFL and also found a home in the hearts and minds of religious and political leaders. The consequences were significant for the ACW as well. During this period of red-baiting, Sara Borinsky "Americanized" her name to Barron, following Edelman's advice to "get rid of the '-sky,'" lest she be labeled a communist.[59]

After 1937, the Amalgamated encountered increasing "difficulty among the Catholic workers," who formed the majority in the cotton garment trade. "Whispering campaigns" inspired by the BFL, a number of employers, and a few local political leaders placed the Amalgamated at the front of a communist conspiracy. Parish priests, ACW activists asserted, also discouraged all forms of labor organization as dangerous attacks on organized religion and urged their members to avoid the CIO. The situation was so se-

rious at the Marlboro factory that Dorothy Jacobs Bellanca sent the organizers copies of a prolabor pamphlet written by Father Francis Haas, a national Catholic leader, entitled "Why and Whither of Labor Unions." Although fearing the pamphlet "a bit too long" and "too highbrow," the ACW
distributed hundreds of copies during its organizational efforts.[60]

The most serious obstacle to the ACW's organizational campaigns,
however, was the fear that a shop might go out of business. Employers themselves raised that prospect to forestall unionization. "Bosses tried the usual
tricks," reported one ACW activist, circulating "the rumor, old as unionism
itself, that the plant would close down." Organizers in other shops agreed
that "the hardest rumors to break down are that the plant will close down
and move out of town." The record was hard to refute, for the city had lost
most of its nationally competitive manufacturers and many of its medium-
sized shops as firms either moved to outlying locations or vied for temporary
competitive advantages among rural areas.[61] The ACW attempted, almost
in vain, to explain to company owners the long-term consequences of such
practices. The industry would disappear, officials from DeDominicis to
Hillman argued. Tying the company's profits to the discovery of the cheapest labor pools would provide only short-term profits, the ACW repeated in
all its literature. Still, the movement of the industry counted among the
ACW's most significant concerns.

During the organizational drive at the Aetna Shirt Company in 1939,
the ACW confronted both the charges of communism and the fears of plant
closing. It issued hundreds of letters that quoted Father Haas as saying, "The
rumor you have heard that the Amalgamated is 'communist' and 'radical' is
absolutely false. Nothing could be farther from the truth." Calling the ACW
"an old established union," the letter even blurred the union's affiliation with
the CIO, describing the ACW as "a very high grade Union, one of the best
in the country either in the C.I.O. or the A.F. of L." It closed by reassuring
the workers that, despite the rumors, the "Aetna Shirt Company can't close
to escape the Amalgamated Union" and that other companies had signed
agreements without closing down their shops.[62]

The ACW tried to maintain its control over the Baltimore market, going so far as to chase companies and contract shops from state to state. But
workers who lost their jobs in the city, and others fearful of doing the same,
regarded inadequate wages as better than no wages at all. No amount of
Amalgamated educational work could dissuade them from standing with
their company, despite the larger economic trends that threatened their jobs.

Finally, persistent internal dissension diminished the united front nec-

168 essary for the consolidation and expansion of the union. The sources of discord were familiar, with ethnicity and skill especially divisive. Absent, however, were the earlier animosities toward women, for women's place in the union had been confirmed, and, at least in the 1930s, few women challenged their subordinate place. Women still took the lead in the union's educational and cultural programs, but there were virtually no reminders that they did so as union sisters with an equal voice in the ACW. Indeed, in stark contrast to the 1920s, the minutes of the Joint Board in the 1930s make no mention of any concern for the special organizational or educational needs of women. Only one entry occurs: immediately after the 1933 formation of the "American local," the Joint Board allocated $1.20 for reimbursement to the "Women's Organizing Committee," which had been essentially responsible for the success of the strike. The committee merged into the American local, and by the mid-1930s more men than women represented the local on the Joint Board. The paltry expenditure for women, moreover, stood in sharp contrast to the substantial funds spent on supporting ethnic activities in the union.[63]

Although immigration restriction and Americanizing forces in society had helped reduce ethnic divisions in the 1920s, the economic competition encouraged by the Depression created new hostilities and revived old ones, too. To be sure, the ethnic tensions that flared were not as intense as those of the prewar era, but they still managed to challenge efforts at remaking the union. Several local leaders complained of anti-Semitism, and the Joint Board conducted several investigations of members in the Italian, Lithuanian, and Bohemian locals, finding some guilty and others not. Fines or formal apologies constituted the penalties for the offenders, and DeDominicis harshly denounced ethnic slurs as part of the "Fascist idea" that "could only hurt" the union. The shift in the local leadership toward Italian and Polish members troubled one of the larger Jewish locals, which maintained a steady barrage of criticism for not receiving what it believed to be fair representation in the union. DeDominicis responded that the absence of a Jewish business agent reflected the decline in the men's tailoring business and that all the union's business agents had to devote themselves to the other segments of the industry. But Local #36, one of the founding locals, was not persuaded and its relationship to the Joint Board remained strained throughout the decade.[64]

Ethnic ties also challenged the Joint Board's enforcement of the production restrictions placed on Baltimore's contractors by the union's national office. Depression conditions allowed petty entrepreneurs to start their own small shops and sometimes forced out-of-work tailors to do so. In the 1930s, Polish- and Lithuanian-owned shops cropped up in East Baltimore, and the ACW found them particularly resistant to union control, despite the union affiliation of their workers. Although many of the workers were dues-paying members, they assisted the contractors by finishing work secretly sent from New York and refused to report the violation to the Joint Board. Bound by ethnic and community loyalties, they felt no special bond to the "New York market." Indeed, the Joint Board leadership often complained that "one of the hardest things" for members "to understand is that they or their shop is a part of a widely scattered industry and that the union is interested in not only their shop or locality but the whole industry."[65]

Changing industrial conditions not only complicated efforts to ensure compliance with union agreements, but also made it difficult to impose discipline on the shopfloor. Some ACW members had never fully relinquished what they saw as their right of immediate redress. During the era of the NRA, for example, employers complained that workers had their own notions about what the Blue Eagle agreements meant and would "lay down on the job" until they received satisfaction. The ACW warned that it would not "tolerate actions of this kind because we hurt our own cause by so doing." The "Roosevelt Recession" of 1937, which ravaged the cotton and men's garment industries and undermined the union gains of 1936 and early 1937, also produced a number of disciplinary problems. Employers, too, continued to challenge their agreements with the ACW, with their violations becoming so flagrant that Hyman Blumberg warned DeDominicis of the need for "tighter control." In response, DeDominicis convened a special meeting to "formulate plans to put a tighter grip on some of the manufacturers who are out to chisel" and instructed all shop chairmen and chairwomen to "be more strict with any strange work that comes in the shop" and report all violations "immediately" to the Joint Board. He also created a Control Committee for the sole purpose of upholding market arrangements and instituted a complex system of "production slips" that would have to be personally signed by Baltimore cutters before any work could be completed in the tailoring shops. This system, he assured the membership, would both serve market needs and prevent local manufacturers from "chiseling." One shop chairman, however, defied the new arrangements, obeying instead what he called "the will of the workers in his shop." Found guilty of insubordination to the union, he was removed from his position.[66]

The Joint Board faced an even graver danger to the union: the emergence of "craft clubs" among union members. First started by the pocket

170 makers, craft clubs were organized by skilled workers seeking to promote their own interests. Initially, the ACW responded favorably to their demands that they should receive larger wage increases than the rest of the membership because they could force those concessions from employers. Other groups followed suit, distinguishing themselves from the mass of unskilled workers and forming craft clubs in Locals #36 and #70. Without union permission, they conducted a series of strategic work stoppages in attempts to win wage adjustments. The incidents caused turmoil in the union and produced irate reactions from employers, who had already signed union agreements. Now rejecting the kind of concessions earlier granted, the ACW repudiated the clubs as "dual organizations" and refused to "create any special privileges for a few and do nothing for the rest." The Joint Board fined those members responsible for the clubs, but relationships between the union and the club members remained tense.[67]

"Keep up a general agitation"

The virtual disappearance of the ACW from the industry in the 1920s had also meant, of course, a decline in the educational activities essential to cementing union loyalties. Even in cities where the ACW continued to be viable, the educational programs had drawn fewer and fewer participants. At the time, union organizers attributed the decline to the rise of commercialized entertainment that offered new forms of excitement and escape. At the national level, the ACW leadership during the 1928 convention dismissed workers' educational programs as a form of "adult education" that hardly reflected the union's goals or needs. Always somewhat skeptical of educational activities, Sidney Hillman barely blinked when the ACW educational director announced that henceforth the New York office would no longer promote educational programs in the various cities. The official policy hardly reflected the sentiments of local-level members, however, and during the 1930s members campaigned vigorously for a new national education department within the union.[68]

Baltimore's ACW leaders saw educational activities as essential to attracting union members and maintaining their allegiance, but what they offered in this regard in the 1930s differed significantly from what they offered in the union's heyday in 1916 to 1920. Back then, evening classes at Johns Hopkins University, in which left-leaning professors discussed political economy, the principles of socialism, and the history of the labor movement, had accounted for much of the educational program. Those activities, com-

bined with special lecture series that touched on such diverse issues as the
moral significance of life and the responsibilities of shop chairwomen and
chairmen, served to link members more fully to the union and to the larger
society. The romanticized discussions of labor's triumphs might have seemed
maudlin or sentimental to national leaders, but they provided Sara Barron,
Jacob Edelman, and other members with enduring lessons in the meaning
of workers' solidarity. In the 1930s, such union veterans insisted on reviving
the ACW's educational programs.[69]

Reinforcing the union idea of unity and mutual support in the membership of the 1930s, these seasoned members believed, required new methods and new messages. Unfamiliar with even the broadest principles of socialism and uncomfortable with the revolutionary rhetoric of a classless
society, the new members were still sharply attuned to class distinctions and
deeply interested in social and economic improvement. They were interested in the New Deal, and not the Socialist Party. In this regard, they hardly
differed from the union's national leadership, which had also departed from
its earlier rhetoric to embrace a "new deal, a square deal for all."

Local organizers sought to broaden the ACW's educational program,
incorporating more cultural events as well as activities that could only be described as sheer entertainment. They extended that broader approach to organizational activities, for the new recruits, although the sons and daughters
of immigrant mothers or fathers, saw themselves as thoroughly American,
free from accents and Old World habits, and were eager for greater economic
freedom and independence. Organizers like Barron regarded "the girls" as
young and uninformed about unions but also more sophisticated about the
ways of the world, with more education and a greater sense of economic possibilities. Joseph Schlossberg described the women of Baltimore's new Local
#70 as "a new generation. . . . No foreigners. No immigrants. American
born! Young America! Born and bred in this country. Educated in American
schools. English is their mother tongue. American games are their amusements. Hardly any radicals among them." Largely at the insistence of Local
#70, the Joint Board hired a drama coach to instruct organizers on how to
appeal to such a constituency in a way that captured their interest and inspired them to join. Local #70 also filmed its activities, from striking and
picketing to its regular weekend excursions, and used these films at organizational meetings. Given the success of this approach, the Joint Board ab-
sorbed the cost (thereby indirectly facilitating the organization of women)
and also copied the idea, with Ulisse DeDominicis eventually insisting on
filming the annual May Day celebrations.[70]

172   The promotion of workers' educational programs received support from the New Deal through the Works Progress Administration, which helped revitalize the labor education movement. Amalgamated members sought to take advantage of those government programs, but the hostility of the city's political leaders toward the Roosevelt administration and the bitter division between the BFL and the Baltimore Industrial Council prevented much federal money from reaching the city for that purpose. The ACW did, however, become convinced that the federal government should take an active role in the education of the working class, a position that the national Amalgamated would also ultimately endorse.[71]

Educational activities, local members agreed, were necessary not only to attract and retain new members, but to revitalize older ones and repair divisions within the union. Since its formation, Local #70 promoted more educational activities than any other local in the union; it also initiated joint sponsorship of lectures, picnics, and dances. At all of these events, there would always be at least one speaker who would remind the audience of the necessity for the union and for worker solidarity. Joint sponsorship of activities led to joint meetings between locals to discuss educational activities and to plan programs. Members of Local #70 were so convinced of the importance of education that they also held seminars on the history of the workers' education movement and invited such longtime advocates of workers' education as Hilda Smith and Tom Tippett. They also initiated a variety of activities with other locals to promote greater cooperation within the union. Finally, they regarded education as necessary to break down both ethnic barriers and the more formidable ones presented by racial differences. As Barron later recalled, the union had to instruct new members about unions, about the New Deal and democracy, and about the "equality of all," regardless of color.[72]

By the end of the 1930s, the women of Local #70 had also persuaded De-Dominicis of the value of educational and cultural activities. Until then, he had not initiated any major educational program under Joint Board sponsorship but had limited his support to words of encouragement for the actions of the locals. In 1938, he called for a more energetic and coordinated program that would educate new members, cultivate others for leadership positions, and, given the internal problems, foster greater harmony and unity within the union. His new interest also resulted from developments at the national level, including the formation of the ACW's Department of Cultural Activities in 1937 and the constant lobbying by the union's Educational Committee for "all necessary help to our local unions' joint boards in the

development of a system of educational and cultural activities." The successful production of the play *Pins and Needles* by the city's branch of the International Ladies' Garment Workers' Union further spurred his interest,
prompting him to declare, "With all the good actors, beautiful girls, and
handsome boys of the Baltimore [Amalgamated] organization, we could do
the same, if not better, in the near future."[73]

The New Deal also helped to transform the message heard by the unions'
new members, as political action merged with the ACW's educational program. There were obvious roots to this development, suggested, for instance,
by Hyman Blumberg's telling striking Baltimore workers in 1932, "Hoover
speaks of 'rugged individualism.' That means stand by yourself, scab on one
another." But the New Deal's activist government and support of labor rights
comported well with the Amalgamated's new unionism, and FDR's reelection campaign in 1936 proved a significant turning point in the local union's
politicization and incorporation into mainstream politics. Political campaigning by union members produced displays of unity and activism that ri-
valed those engendered by the picket line. Until 1936, the Joint Board rarely
engaged in local or national politics, beyond occasionally sending petitions
or telegrams to local and state representatives and fitfully endorsing Socialist candidates in local elections. In 1936, the Joint Board, at the prompting
of the General Office and the insistence of local members, set up a special
committee to help reelect the president. "The most important question,"
DeDominicis declared, "is the re-election of President Roosevelt, and we
must help do the job. If he is reelected, there will be a possibility to have good
sound progressive legislation passed if not labor will be put in a sad plight.
We must see that people register, have shop chairmen's meetings, and have
mass meetings and keep up a general agitation." The ACW rank-and-file enthusiastically agreed, many announcing that this would be their first non-
Socialist vote and all authorizing the Joint Board manager to "start on this
campaign at once, to incur any expense he deems necessary to support President Roosevelt for re-election to the presidency of the United States."[74]

A flurry of activity followed. Women members organized under the banner "Amalgamated Women for Roosevelt," an action that recalled some of
their earlier gender-based activism. Even their union brothers conceded they
were in the forefront of the reelection activities. They canvassed door-to-
door, distributing FDR pamphlets, buttons, and ribbons. They organized
parades and parties, usually sponsored jointly with other locals, and raised
money for the Democratic Party by holding "ACW-FDR" dances. They
planned the ACW's main event for the reelection campaign: a mass rally in

174   October 1936, when thousands of workers, waving ACW and CIO flags and placards, lined the downtown streets to hear Hillman, Blumberg, and David Dubinsky sing FDR's praises. Barron cast her first non-Socialist vote in November and later recalled the ACW's role fondly: "We had lots of parades and lots of spirit."[75]

The Baltimore ACW spent almost $2,000 on the reelection effort, a huge sum given the union's limited treasury. Only the expenditure for the annual May Day celebration approached that record, and the members even voted to use more funds to hold victory balls and victory picnics after FDR's impressive triumph.[76]

Thereafter, the ACW maintained a more pronounced political profile, issuing political opinions to the press and supporting FDR at nearly every turn, even his court-packing plan and his support of David Lewis against the reelection of Senator Millard Tydings in 1938, both of which alienated many of FDR's loyal political supporters in Baltimore. The ACW took the lead in the city in promoting the candidacy of Lewis against the "reactionary" Tydings, donating a sizable contribution to his campaign and organizing a series of rallies and meetings to honor Lewis as a champion of organized labor. Although Lewis was defeated as an "outsider"—a White House candidate rather than a homegrown one—he rallied the forces of organized labor in the city. The ACW and the Baltimore Industrial Council worked through the Labor Non-Partisan League and helped to attract new sources of labor support. "As usual," Barron reported to the *Advance,* "the Amalgamated has assumed most of the responsibilities" in organizing the Labor Non-Partisan League in Baltimore, with DeDominicis serving as secretary-treasurer and succeeding in bringing most of the city's unions—both American Federation of Labor and CIO—into the organization. Politics had become an integral part of the union, and labor loyalty took on a distinctively partisan tone.[77]

The ACW's process of politicization could be seen in other forms as well. The Joint Board even invited Eleanor Roosevelt to be the guest of honor at its May Day parade in 1937, an act of more than symbolic significance for a union that traditionally had separated politics from industrial democracy. After 1937, many of the union's locals transformed their existing educational committees into educational and political committees. The activities these committees supported in their bimonthly meetings further illustrated the union's incorporation of a political perspective, for they frequently sponsored lectures by such politicians as congressman Thomas D'Alesandro, himself a former member of the Italian Local #51. ACW members' entrance into the political arena underscored their new attachment to the party of FDR. They took particular pride in the 1939 election of Edelman, a former Sonneborn cutter from Local #15 and the Amalgamated's attorney, to a seat on the Baltimore City Council—"the result," reported the *Advance,* "of militant political action by the Baltimore Joint Board and other labor and progressive groups in the city." Finally, the ACW, more than any other union in the city, used the slogans of FDR's New Deal to attract new members. Although all unions, even those affiliated with the BFL, legitimized their organizational campaigns by claiming that "Roosevelt Said Organize," few incorporated the programs and policies of the New Deal into their educational and cultural activities as fully as the Amalgamated did. ACW members figured prominently among groups lobbying for public housing or other New Deal reforms. They embraced the New Deal as an opportunity to realize a "progressive agenda," and they identified fully with a vision of a better deal for the working class.[78]

"The true picture"

By 1939, the ACW had succeeded in rebuilding a union. Union membership was a family and community responsibility and opportunity. Members were expected to do more than pay dues: they were urged to vote Democratic; attend union picnics, dances, and lectures; protest fascism; and support the Spanish civil war. The ACW sponsored active bowling leagues and movie clubs. Every local held at least one educational or cultural event each month, and members read and discussed books together. They constructed lasting friendships and loyal bonds to the union. They were essentially a union of workers, who wanted a fairer deal on the shopfloor. Their dedication on the picket line and their willingness to strike earned them the respect even of their foes in the BFL. DeDominicis spoke frequently and fondly of his "army of clothing workers" as a "disciplined fighting unit" with a thorough understanding of the importance of workers' "industrial power."[79]

To celebrate what it saw as its "return" to the city's industry, the Baltimore ACW moved in October 1937 into more spacious headquarters on Redwood Street in West Baltimore—"an ideal place for local unions to hold their meetings and social activities." The leadership remained hopeful through the rest of the decade, though their optimism was badly bruised by the Roosevelt Recession, and the structural changes that had occurred in the

176 1920s and 1930s were foreboding: the city's clothing industry bore little resemblance to its earlier shape, and the continued trends toward contract shops and runaway shops offered little hope to Baltimore's ACW.

Two months after the move to new headquarters, DeDominicis called a special meeting of the Joint Board to discuss the problem the union faced in the Baltimore market. "The majority of the shops are closed," he reported, "and those working are on part time." Conditions remained unchanged in February 1938: "very few shops are at work in either the ready-made or mail order houses." By spring, with the local garment industry in a "very poor" state, Sara Barron reported that union leaders were spending much of their time pressing public officials to establish emergency relief stations at union headquarters and "helping our members in matters pertaining to the unemployment insurance benefits." By fall of that year, "with conditions in our market . . . not yet improved," local ACW officials described "the unemployment situation" as "a serious problem" and conceded that "the outlook is not very bright." Loyal union members, "though . . . not working," continued to plan and hold educational and social programs.[80]

At the end of 1938, Barron reported a poignant story that dramatically illustrated the course of the industry and the union in Baltimore. One of the city's few remaining large manufacturers, Baltimore Clothes, went out of business, costing five hundred ACW members their jobs. The Joint Board had worked with management for three years to forestall liquidation, and DeDominicis now had to call a meeting to break the "sad news." His unpleasant task was made worse, Barron noted, for the shop had been the first "to respond to the union's call in 1932 and has stood loyally by the union 100%, ready to defend and sacrifice for the organization whenever called upon." After hearing of the company's closing, the workers, though "desperate" and without "prospects for work," responded by voting "their appreciation to the Joint Board for all they had done to keep the shop operating as long as it had." Then "the workers, in saying farewell to each other, cried and kissed one another but pledged to the union that they would remain loyal members." Asked to say a few encouraging words, DeDominicis could only urge them "to be as courageous in the future as they have been in the past."[81]

Both Blumberg and Hillman visited the city to survey the industrial landscape. They were impressed with the "fighting spirit" and the "loyalty" of the members, but they were stunned by the assessment DeDominicis offered of "the true picture of the Baltimore market." The Baltimore membership continued to do its part to uphold regional agreements, maintaining price levels that kept out business from New York but that also made "the **177** shops quite empty" and "workers everywhere" in need of more work. De-Dominicis then tallied the number of major firms that had left the city, beginning in 1933 with Schoeneman: the total was fourteen. He concluded, "We need some reliable and solid manufacturers to pull us out of the wilderness."

The Amalgamated had rebuilt the union, but, as DeDominicis sadly observed, "we lost the industry."[82]

EPILOGUE

The decline in Baltimore's garment industry that so troubled Ulisse De-Dominicis in the late 1930s continued in succeeding years. Even World War II had little positive impact, so unlike World War I. Few large companies remained in the city to take advantage of government contracts. Greif, the largest, had war production valued in excess of $15 million but actually reduced the number of employees at its Homeland Avenue plant from 1,030 before the war to 870; Cohen, Goldman & Company decreased its prewar workforce of 800 by more than 10 percent, even while annually producing 125,000 navy coats. A few medium-sized firms, such as Haas Tailoring Company and Marlboro Shirt Company, did expand because of government business, but most of the city's garment manufacturers had constant or decreasing workforces during the war. Efforts of the War Manpower Commission to shift labor into Baltimore's airplane manufacturing, shipbuilding, and other war industries aggravated matters, convincing DeDominicis that the city's clothing industry faced "a slow, very pitiful agony, and then death." By 1947 Baltimore's garment workers numbered nearly 20 percent fewer than at the end of the 1930s.[1]

In the 1950s and 1960s, the insistent internationalization of the garment industry further stripped Baltimore of both firms and jobs, and at rates greater than those in the industry nationally. Particularly disturbing was the 1950 liquidation of Cohen, Goldman & Company, a New York firm ranking among the ten leading producers of men's clothing; its Baltimore factory was a mainstay of both the local garment industry and the Amalgamated Clothing Workers (ACW), which had organized it during the great strike of 1932. In 1951, Erlanger Brothers closed its huge manufacturing complex at Pratt and Greene Streets and sold its famous B.V.D. trademark. In certain ways, the flight of the garment industry mirrored other developments in the city, leaving bare outlines of once successful businesses and neighborhoods. Empty houses in neighborhoods divided by race and vacated factory buildings in the loft district became visible scars in the urban landscape.

A few firms, notably A. Sagner & Sons, prospered in the 1950s, thanks to efficient production, effective merchandising, and a close relationship with the ACW. Indeed, Stanley Sagner negotiated with the Amalgamated directly, bypassing the group bargaining of the Clothing Manufacturers' Association, and often supported union positions opposed by the association. Still, the larger industrial trend was a downward turn, and even the Sagner firm eventually succumbed to foreign competition. In 1959 a national conglomerate, Genesco, purchased the Greif company, and in the 1960s J. Schoeneman, the Marlboro Shirt Company, Lamm Brothers, Lebow Brothers, and other Baltimore clothiers fell to similar takeovers by outside interests—all significant signs of the decline of the industry in Baltimore. Although some of the firms continued to produce clothes in the city, others closed their facilities. The Wohlmuth Company, where Sara Barron had first worked in 1914, was liquidated in 1970. Greif itself abandoned Baltimore in 1983, confirming the *News-American*'s account of the city's "dying industry."[2]

The ACW, which, as discussed in Chapter 6, had revitalized itself in the 1930s despite the industry's decline, gaining new members, influence, and legitimacy locally as well as nationally, continued to work vigorously in the postwar years to promote its members' interests and the industry's stability. Persistent organizational activity even brought the recalcitrant Greif company and the runaway shops of Schoeneman under union contracts in 1943 and 1950, respectively. "Amicable negotiations" unionized A. Sagner & Sons in 1950 and improved wages, working conditions, and benefits. In 1951 Raleigh Clothes, convinced of "the value of the Amalgamated constructive policies," agreed to its first union contract for its five hundred employees. And other firms, such as the Londontown Manufacturing Company and the

180 Townley Shirt Co., previously regarded by the union as an "open-shop fortress," accepted ACW contracts later in the decade. All such work was largely accomplished by the patient and persuasive DeDominicis, often assisted by Barron, who was on the Baltimore Joint Board. With the industry in decline, DeDominicis also had to fight a rearguard action, as when he negotiated severance pay for the B.V.D. workers. "Clothing workers all over the country," he lamented, faced "very poor" times.[3]

In 1961, after a long illness, DeDominicis died at age 65, ending a lengthy career that began when he was a sixteen-year-old tailor at Schloss Brothers. He had become a national organizer at age twenty-four and was elected an ACW vice president and member of the national General Executive Board in 1948, even as he served as manager of the Baltimore Joint Board from 1933 until his death. As Hyman Blumberg mourned, "Ulisse was the cement that held the union together in Baltimore for 28 years." Even the *Baltimore Sun,* which had previously railed against DeDominicis's "radicalism," noted that he had earned "the affection and the esteem of both workers and management" and eulogized him for his "determination to obtain a harmonious relationship between clothing workers and manufacturers in Baltimore that would be to the best interest of the workers, the employers, and the community at large."[4]

Like DeDominicis, other Baltimore ACW pioneers gradually passed from the scene. Dorothy Jacobs Bellanca had preceded him in 1946, her death provoking an outpouring of grief throughout the labor movement. Blumberg followed him, leaving few Baltimore leaders in the union. Mamie Santora had retired from her extensive national organizing activities in 1956 to live in Baltimore until her death at age ninety-five in 1984. Four months later, Jacob Edelman died at age eighty-eight, a veteran of thirty-two years on the Baltimore City Council, countless humanitarian activities, and seven decades of service to the Amalgamated. Sara Barron officially retired in 1972 but remained a vigorous activist, even lobbying Congress for equal rights legislation, until she died in 1992.[5]

After DeDominicis's death in 1961, the General Executive Board revoked the charter of the Baltimore Joint Board and merged it with the Maryland-Virginia-Pennsylvania Regional Joint Board, which represented some six thousand Schoeneman and Greif employees in thirteen locals, most of them in smaller towns in the region but some in Baltimore. Members represented by the Baltimore board had numbered about the same but worked for more than forty employers, indicating the predominance of smaller firms in the city. Sam Nocella, manager of the tristate Joint Board, assumed lead-

ership of the new Baltimore Regional Joint Board and tried to deflect attention from the obvious continuing decline of the Baltimore market: the merger, he maintained, would "not take away anything from the Baltimore Joint
Board, because the richness of its tradition will still be there. The new people from the outlying areas will be able to learn something from the older
people in Baltimore, and I am hopeful that the older people will learn something from the new people too." At least some of the few remaining old-
timers, however, felt differently. They had worked hard for their own Joint
Board, had watched patiently but not happily as the union shifted business
to Rochester and New York City in the 1920s and 1930s, and now suffered
another indignity as one of the union's founding locals lost its charter.[6]

Still, Nocella remained optimistic and continued the cooperative course
set by his predecessors. While striving to organize the scattered small clothing plants in the region, he was especially interested in promoting broad participation of workers through what he called "an education program . . . in
order that they can fully understand that they can make their greatest gains
only through their union." He described the Amalgamated as "my university." Sensitive to social issues, a stance he regarded as appropriate for a union
80 percent of whose members were women, Nocella also campaigned for civil rights and other reforms in society and established child care centers, health
services, and recreational and educational facilities for ACW members.[7]

His greatest accomplishment, rich in symbolism as well, came when the
Baltimore ACW bought the Phoenix Club at 1505 Eutaw Place in fashionable Bolton Hill in 1959. Blumberg described the club as formerly "an exclusive institution for the very rich" and "forbidden territory for the clothing workers." Indeed, its prominent German Jewish membership earlier in
the century had included Sonneborn, Schoeneman, Schloss, Strouse, and
other leading garment manufacturers. The Amalgamated razed the club and
in 1964 built a modern building housing the Joint Board offices and rooms
for educational, social, and recreational activities: "a rich man's hideaway
here is now a working man's haven." The most popular feature was the Hyman Blumberg Center for Retired Members, which attracted more than six
hundred retirees to its opening. It was a new building, but most attention
again seemed focused on the past, as old-timers reminisced about the great
Sonneborn strike that had launched the union exactly half a century before.
The *Advance* reported the occasion as "a reunion as well as a dedication."[8]

Meetings of Baltimore's active ACW members concentrated increasingly on
"unemployment, automation, and the import problem." Although nation-

182 al union officials assured locals, "We don't intend to sit by and see our industry annihilated by international sweatshops," larger economic developments limited their prospects for success. With imports of clothing mounting exponentially, the General Executive Board had explained the problem as early as 1959: The intense competition among the many small firms left the garment industry with low profit margins, high business mortality, and pressure to cut costs. "Before the advent of the Amalgamated, the workers . . . bore the major brunt of this competitive pressure through starvation wages and sweatshop conditions . . . . We now find that the hard-won labor standards of our members, and ultimately their jobs, are threatened by these very same evils imported from abroad."[9]

A union of immigrants, the ACW did not engage in immigrant-bashing even as it campaigned for restrictions on imports. It focused instead on the fate of American industry and the economic opportunity and security of all workers. The competitive advantage of imported apparel, noted ACW leaders, derived from "substandard wages and degrading working conditions" in other lands. As a speaker at the Amalgamated's fiftieth anniversary national convention noted in 1964, "domestic runaways who specialize in obtaining an unfair labor cost advantage by moving to communities which are hostile to unions, have been extending their area of activity. Many have become international runaways, setting up their own apparel factories overseas for export to the United States." In 1975 the *Advance* described U.S. "runaway multinational corporations" as producing "sweatshops abroad and unemployment in the United States." Their relentless pursuit of low-cost labor and constant shifting of operations to new areas with lower wage scales produced, the *Advance* asserted, "economic chaos and social injustice." Indeed, by focusing on the issues of economic chaos and injustice, the newspaper was merely reaffirming the union's constant principles of providing industrial stability and rationality in return for a measure of economic dignity.[10]

Like ACW members elsewhere, Baltimore's unionists condemned these developments and attempted to influence public opinion, waging a campaign against foreign production and imports that was being waged throughout most of America's industries, from automobiles to steel. For the clothing industry, the largest national demonstration occurred on November 11, 1974, "Amalgamated Day," when a work stoppage combined with mass rallies of one hundred thousand ACW members to protest the internationalization of the industry. "Low-wage sweatshop imports," ACW officials calculated, had caused 150 manufacturers employing eleven thousand workers to liquidate in the previous four years alone. Nocella led a union **183** march in Washington, D.C., that drew twenty-five hundred Amalgamated members, including several busloads of Baltimore workers, from the ranks represented by the Baltimore Regional Joint Board. In Baltimore, another fifteen hundred Amalgamated members rallied at the Charles Center Plaza before parading through what remained of the loft district. In both Baltimore and Washington, D.C., workers carried draped coffins symbolizing the death of the once vibrant industry and its workforce. A band playing the funeral march emphasized the somber realities.[11]

As conditions continued to deteriorate, the Amalgamated adopted another tactic as well. Under attack from external forces, unions, like businesses, have often turned to mergers to consolidate their economic position and preclude further erosion in size and status. Such had been the case, for example, at the turn of the century, when industrial changes pointed up the inadequacies of narrowly defined craft unions, and workers and unions alike struggled with reconciling new jobs, new skills, and new industries within the jurisdictional confines of the American Federation of Labor. The attempt to address those issues resulted in the consolidation of unions, producing an amalgam of groups with such lengthy names as the "International Association of Marble, Slate and Stone Polishers, Rubbers and Sawyers, Tile and Marble Setters Helpers and Terrazzo Helpers."[12] The formation of the Amalgamated itself along quasi-industrial lines—and its very name—had been an attempt to secure worker solidarity despite the hierarchy of skills that privileged cutters and tailors over other workers in the garment industry and despite divisions over ethnicity and gender.

Now responding to the sharp decline in the number of jobs in the clothing industries, the ACW merged with other unions in an effort to retain some beneficial influence. In 1976, the ACW and the textile workers merged to form the Amalgamated Clothing and Textile Workers Union (ACTWU). By 1989, however, that union represented only about 250,000 clothing *and* textile workers in the United States, Canada, and Puerto Rico—or only 70,000 more than the number of garment workers the ACW had represented in the United States alone in 1920 and 50,000 fewer than the organized textile workers had claimed in 1937. The globalization of the production of clothes only accelerated after the 1970s, and the decline in the clothing industry mirrored the general dropoff in manufacturing jobs at the national level. International competition combined with outsourcing in a low-paid global workforce to result in sharp challenges to American-made clothing, shoes, electronics, automobiles, and steel. In 1995, the ACTWU

184 and the International Ladies' Garment Workers' Union merged to become the Union of Needletrades, Industrial, and Textile Employees, or UNITE, with a worldwide membership of only about three hundred thousand.[13]

The new union's first battle has been the seemingly eternal problem of sweatshops. Indeed, UNITE has faced an unusual turn of events in the history of the garment industry. In 1995, the U.S. Labor Department reported an unexpected rise in the number of jobs in the clothing industry in the United States, reversing a decades-old trend. Citing automation and technological advances, primarily the use of computerization, laser cutting devices, and bar codes, the Labor Department noted a "reviving" American clothing industry in the late 1980s and early 1990s—but it is a revival that has produced an increasing number of sweatshops. The Labor Department reported that the United States has fewer than one thousand manufacturers but as many as twenty-two thousand subcontractors, most of them petty entrepreneurs bidding for jobs at the expense of labor and many of them violating minimum-wage, worker safety, and other labor laws. Confirming the "growing problem," Secretary of Labor Robert B. Reich described working conditions in U.S. garment shops "that many Americans would find appalling even in the Third World." An organizer for UNITE further exclaimed that the "sweatshops that gave birth to our union . . . are now back with a vengeance."[14]

In Baltimore, not only is the once-bustling loft district free from the hum of sewing machines, as some of the large factories have been transformed into offices and condominiums, but even the medium-sized firms have all but disappeared. In 1982 the Census Bureau reported a scant eleven hundred workers producing men's clothes in the city and only eight shops with more than twenty workers. Counting the several states that now constitute the "Baltimore region" and the union merger, union membership numbered just over six thousand in the mid-1990s, a decline of nearly 70 percent since Sam Nocella led worker demonstrations in the 1970s.

Now Carmen Papale, Baltimore born and raised, heads the regional board. He has continued its tradition of "realistic" labor-management relations, even helping organize the Maryland Alliance to promote better labor-management relations. In addition, in much the same way the ACW helped the Sonneborn company in the 1920s, he has contributed efforts essential to the retention and successful reorganization of such firms as Jos. A. Bank and English American Tailoring in the early 1990s.[15]

Indeed, the outlines of the story of the Baltimore ACW have remained the same throughout the twentieth century. The union sometimes became an essential part of some companies' planning, production, and marketing—working with management to create an efficient and cooperative industry that recognized the importance of workers, the value of the union, and the profitability of the industry. In 1997, for example, Jos. A. Bank Clothiers signed a three-year contract with UNITE. Bank's CEO, Timothy Finley, conceded that he was defying "industry trends" by not closing the sewing factory on North Avenue, firing its four hundred workers, and outsourcing production to the Caribbean or Mexico, but he said his decision, made after negotiations with UNITE's Papale, was not simply a short-term dollars-and-cents one. Rather it reflected a more strategic vision of the company's future, one that recognized not only that domestic manufacturing insulates Bank from fluctuations in the value of the dollar and enables it to respond to market changes more rapidly than if its clothes were made overseas by a contractor, but also that the company's long-term profitability lies in the efficiency, predictability, and quality work of its "good labor force." Moreover, the garment workers at the Bank factory still reflect the profile firmly established earlier: predominantly female and largely immigrant. Speaking a total of fourteen languages, the workforce "is like a United Nations," said Theresa Watson, a union shopfloor official.[16]

Other companies, however, have rejected such cooperation with the union and its members, preferring to compete in a chaotic industry without making accommodations to labor. Indeed, it was the union and its wages and benefits contract that London Fog cited in 1994 as the primary reason for its closing several plants in Baltimore and elsewhere in Maryland. In 1997, just days after Jos. A. Bank signed its new union contract, London Fog closed its last Baltimore factory, its sole remaining U.S. factory, again citing labor costs for the company's decision to place "the remaining portion of our business with offshore contractors."[17]

Firmly convinced that labor and management must work together for the nation's future and also determined that management must "give our people respect," Papale retains the ACW's belief in the redemptive power of the union—now UNITE—in an industry still characterized by sweatshops, low pay, and little job security.[18]

NOTES

Introduction

1. *Baltimore Sun,* Aug. 16 and Oct. 1 and 29, 1995, May 2, July 16 and 19, Aug. 12, 1996.

2. Ibid., Oct. 29, 1995, Aug. 9, 1996.

3. Ibid., June 4 and 19, July 30, Aug. 8, 13, and 24, Sept. 26 and 27, Oct. 21, 1994.

4. Ibid., Jan. 26, 1908.

5. Minutes of the General Executive Board, Aug. 25–8, 1931, Box 165, Folder 15, Amalgamated Clothing Workers of America Papers, Catherwood Library, Industrial Labor Relations School, Cornell University, Ithaca, N.Y.

6. For the best discussion of the continuities and distinctions between the recent and traditional approaches to labor history, see David Brody, *Workers in Industrial America: Essays on the Twentieth Century Struggle* (New York: Oxford University Press, 1993), 135–54.

7. For a discussion of the traditional ways Jewish women workers behaved, see Susan A. Glenn, *Daughters of the Shtetl: Life and Labor in the Immigrant Generation* (Ithaca, N.Y.: Cornell University Press, 1990), esp. 207–42. For another perspective on the diversity of women's activism, and one more in keeping with my findings, see Annelise Orleck, *Common Sense and a Little Fire: Women and Working-Class Politics in the United States, 1900–1965* (Chapel Hill: University of North Carolina Press, 1995).

8. Robert J. Schaefer, "Educational Activities of the Garment Unions, 1890–1948" (Ph.D. diss., Columbia University, 1951); Steven Fraser, *Labor Will Rule: Sidney Hillman and the Rise of American Labor* (New York: Free Press, 1991), esp. chaps. 3 and 4; Charles Elbert Zaretz, *The Amalgamated Clothing Workers of America: A Study in Progressive Trades-Unionism* (New York: Ancon, 1934); Sara Barron, interview by author, Feb. 17, 1986.

9. See Fraser's description of Italian male workers in *Labor Will Rule,* 107–13.

10. *Labor Leader* (Baltimore), Feb. 26, 1916.

Chapter 1: Toilers and Sweaters

1. Charles Hirschfeld, *Baltimore, 1870–1900: Studies in Social History,* The Johns Hopkins University Studies in Historical and Political Science (Baltimore: Johns Hopkins Press, 1941), 9–31, 37–53; Bureau of the Census, *Twelfth Census of the United States: Manufacturing* (Washington, D.C.: Government Printing Office, 1901), 2:276; Edward K. Muller and Paul A. Groves, "The Changing Location of the Clothing Industry: A Link to the Social Geography of Baltimore in the Nineteenth Century," *Maryland Historical Magazine* 71 (fall 1976): 403–4; Eleanor Bruchey, "The Industrialization of Maryland, 1860–1914," in *Maryland: A*

188 *History, 1632–1974,* ed. Richard Walsh and William Lloyd Fox (Baltimore: Maryland Historical Society, 1974), 408–30; Sherry H. Olson, *Baltimore: The Building of an American City* (Baltimore: Johns Hopkins University Press, 1980), 198–244. It is also important to note that the port's volume of trade similarly expanded, and Baltimore's national ranking rose from fifth to third.

2. Olson, *Baltimore,* 249–53; Patricia Ann McDonald, "Baltimore Women, 1870–1900" (Ph.D. diss., University of Maryland, College Park, 1976), 16–7, 24.

3. McDonald, "Baltimore Women," 24–6, 32–7, 44.

4. Hirschfeld, *Baltimore, 1870–1900,* 32–44; Bureau of the Census, *Twelfth Census of the United States,* 236. For a convenient summary of the emergence of the American ready-made clothing industry, see Philip Scranton, "The Transition from Custom to Ready-to-Wear Clothing in Philadelphia, 1890–1930," *Textile History* 25 (1994): 244–6.

5. Muller and Groves, "Changing Location," 408–11; Bureau of the Census, *Eighth Census of the United States, 1860: Manufactures* (Washington, 1865), 40; Henry A. Corbin, *The Men's Clothing Industry: Colonial Through Modern Times* (New York, 1970), 19; Joel Seidman, *The Needle Trades* (New York: Farrar & Rinehart, Inc., 1942), 7–20; Abraham Imberman, "Report on Men's Clothing Industry," sponsored by the Works Progress Administration (Baltimore: State Printers, 1945), 9–14; Zaretz, *The Amalgamated Clothing Workers of America,* 13–49 (see intro., n. 8); Hirschfeld, *Baltimore, 1870–1900,* 41–2, 57–9. Although it discusses more than the clothing industry, see also Philip Kahn Jr., *A Stitch in Time: The Four Seasons of Baltimore's Needle Trades* (Baltimore: Maryland Historical Society, 1989), chaps. 1 and 2.

6. Jo Ann E. Argersinger, "To Discipline an Industry: Workers, Employers, and the ACWA in Baltimore" (paper presented at the annual meeting of the Social Science History Association, Chicago, Nov. 1985); Argersinger, "The City That Tries to Suit Everybody: Baltimore's Clothing Industry," in *The Baltimore Book,* ed. Elizabeth Fee, Linda Shopes, and Linda Zeidman (Philadelphia: Temple University Press, 1991), 80–3; Muller and Groves, "Changing Location," 417–20. For excellent discussions of the nature of the clothing industry, see two works by Steven Fraser, "Combined and Uneven Development in the Men's Clothing Industry," *Business History Review* 57 (winter 1983): 522–47, and his superb biography of Sidney Hillman, *Labor Will Rule* (see intro., n. 8), esp. 26–39.

7. *Baltimore Sun,* Nov. 12, 1895.

8. Argersinger, "To Discipline an Industry"; *Baltimore Sun,* July 1, 1892; Imberman, "Men's Clothing," 10–4; M. H. Rosemond, "Mass Production Cuts Costs in Manufacturing Men's Suits," *Manufacturing Industries* 14 (July 1927): 60–1.

9. Bureau of the Census, *Twelfth Census of the United States, Special Reports: Occupations* (Washington, D.C.: Government Printing Office, 1904), 429, 430–1, 494; Hirschfeld, *Baltimore, 1870–1900,* 45; Industrial Survey of Baltimore, *The Industrial Survey of Baltimore: Report of Industries Located within the Baltimore Metropolitan District* (Baltimore, 1914) and *Baltimore: As It Was, As It Is, As It Will Be* (Baltimore, 1914); Isaac M. Fein, *The Making of an American Jewish Community: The History of Baltimore Jewry from 1773 to 1920* (Philadelphia: Jewish Publications Society of America, 1971); Isidor Blum, *The Jews of Baltimore* (Baltimore: Historical Review Publishing, 1910).

10. "Baltimore: Its Manufacturing Market," *Apparel Manufacturer,* Aug. 1945: 71–3, in the Vertical File, Enoch Pratt Free Library, Baltimore (hereafter referred to as EPFL); Hirschfeld, *Baltimore, 1870–1900,* 41–2.

11. Rosemond, "Mass Production," 60; Zaretz, *The Amalgamated,* 20–2; Imberman, "Men's Clothing," 73–82.

12. Bruchey, "Industrialization of Maryland," 413–4, 425–31; *Industrial Survey of Baltimore,* v, 34. For an excellent overview of Baltimore's political, social, and economic landscapes, see Robert J. Brugger, *Maryland: A Middle Temperament, 1634–1980* (Baltimore: Johns Hopkins University Press, 1988), esp. 345–54.

13. Bureau of the Census, *Ninth Census of the United States: Population* (Washington, D.C.: U.S. Government Printing Office, 1872), 1:xx; Bureau of the Census, *Tenth Census of the United States: Population* (Washington, D.C.: U.S. Government Printing Office, 1881), 1:xc; Bureau of the Census, *Eleventh Census of the United States: Population* (Washington, D.C.: U.S. Government Printing Office, 1891), 1:434, 439; Bureau of the Census, *Twelfth Census of the United States: Population* (Washington, D.C.: U.S. Government Printing Office, 1901), 1:454–5, 620–3.

14. Hirschfeld, *Baltimore, 1870–1900,* 23–7; Muller and Groves, "Changing Location," 412, 419; Bureau of Industrial Statistics and Information of Maryland (hereafter referred to as BIS), *Third Biennial Report, 1888–89* (Annapolis, Md., 1889), 121; BIS, *Third Annual Report, 1894* (Baltimore, 1895) and *Fifth Annual Report, 1896* (Baltimore, 1897), 58–60; *Baltimore Sun,* Sept. 26, 1893; Fein, *The Making of an American Jewish Community,* 167; McDonald, "Baltimore Women," 15.

15. *Baltimore Sun,* Nov. 12, 1895; *Baltimore Critic,* June 11 and 18, 1892.

16. BIS, *Third Annual Report, 1894,* 80–114. All the annual reports of the BIS were examined.

17. Hirschfeld, *Baltimore, 1870–1900,* 59; Argersinger, "To Discipline an Industry"; *Baltimore Critic,* June 11, 25, 1892; Fraser, *Labor Will Rule,* 27–38; BIS, *Third Annual Report, 1894* and *Fifth Annual Report, 1896;* Zaretz, *The Amalgamated,* 36–50.

18. Argersinger, "Baltimore's Clothing Industry," 83–4; BIS, *Fifth Annual Report, 1896;* Hirschfeld, *Baltimore, 1870–1900,* 57–9; *Baltimore Critic,* June 18, 1892.

19. BIS, *Third Annual Report, 1894* and *Fifth Annual Report, 1896;* Jo Ann E. Argersinger, "When Women Organize: Workers, Employers, and the ACW" (paper presented at the Society for Historians of the Gilded Age and Progressive Era, American Historical Association, New York, Dec. 1990). The poem is also reproduced in Roderick N. Ryon, "'Human Creatures' Lives': Baltimore Women and Work in Factories, 1880–1917," *Maryland Historical Magazine* 83 (winter 1988): 346–64, which provides an overview of women's occupations and the conditions of work. The poem, entitled "Song of the Shirt," was written in 1843, according to the BIS. For an exceptional discussion of the "family culture of work," see Glenn, *Daughters of the Shtetl,* 64 (see intro., n. 7). See also Judith E. Smith, *Family Connections: A History of Italian and Jewish Immigrant Lives in Providence, Rhode Island* (Albany, N.Y.: SUNY Press, 1985). For the family wage economy in Baltimore, see the detailed reports of household wages, food prices, and housing costs in McDonald, "Baltimore Women," 25–6, 34–6. In McDonald's sample of Baltimore working-class families in 1900, a majority had three or more wage earners.

20. Joan M. Jensen, "Needlework as Art, Craft, and Livelihood Before 1900," in *A Needle, A Bobbin, A Strike: Women Needleworkers in America,* ed. Joan M. Jensen and Sue Davidson (Philadelphia: Temple University Press, 1984), 3–17; BIS, *First Annual Report, 1892* and *Third Annual Report, 1894; Baltimore Sun,* Jan. 22, 1883; Cynthia R. Daniels, "Between Home

190 and Factory: Homeworkers and the State," in *Homework: Historical and Contemporary Perspectives on Paid Labor at Home,* ed. Eileen Boris and Cynthia R. Daniels (Chicago: University of Illinois Press, 1989), 13–29.

21. BIS, *Fifth Annual Report, 1896.*

22. For a thoughtful discussion of Progressive Era investigators attempting to deal with women at the workplace, see Glenn, *Daughters of the Shtetl,* 115–7. See also James B. Crooks, *Politics and Progress: The Rise of Urban Progressivism in Baltimore, 1895 to 1911* (Baton Rouge: Louisiana State University Press, 1968), 189–90. The quote is from BIS, *Fifth Annual Report, 1896.*

23. Leonora Barry quoted in Carolyn Daniel McCreesh, "On the Picket Line: Militant Women Campaign to Organize Garment Workers, 1880–1917" (Ph.D. diss., University of Maryland, College Park, 1975), 43.

24. *Baltimore Critic,* Aug. 25, 1888, Mar. 2 and May 11, 1889, Apr. 11, 1891; "Myrtle Assembly to Friend," in BIS, *Third Biennial Report, 1888–89,* 25–6. See also Ryon, "Human Creatures' Lives," 354.

25. Sara Barron, interview by author, Feb. 17, 1986. Much has been written about the role of class and gender in the doctrine of separate spheres and the "special character of women" in "women's sphere." For this study, the work of Kathy Peiss in *Cheap Amusements: Working Women and Leisure in Turn-of-the-Century New York* (Philadelphia: Temple University Press, 1986) offers particularly useful guidelines and insights.

26. BIS, *Third Annual Report, 1894, Fifth Annual Report, 1896,* and *Ninth Annual Report, 1900;* Hirschfeld, *Baltimore, 1870–1900,* 57–9, 62–3, 75–6; Argersinger, "Baltimore's Clothing Industry," 85–6.

27. "Baltimore: Its Manufacturing Market," 71–2; BIS, *First Annual Report, 1892.*

28. Both the *Baltimore Sun* and *Baltimore American* daily newspapers were examined for this period. See also BIS, *Third Annual Report, 1894, Fifth Annual Report, 1896, Ninth Annual Report, 1900,* and *Tenth Annual Report, 1901,* and Crooks, *Politics and Progress,* 189–92.

29. *Baltimore Critic,* Sept. 21, 1889.

30. *Baltimore American,* July 3 and June 30, 1892; *Baltimore Sun,* Aug. 3, 1892; McCreesh, "On the Picket Line," 71.

31. *Baltimore Critic,* July 2 and 23, 1892; *Baltimore Sun,* July 20 and Aug. 24, 1892.

32. *Baltimore Sun,* July 6, 1892.

33. Ibid., Aug. 17, 1892; *Baltimore Critic,* June 25, 1892.

34. *Baltimore Critic,* July 16 and 23 and Aug. 20, 1892; *Baltimore Sun,* Aug. 16, 1892; BIS, *Fifth Annual Report, 1896; Baltimore American,* June 20, 1892.

35. BIS, *First Annual Report, 1892; Baltimore American,* June 28 and 30, July 2, 3, 6, and 8, 1892; *Baltimore Sun,* Aug. 25 and Sept. 15 and 20, 1892; *Baltimore Critic,* Aug. 20, 1892.

36. *Baltimore Sun,* Jan. 15, 1894; BIS, *Third Annual Report, 1894* and *Twelfth Annual Report, 1903;* Crooks, *Politics and Progress,* 166–7.

37. BIS, *Fourth Annual Report, 1895* and *Fifth Annual Report, 1896; Baltimore Sun,* Nov. 21, 1894.

38. *Baltimore Sun,* Nov. 21, 1894; Hirschfeld, *Baltimore, 1870–1900,* 54–5; BIS, *Fifth Annual Report, 1896.*

39. *Baltimore Sun,* May 2–4 and 9, 1895.

40. *Baltimore American,* Feb. 18 and 19, 1896; BIS, *Fifth Annual Report, 1896.*

41. *Baltimore Sun,* Feb. 25 and 27, 1896.

42. Ibid., Mar. 10 and 17, 1896.

43. Ibid., Feb. 25 and Mar. 10, 1896; BIS, *Fifth Annual Report, 1896.*

44. *Baltimore American,* Feb. 20 and 25, 1896; *Baltimore Sun,* Mar. 14 and 31, 1896; BIS, *Fifth Annual Report, 1896.*

45. *Baltimore Sun,* Mar. 31, 1896; BIS, *Fifth Annual Report, 1896.*

46. BIS, *Fifth Annual Report, 1896.*

47. BIS, *Ninth Annual Report, 1900.*

48. BIS, *Tenth Annual Report, 1901.*

CHAPTER 2: FORMING LABOR'S NEW VOICE

1. "Oral History Interview with Sara Barron by Barbara Wertheimer, June 4, 1976, Baltimore, Maryland," New York State School of Industrial and Labor Relations, New York City Division of Cornell University.

2. Bureau of the Census, *Thirteenth Census: Manufacturers, 1910* (Washington, D.C.: Government Printing Office, 1911), 480, 482, and *Twelfth Census, Special Reports: Occupations,* 429, 430–1 (see chap. 1, n. 9); *Baltimore Sun,* Jan. 26, 1908.

3. BIS, *Ninth Annual Report, 1900;* Hirschfeld, *Baltimore, 1870–1900,* 44–5, 58–9, 62 (see chap. 1, n. 1).

4. BIS, *Eleventh Annual Report, 1902* and *Thirteenth Annual Report, 1904;* *Baltimore Sun,* Aug. 27, 1902.

5. *Baltimore Sun,* Aug. 27, 1902. See also Crooks, *Politics and Progress,* chap. 7 (see chap. 1, n. 22).

6. Senate, *Reports of the Immigration Commission: Immigrants in Industries. Part 6: The Clothing Manufacturing Industry,* 61st Cong., 2d sess., 1911, S. Doc. 633, 413–5; Senate, *Report on Condition of Woman and Child Wage-Earners in the United States. Volume II: Men's Ready-Made Clothing,* 61st Cong., 2d sess., 1911, S. Doc. 645, 53, 195–8, 415, 419–29, 438–40.

7. Matthew Josephson, *Sidney Hillman, Statesman of American Labor* (Garden City, N.Y.: Doubleday, 1952), 50–7, 111–2; Zaretz, *The Amalgamated,* 94–9, 134–5 (see intro., n. 8); Fraser, "Sidney Hillman and the Origins of the 'New Unionism,' 1890–1933" (Ph.D. diss., Rutgers University, 1983), 97; Nina Lynn Asher, "Dorothy Jacobs Bellanca: Feminist Trade Unionist, 1894–1946" (Ph.D. diss., State University of New York at Binghamton, 1982), 48–56; Seidman, *Needle Trades,* 87–9 (see chap. 1, n. 5); *The Garment Worker* (New York), 1902; *Baltimore Sun,* Nov. 12 and 13, 1895, Feb. 27, 1896.

8. Fraser, *Labor Will Rule,* 43 (see intro., n. 8).

9. Crooks, *Politics and Progress,* 81, 160, 176, 198, 228.

10. For an eloquent description of the distinction between Orthodox and German Jews in Baltimore, using the example of the *mikve,* among others, see Brugger, *Middle Temperament,* 351 (see chap. 1, n. 12).

11. Fraser, "Sidney Hillman," 96–100; Glenn, *Daughters of the Shtetl,* 177–82 (see intro., n. 7); Moses Rischin, *The Promised City: New York's Jews, 1870–1914* (Cambridge, Mass.: Harvard University Press, 1962), 166.

12. *Labor Leader* (Baltimore), Jan. 13 and June 29, 1912.

13. *Baltimore Sun,* Oct. 27 and Nov. 14, 17, 25, and 27, 1905; *Baltimore American,* Nov. 25, 1905; BIS, *Fourteenth Annual Report, 1905.*

14. *Weekly Bulletin of the Clothing Trades* (New York), Dec. 17, 24, and 31, 1909, Jan. 7 and 14, 1910; *Baltimore American,* Dec. 19, 1909.

15. Jacob Edelman, oral history interview by Bertha Libauer, Nov. 2, 1975, Jewish Historical Society of Maryland; Jacob Edelman, interview by author, June 18, 1983; *Baltimore American,* Nov. 24, 1905.

16. *Baltimore Sun,* May 2 and Aug. 2 and 31, 1913.

17. Ibid., Aug. 2–4 and 31, July 31, and Apr. 26, 1913.

18. Edelman, interview by author; Seidman, *Needle Trades,* 128–30; David Montgomery, *The Fall of the House of Labor: The Workplace, the State, and American Labor Activism, 1865–1925* (Cambridge: Cambridge University Press, 1987), 199–22; Fraser, *Labor Will Rule,* 83–4; Zaretz, *The Amalgamated,* 84–9.

19. Edelman, interview by author; Sara Barron, interview by author, Feb. 17, 1986; Asher, "Dorothy Jacobs Bellanca," 60, 66–7; *Weekly Bulletin of the Clothing Trades* (New York), May 27, 1910. For the great New York strike, see Maxine Schwartz Seller, "The Uprising of the Twenty Thousand: Sex, Class, and Ethnicity in the Shirtwaist Makers' Strike of 1909," in *"Struggle a Hard Battle": Essays on Working-Class Immigrants,* ed. Dirk Hoerder (DeKalb: Northern Illinois University Press, 1986), 254–79; Ann Schofield, "The Uprising of the 20,000: The Making of a Labor Legend," in *A Needle, A Bobbin, A Strike,* ed. Jensen and Davidson, 167–82 (see chap. 1, n. 20); and Meredith Tax, *The Rising of the Women: Feminist Solidarity and Class Conflict, 1880–1917* (New York: Monthly Review Press, 1980), chap. 8.

20. *Baltimore Evening Sun,* Jan. 18, 21, 22, 24, and 25, 1913; *Baltimore American,* Jan. 19 and 22, 1913; *Baltimore Sun,* Jan. 20, 1913; Jacob Edelman, oral history interview by Libauer.

21. *Baltimore Evening Sun,* Jan. 21, 22, 24, and 25, 1913; *Baltimore Sun,* Feb. 2, 1913.

22. *Baltimore Evening Sun,* Jan. 18 and 20, 1913.

23. *Baltimore American,* Jan. 30, 1913; *Baltimore Evening Sun,* Jan. 28, Feb. 4 and 7, and Mar. 10, 1913; *Baltimore Sun,* Feb. 2, 1913.

24. *Baltimore Evening Sun,* Jan. 21 and 23, 1913; Edelman, oral history interview by Libauer.

25. *Baltimore Sun,* Jan. 20, Feb. 2, and Mar. 13, 1913; *Baltimore American,* Jan. 30 and Mar. 14, 1913.

26. *Baltimore Evening Sun,* Jan. 28 and Mar. 13, 1913; *Baltimore Sun,* Mar. 13–5, 1913; *Baltimore American,* Mar. 14, 1913.

27. *Baltimore Sun,* Mar. 22–4, 1913.

28. Edelman, oral history interview by Libauer.

29. *Documentary History of the Amalgamated Clothing Workers of America, Special Convention, 1914* (New York: ACWA, 1914), 23, 33–7 (hereafter referred to as *ACW Documentary History*); Argersinger, "To Discipline an Industry" (see chap. 1, n. 6); Elias Lieberman, "In the Field of Jewish Labor," *Jewish Times* (Baltimore), May 14, 1920; Josephson, *Hillman,* 93–108.

30. Henry Sonneborn Jr., oral history interview by Moses Aberbach, Feb. 14, 1972, Jewish Historical Society of Maryland; Josephson, *Hillman,* 111–5; Zaretz, *The Amalgamated,* 134; *ACW Documentary History, Special Convention, 1914,* 56–60; *Baltimore Sun,* Oct. 28 and Nov. 21, 23, and 24, 1914. Sonneborn's self-described "very progressive business" had by 1914 developed a system in which seventy-eight different operations were required to make a pair of pants, compared to but four at the turn of the century. See *Styleplus-Home Magazine* 1 (May 1914): 3, in the Rudolph Sonneborn Papers, Jewish Historical Society of Maryland. For Taylorism, see Daniel Nelson, *Frederick W. Taylor and the Rise of Scientific Management* (Madison: University of Wisconsin Press, 1980).

31. *Baltimore Sun,* Oct. 9 and 22, 1914; *Labor Leader* (Baltimore), Apr. 10, 1915; Joseph-

son, *Hillman,* 113–5; *ACW Documentary History, Special Convention, 1914,* 55–9. See also Fraser, *Labor Will Rule,* 101–2.

32. Edelman, interview by author; Barron, interview by author; Argersinger, "To Discipline an Industry"; Josephson, *Hillman,* 114–5.

33. Barron, interview by author; Asher, "Dorothy Jacobs Bellanca," 78; *Advance,* Sept. 15, 1946.

34. Edelman, interview by author; Zaretz, *The Amalgamated,* 217; Josephson, *Hillman,* 113–5; *ACW Documentary History, Special Convention, 1914,* 56–9; Argersinger, "To Discipline an Industry." See also Fraser, *Labor Will Rule,* 102.

35. *Baltimore Sun,* Nov. 23–4, 1914; *ACW Documentary History, Special Convention, 1914,* 56–9.

36. Edelman, interview by author; Elizabeth Kessin Berman, "Threads of Life: Overcoming the Conflicts between Jewish Employers and Jewish Workers in Baltimore's Garment Industry," in *Threads of Life: Jewish Involvement in Baltimore's Garment Industry* (Baltimore: Jewish Historical Society of Maryland, 1991), 9–17, esp. 16.

37. *ACW Documentary History, Special Convention, 1914,* 60; Josephson, *Hillman,* 114–5. For Jacob Moses, see Crooks, *Politics and Progress,* 75–6, 80, 81, 190, 196, 197, 203, 204, 230.

38. My understanding of the ACW's brand of "new unionism" owes much to the exceptional work of Steve Fraser; see esp. *Labor Will Rule,* chaps. 3 and 4. The quote from Dorothy Jacobs is from *ACW Documentary History, Third Biennial Convention, 1918,* 265.

39. See "Minutes of the Baltimore District Council, September 13–December 21, 1935," Box 37, Folder 20, Papers of the Joint Boards and Local Unions, Amalgamated Clothing Workers of America Papers, Catherwood Library, Industrial Labor Relations School, Cornell University, Ithaca, N.Y. (hereafter referred to as ACWA Papers), and the original preamble and constitution in *Baltimore Joint Board Minutes, 1932 to December 1935,* Regional Office, Union of Needletrades, Industrial, and Textile Employees (UNITE), Baltimore (hereafter referred to as *BJB Minutes, 1932–1935*). UNITE was formed in 1995 by a merger between the Amalgamated Clothing and Textile Workers Union and the International Ladies' Garment Workers' Union.

40. *ACW Documentary History, Special Convention, 1914,* 56–9; Asher, "Dorothy Jacobs Bellanca," 83–6, 91.

41. Imberman, "Men's Clothing," 12–3 (see chap. 1, n. 5); Fraser, "Sidney Hillman," 35–6; "Baltimore: Its Manufacturing Market" (see chap. 1, n. 10). See also Kahn, *Stitch in Time,* 108–9 (see chap. 1, n. 5).

42. H. Madanick to Sidney Hillman, Feb. 15 and Sept. 15, 1915, Box 3, Folder 37, Hillman Correspondence, ACWA Papers; H. Madanick to Joseph Schlossberg, Oct. 15, 1915, Box 45A, Folder 3, and David Wolf to Schlossberg, Dec. 15, 1915, Box 45A, Folder 2, Papers of the Joint Boards and Local Unions, ACWA Papers.

43. August Bellanca to Joseph Schlossberg, Sept. 2 and 6, 1915, Box 8, Folder 25, Schlossberg Correspondence, ACWA Papers.

44. P. Sinkus to Schlossberg, Oct. 21, 1915, Box 45A, Folder 2, Wolf to Schlossberg, Dec. 20, 1915, Box 45A, Folder 2, and Madanick to Schlossberg, Oct. 9 and 15, 1915, Box 45A, Folder 3, Papers of the Joint Boards and Local Unions, ACWA Papers; Madanick to Hillman, July 12 and Oct. 4, 1915, Box 3, Folder 37, Hillman Correspondence, ACWA Papers; *ACW Documentary History, Special Convention, 1914,* 100; *Labor Leader* (Baltimore), Jan. 15, 1916; Asher, "Dorothy Jacobs Bellanca," 79–81.

45. Madanick to Hillman, Oct. 4, 1915, Box 3, Folder 37, Hillman Correspondence, ACWA Papers; Bellanca to Schlossberg, Sept. 6, 1915, Box 8, Folder 25, Schlossberg Correspondence, ACWA Papers.

46. Fraser, *Labor Will Rule,* 99.

47. *Baltimore Sun,* Feb. 2, 17, 18, and 22 and Aug. 18, 21, 26–8, and 30–1, 1916; Henry Sonneborn Jr., oral history interview by Aberbach.

48. Brugger, *Middle Temperament,* 457–62 (see chap. 1, n. 12); Joseph L. Arnold, "Suburban Growth and Municipal Annexation, 1748–1918," *Maryland Historical Magazine* 73 (summer 1978): 109–28; Olson, *Baltimore* (see chap. 1, n. 1).

49. Edelman, interview by author; Imberman, "Men's Clothing," 142; *ACW Documentary History, Second Biennial Convention, 1916,* 162–71; Madanick to Schlossberg, Feb. 23, 1916, Box 8, Folder 25, Schlossberg Correspondence, ACWA Papers.

50. Barron, interview by author; "Minutes of the Baltimore District Council No. 3, January 3 to Dec. 16, 1916," 4–5, Box 37, Folder 20, Papers of the Joint Boards and Local Unions, ACWA Papers.

51. On February 28, 1916, August Bellanca wrote Schlossberg that "the situation of the Greif strike is very complicated at the present time. We do not only have to fight L. Greif & Bro., but it is a fight against the Baltimore Federation of Labor and the Industrial Workers of the World, who are supporting the Baltimore Federation of Labor" (Box 8, Folder 25, Schlossberg Correspondence, ACWA Papers).

52. *ACW Documentary History, Second Biennial Convention, 1916,* 162–71; Madanick to Schlossberg, Feb. 23, 1916, Box 8, Folder 4, Papers of the Joint Boards and Local Unions, ACWA Papers; Bellanca to Schlossberg, Feb. 28, 1916, Box 8, Folder 25, Schlossberg Correspondence, ACWA Papers; Madanick to Hillman, Jan. 29, 1916, Box 3, Folder 37, Hillman Correspondence, ACWA Papers; Senate, *Reports of the Immigration Commission. Immigrants in Industries. Part 6: Clothing Manufacturing,* 426.

53. Barron, interview by author; "Minutes of the Baltimore District Council No. 3, January 3 to Dec. 16, 1916," 3–10, Box 37, Folder 20, Papers of the Joint Boards and Local Unions, ACWA Papers; Madanick to Hillman, Jan. 21 and 29, 1916, Box 3, Folder 37, Hillman Correspondence, ACWA Papers; *Baltimore Sun,* Feb. 2, 1916.

54. *Baltimore Sun,* Feb. 2, 1916.

55. "Minutes of the Baltimore District Council No. 3, January 3 to Dec. 16, 1916," Box 37, Folder 20, Papers of the Joint Boards and Local Unions, ACWA Papers; Wolf to Schlossberg, Feb. 1, 1916, Box 45A, Folder 4, Papers of the Joint Boards and Local Unions, ACWA Papers; Dorothy Jacobs to Schlossberg, July 20, 1916, Box 8, Folder 26, Schlossberg Correspondence, ACWA Papers; *Baltimore Sun,* Feb. 2–4, 1916.

56. *Baltimore Sun,* Feb. 4, 1916.

57. "Minutes of the Baltimore District Council No. 3, January 3 to Dec. 16, 1916," esp. 4–6, Box 37, Folder 20, Papers of the Joint Boards and Local Unions, ACWA Papers; *Baltimore Sun,* Feb. 17, 1916.

58. Hyman Blumberg to Schlossberg, May 17 and June 2, 1916, Box 9, Folder 2, and Dorothy Jacobs to Schlossberg, July 20, 1916, Box 8, Folder 26, Schlossberg Correspondence, ACWA Papers; "Minutes of the Baltimore District Council No. 3, January 3 to Dec. 16, 1916," 5, Box 37, Folder 20, Papers of the Joint Boards and Local Unions, ACWA Papers.

59. *Baltimore Sun,* Feb. 22 and 23, 1916; *Labor Leader* (Baltimore), Feb. 26, 1916.

60. *Baltimore Sun,* Feb. 22 and 23, 1916; "Minutes of the Baltimore District Council No.

3, January 3 to Dec. 16, 1916," 7- 8, Box 37, Folder 20, Papers of the Joint Boards and Local Unions, ACWA Papers; *Labor Leader* (Baltimore), Mar. 4, 1916.

61. *ACW Documentary History, Second Biennial Convention, 1916,* 166–71; *Baltimore Sun,* Feb. 28, 1916.

62. Dorothy Jacobs to Schlossberg, Aug. 20 and Dec. 10, 1916, Box 8, Folder 26, Schlossberg Correspondence, ACWA Papers; Madanick to Schlossberg, Feb. 23, 1916, Box 45A, Folder 4, and "Minutes of the Baltimore District Council No. 3, January 3 to Dec. 16, 1916," Box 37, Folder 20, Papers of the Joint Boards and Local Unions, ACWA Papers. See also *Baltimore Sun,* Feb. 29, Mar. 16, Apr. 4, and Dec. 4, 1916.

63. "Minutes of the Baltimore District Council No. 3, January 3 to Dec. 16, 1916," 10–24, Box 37, Folder 20, Papers of the Joint Boards and Local Unions, ACWA Papers; "Ulisse De-Dominicis," Box 242, Folder 1, ACWA Biographical File, ACWA Papers.

64. "Minutes of the Baltimore District Council No. 3, January 3 to Dec. 16, 1916," 25–30, Box 37, Folder 20, Papers of the Joint Boards and Local Unions, ACWA Papers.

65. *Baltimore Sun,* July 4, 6–8, and 13 and Aug. 8, 10–3, and 15–8, 1916; "Minutes of the Baltimore District Council No. 3, January 3 to Dec. 16, 1916," Box 37, Folder 20, Papers of the Joint Boards and Local Unions, ACWA Papers; Jacobs to Schlossberg, July 20, 1916, Box 8, Folder 26, Schlossberg Correspondence, ACWA Papers; *Labor Leader* (Baltimore), July 1 and 8, 1916. Ferguson further characterized the UGW cutters as "natives of this city" who were "sober, industrious, and conservative" (*Labor Leader,* July 8, 1916).

66. Jacobs to Schlossberg, July 20, 1916, Box 8, Folder 26, Schlossberg Correspondence, ACWA Papers.

67. Schlossberg to Felix Clothing Co., Oct. 14, 1916, Box 37, Folder 23, "Minutes of the Baltimore District Council No. 3, January 3 to Dec. 16, 1916," Box 37, Folder 20, Papers of the Joint Boards and Local Unions, ACWA Papers; Josephson, *Hillman,* 144–6. See also Fraser, *Labor Will Rule,* 102–5, and Asher, "Dorothy Jacobs Bellanca," 87–9.

68. *Baltimore Sun,* Aug. 15–8 and 21, 1916; Josephson, *Hillman,* 145–6; *Labor Leader* (Baltimore), Sept. 2, 1916. The UGW boycott continued despite the apparent settlement of the strike. See Strouse & Brothers to ACWA, Oct. 24, 1916, and Eli Strouse to ACWA, Mar. 25, 1917, Box 37, Folder 23, Papers of the Joint Boards and Local Unions, ACWA Papers; Eli Strouse to Hillman, Nov. 15, 1916, Box 6, Folder 26, Hillman Correspondence, ACWA Papers.

69. *Baltimore Sun,* Aug. 21, 1916; *Labor Leader* (Baltimore), Aug. 12, 1916.

70. "Minutes of the Baltimore District Council No. 3, January 3 to Dec. 16, 1916," 24–8, Box 37, Folder 20, Papers of the Joint Boards and Local Unions, ACWA Papers; *Baltimore Sun,* Aug. 26, 1916.

71. *Baltimore Sun,* Aug. 26 and 27, 1916; *Labor Leader* (Baltimore), Sept. 2, 1916; *ACW Documentary History, Third Biennial Convention, 1918,* 81–6; Josephson, *Hillman,* 147–8; Barron, interview by author.

72. *Baltimore Sun,* Aug. 27, 1916; *Labor Leader* (Baltimore), Sept. 2, 1916. For a suggestive analysis of union competition and the 1916 strikes, see Dana Frederic Gillian, "The Greif, Strouse, and Sonneborn Strikes of 1916: Ethnicity and Industrial Unionism in the Amalgamated Clothing Workers of America" (master's thesis, Johns Hopkins University, 1986).

73. "Minutes of the Baltimore District Council No. 3, January 3 to Dec. 16, 1916," 27–32, Box 37, Folder 20, Papers of the Joint Boards and Local Unions, ACWA Papers.

CHAPTER 3: TO DISCIPLINE AN INDUSTRY

1. *Public Ownership* article reprinted in the *Advance,* Mar. 1, 1918; "Statement by Sidney Hillman," Dec. 13, 1920, "Statement by Sidney Hillman," Dec. 14, 1920, Box 122, Folder titled "Textile Industry: ACW Press Releases, 1920–21," Mary Heaton Vorse Papers, Archives of Labor History and Urban Affairs, Walter Reuther Library, Wayne State University, Detroit, Mich. (hereafter referred to as the Reuther Library). See also *Advance,* July 6, 1917.

2. "Statement by Sidney Hillman," Dec. 13, 1920, Box 122, Folder titled "Textile Industry: ACW Press Releases, 1920–21," Mary Heaton Vorse Papers, Reuther Library; Nathan Shaviro, "Labor Leader: Hillman of the CIO," *Survey Graphic* (June 1937), in the Herman Wolf Collection, Box 13, Folder titled "Textile Workers," Mary Heaton Vorse Papers, Reuther Library. For an important discussion of the "new unionism" and its relationship to the New Deal, see Fraser, "Dress Rehearsal for the New Deal: Shop-Floor Insurgents, Political Elites, and Industrial Democracy in the Amalgamated Clothing Workers," in *Working-Class America: Essays on Labor, Community, and American Society,* ed. Michael H. Frisch and Daniel J. Walkowitz (Urbana: University of Illinois Press, 1983), 228–32. Also see Zaretz, *The Amalgamated,* 102–5 (see intro., n. 8), and Fraser, *Labor Will Rule,* 136–40 (see intro., n. 8).

3. *Advance,* Feb. 18, 1918. For treatments of welfare capitalism, see Stuart D. Brandes, *American Welfare Capitalism, 1880–1940* (Chicago: University of Chicago Press, 1976); David Brody, "The Rise and Decline of Welfare Capitalism," in *Workers in Industrial America: Essays on the Twentieth-Century Struggle,* ed. David Brody (New York: Oxford University Press, 1980), 48–81.

4. For a useful analysis of personnel departments and managerial innovation, see Richard Gillespie, *Manufacturing Knowledge: A History of the Hawthorne Experiments* (Cambridge: Cambridge University Press, 1991), 30–6.

5. *ACW Documentary History, Fifth Biennial Convention, 1922,* apps.; "Minutes and Reports—Report of the Work of the Board of Control of Labor Standards for Army Clothing through December 15, 1917" and Harry Myers to Sidney Hillman, Apr. 17, 1917, Box 5, Folder 12, Hillman Correspondence, and Hyman Blumberg to Joseph Schlossberg, Oct. 20, 1917, Box 9, Folder 2, Schlossberg Correspondence, ACWA Papers (see chap. 2, n. 39); Fraser, *Labor Will Rule,* 115. For government labor policy during World War I, see Valerie Jean Conner, *The National War Labor Board: Stability, Social Justice, and the Voluntary State in World War I* (Chapel Hill: University of North Carolina Press, 1983), and Melvyn Dubofsky, "Abortive Reform: The Wilson Administration and Organized Labor, 1913–20," in *Work, Community, and Power: The Experience of Labor in Europe and America, 1900–1925,* ed. James E. Cronin and Carmen Sirianni (Philadelphia: Temple University Press, 1983), 197–220.

6. *Baltimore Sun,* Sept. 19, 1917; Hyman Blumberg to Schlossberg, May 3, 1918, Box 9, Folder 2, Schlossberg Correspondence, ACWA Papers.

7. *Advance,* May 18, June 22, Sept. 28, and Oct. 19 and 26, 1917; H. Madanick to Hillman, Jan. 21, 1916, Box 3, Folder 37, Hillman Correspondence, ACWA Papers; Blumberg to Schlossberg, May 3, 1918, Box 9, Folder 2, Schlossberg Correspondence, ACWA Papers.

8. *Advance,* Apr. 12, 1918; Blumberg to Schlossberg, May 3, 1918, Jacobs to Schlossberg, Apr. 20, 1918, Box 8, Folder 26, Schlossberg Correspondence, ACWA Papers (see chap. 2, n. 39).

9. *Baltimore American,* Apr. 27 and 28, 1918; *Advance,* Apr. 26 and May 10 and 24, 1918; *Baltimore Evening Sun,* Apr. 26 and 27 and May 15, 1918.

10. *Advance,* May 10, 24, and 31, 1918.

11. Ibid., Apr. 12 and May 31, 1918.

12. *Labor Leader* (Baltimore), Apr. 28, 1917; *Advance,* July 13, Oct. 26, Nov. 30, and Dec. 28, 1917, Mar. 5, 1920; Blumberg to Schlossberg, Nov. 20, 1917, Box 9, Folder 2, Schlossberg Correspondence, ACWA Papers. For more information on the Philip Kahn Company, see Kahn, *Stitch in Time* (which was written by Philip Kahn Jr.), esp. xvii–xix, 106, 107 (see chap. 1, n. 5).

13. *Advance,* July 6 and 27, 1917, Mar. 29, 1918; *Baltimore Trades Unionist,* Mar. 1918, in the Vertical File, EPFL. See also a history of the Baltimore Federation of Labor, which discusses the "forced" resignation of Ferguson, in *The Baltimore Federationist,* Dec. 20, 1939. In 1920 Ferguson was ousted altogether from the Baltimore Federation of Labor for his strikebreaking activities. He then pledged to join the city's Employer Association. See *Baltimore American,* Dec. 2, 9, and 23, 1920.

14. Jacob Edelman, interview by author, June 18, 1983; *Advance,* June 22 and July 13, 1917, Feb. 1, 1918.

15. "The Shop Chairman and His Job," in *How the Union Works,* pamphlet in Box 290, Folder 3, Papers of the Joint Boards and Local Unions, ACWA Papers; *Advance,* Mar. 1, 1918.

16. *Advance,* July 13, 1917. See also Fraser, *Labor Will Rule,* 102–10.

17. Edelman, interview by author; Fraser, "Sidney Hillman," 85–95 (see chap. 2, n. 7); Zaretz, *The Amalgamated,* 240–4.

18. Adolph Roten of Henry Sonneborn & Co., Inc., to Sidney Hillman, n.d., 1917, and Eli Strouse to Hillman, Dec. 18, 1919, Box 6, Folder 12, Hillman Correspondence, ACWA Papers.

19. *Advance,* Jan. 4, 1918; Strouse to Hillman, Dec. 18, 1919, Box 6, Folder 12, Hillman Correspondence, ACWA Papers; Hillman to Schlossberg, Feb. 19, 1915, Box 45A, Folder 2, Papers of the Joint Boards and Local Unions, ACWA Papers; Henry Sonneborn Jr., oral history interview by Aberbach (see chap. 2, n. 30). See also Siegmund Sonneborn, "Price Factors in Men's Ready to Wear Clothing," *American Academy of Political and Social Science Annals* 89 (May 1920): 61–6.

20. Roten to Hillman, n.d., 1917, Box 6, Folder 12, Hillman Correspondence, ACWA Papers; David Wolf to Joseph Schlossberg, Feb. 1, 1916, Box 45A, Folder 4, Papers of the Joint Boards and Local Unions, ACWA Papers; Hyman Blumberg to Joseph Schlossberg, June 18, 1916, Box 9, Folder 2, Schlossberg Correspondence, ACWA Papers.

21. Strouse to Hillman, Oct. 3, 1919, Box 6, Folder 26, and Dec. 18, 1919, Box 6, Folder 12, Hillman Correspondence, ACWA Papers; Bellanca to Schlossberg, Feb. 28, 1917, Box 8, Folder 25, Schlossberg Correspondence, ACWA Papers.

22. *Jewish Times* (Baltimore), June 25, 1920; *Advance,* Nov. 5, 1920; Edelman, interview by author.

23. J. A. Bekampis to Schlossberg, Jan. 22 and June 5, 1918, Box 8, Folder 24, Schlossberg Correspondence, ACWA Papers.

24. *Advance,* June 15, Sept. 7 and 14, and Oct. 5, 1917; Fred Buresji to Schlossberg, Mar. 26, 1917, Box 9, Folder 17, Schlossberg Correspondence, ACWA Papers.

25. Frank Bellanca to Schlossberg, Feb. 12, 1914; Dorothy Jacobs to Schlossberg, Sept. 17, 1916, Box 8, Folder 26, Schlossberg Correspondence, ACWA Papers; Fraser, "Sidney Hillman," 99–100. For other examples of these organizational problems, see August Bellanca to Schlossberg, Mar. 15 and Apr. 14 and 19, 1916, Box 8, Folder 25, Schlossberg Correspondence, ACWA Papers.

198   26. As quoted in Fraser, "Sidney Hillman," 89. See also Howard Barton Myers, "The Policing of Labor Disputes in Chicago: A Case Study" (Ph.D. diss., University of Chicago, 1929).

27. Adolph Roten to Hillman, 1917, Box 6, Folder 12, Hillman Correspondence, ACWA Papers. In another letter to Hillman, the Sonneborn company specifically complained of the "lack of cooperation" on the part of the Jewish workers and the "loafing on the part of the others [i.e., Italians]" (Sonneborn to Hillman, Nov. 22, 1917, Box 6, Folder 12, Hillman Correspondence, ACWA Papers). Jacob Edelman also distinguished between the "laying down" of the Italian workers and the difficulties the union and the foreman had in bringing the "Jewish boys and the Lithuanians into line" (Edelman, interview by author).

28. Mamie Santora to Mrs. August Bellanca (Dorothy Jacobs married August Bellanca in 1918), Sept. 2, 1924, Box 23, Folder 9, Dorothy Jacobs Bellanca Papers, ACWA Papers.

29. Edelman, interview by author; *ACW Documentary History, Fourth Biennial Convention, 1920,* 94.

30. *ACW Documentary History, Fourth Biennial Convention, 1920; ACW Documentary History, Fifth Biennial Convention, 1922*; Robert J. Schaefer, "Educational Activities," 97–104, 110–1 (see intro., n. 8). Although education had its champions in the Amalgamated, Sidney Hillman was not among them. He believed that although education about the union was necessary, more general workers' education movements were of limited usefulness. The local unions, however, were consistently strong advocates of comprehensive educational programs for ACW members. This was true of Baltimore and of other cities as well. See Schaefer for descriptions of activities at the national level and in other cities.

31. *Advance,* Feb. 8, 1918 (quoted from the General Executive Board's report to the ACW's second biennial convention). See also Broadus Mitchell, "Amalgamated Education in Baltimore," *Advance,* Aug. 26, 1921.

32. Schaefer, "Educational Activities," 110; Sara Barron, interview by author, Feb. 17, 1986; "Oral History Interview with Sara Barron" (see chap. 2, n.1); Edelman, interview by author. (Both Barron and Edelman were members of the Young People's Socialist League.) The membership lists of the Workmen's Circle are at the Jewish Historical Society of Maryland, and summaries of the union classes and lectures held in Baltimore were printed in the *Advance* and included in Joint Board Minutes.

33. Schaefer, "Educational Activities," 67, 74–82; Argersinger, "To Discipline an Industry" (see chap. 1, n. 6); *Advance,* Feb. 8, 1918, Aug. 26, 1921; Zaretz, *The Amalgamated,* 235–6.

34. *ACW Documentary History, Second Biennial Convention, 1916*; Schaefer, "Educational Activities," 67.

35. *Advance,* Feb. 1 and 15, 1918, Apr. 20 and June 29, 1917; Barron, interview by author; Jacobs to Schlossberg, Nov. 26, 1917, Box 8, Folder 26, Schlossberg Correspondence, ACWA Papers.

36. Edelman, interview by author; *Advance,* Mar. 5, 1920.

37. Jacobs to Jacob Potofsky, Oct. 30, 1917, Box 45A, Folder 7, Papers of the Joint Boards and Local Unions, ACWA Papers; *Advance,* May 4 and 18, 1917.

38. *Advance,* Feb. 15, 1918; J. A. Bekampis to Schlossberg, Nov. 5, 1917, Box 8, Folder 24, Schlossberg Corresondence, ACWA Papers.

39. *Advance,* Feb. 15, Mar. 1 and 22, and Apr. 5 and 12, 1918.

40. Edelman, interview by author; *Jewish Times* (Baltimore), Dec. 19, 1919; *Advance,* Apr. 5, 1918.

41. *Advance,* Aug. 26, 1921; Broadus Mitchell, letter to author, Sept. 19, 1975. Mitchell confided to his mother that his educational work was "wearing if useful" and particularly objected to speaking in Baltimore's "miserable little halls filled with smoke." See letters to mother, undated, in the Samuel Chiles Mitchell Papers, Folder 135, Southern Historical Collection, University of North Carolina, Chapel Hill.

42. *Advance,* Feb. 27, 1920.

43. Edelman, interview by author; Barron, interview by author.

44. Schaefer, "Educational Activities," 3–29, 97–104.

45. Jacobs to Schlossberg, July 20 and Nov. 5 and 26, 1916, Box 8, Folder 26, Schlossberg Correspondence, ACWA Papers; *Advance,* June 29 and Sept. 14 and 28, 1917.

46. Edelman, interview by author; Barron, interview by author.

47. "Oral History Interview with Sara Barron"; Edelman, interview by author; Barron, interview by author.

48. For especially good examples of the ACW's educational programs, see "A.C.W.A. Songs for the Workers," Box 2, Folder 8, Edith L. Christenson Papers, Reuther Library, and the Papers of the American Labor Education Service (esp. Boxes 52, 53, 58, and 59) and the Papers of the Textile Workers Union of America, State Historical Society of Wisconsin, Madison.

49. *Baltimore Sun,* Oct. 21, 1937; *Advance,* Nov. 1937; Edelman, interview by author; Minutes of the Baltimore Joint Board, Aug. 16, 1937, *BJB Minutes, 1932–1935* (see chap. 2, n. 39). For a suggestive article on Baltimore's union halls in an earlier period, see Roderick N. Ryon, "Craftsmen's Union Halls, Male Bonding, and Female Industrial Labor: The Case of Baltimore, 1880–1917," *Labor History* 36 (spring 1995): 211–31.

50. Blumberg to Schlossberg, May 17, 1916, Box 9, Folder 2, Schlossberg Correspondence, ACWA Papers.

CHAPTER 4: THE "FORGOTTEN" WORKERS

1. Eldon LaMar, *The Clothing Workers in Philadelphia: History of Their Struggles for Union and Security* (Philadelphia: Philadelphia Joint Board, Amalgamated Clothing Workers, 1940), 129.

2. *Advance,* Apr. 8, May 6, and Feb. 4, 1927.

3. Ibid., May 6, 1927.

4. Senate, *Report on Condition of Woman and Child Wage-Earners,* 2:184 (see chap. 2, n. 6); Jo Ann E. Argersinger, *Toward a New Deal in Baltimore: People and Government in the Great Depression* (Chapel Hill: University of North Carolina Press, 1988), chaps. 1 and 6; *Baltimore Sun,* Nov. 21, 1905. The Senate report, prepared from data taken in 1908, must be read carefully, for its data on men's wages refer only to men working in occupations that also employed women, thereby omitting the highest-paid and exclusively male occupations, such as cutter.

5. *Baltimore Sun,* Aug. 18 and Sept. 1, 1916. See also clippings under "Clothing Industry" in the Vertical File, EPFL.

6. "Oral History Interview with Barron" (see chap. 2, n. 1); Sara Barron, interview by author, Feb. 17, 1986.

200   7. For the most comprehensive and sophisticated overview of the variety of women's wage-earning experience, see Alice Kessler-Harris, *Out To Work: A History of Wage-Earning Women in the United States* (New York: Oxford University Press, 1982); for a rich exploration of the value and meaning of women's work culture, see Susan Porter Benson, *Counter Cultures: Saleswomen, Managers, and Customers in American Department Stores, 1890–1940* (Urbana: University of Illinois Press, 1988) and Peiss, *Cheap Amusements* (see chap. 1, n. 25).

8. Peiss, *Cheap Amusements,* 34–48; Barron, interview by author; *Advance,* Mar. 8, 1918; clippings in Vertical File, EPFL.

9. "Oral History Interview with Barron."

10. Barron, interview by author.

11. See Glenn, *Daughters of the Shtetl,* 143–66 (see intro., n. 7). For early examples of such cooperative behavior in Baltimore workrooms, see the suggestive reports in the *Weekly Bulletin of the Clothing Trades* (New York), Dec. 17 and 24, 1909.

12. Barron, interview by author; Jacob Edelman, interview by author, June 18, 1983; Senate, *Report on Condition of Woman and Child Wage-Earners,* 2:180–94; Mary Van Kleeck, "Women and Children Who Make Men's Clothing," *The Survey* 26 (Apr. 1911): 65–9. In *The Employment of Women in the Clothing Trade* (New York: AMS Press, 1968; reprinted from 1902), Mabel Hurd Willett found little evidence of consistency in the employment of women in the men's clothing industry, only suggesting that the ethnicity of owners held some influence in the division of labor (67–72). See also Glenn, *Daughters of the Shtetl,* 112–31.

Much work remains to be done on gender and the division of labor, although a few significant studies have been conducted: Ruth Milkman, *Gender at Work* (Urbana: University of Illinois Press, 1987) and "Redefining 'Women's Work': The Sexual Division of Labor in the Auto Industry during World War II," *Feminist Studies* 8 (summer 1982): 337–72; Sarah Eisenstein, *Give Us Bread, but Give Us Roses: Working Women's Consciousness in the United States, 1890 to the First World War* (London: Routledge and Kegan Paul, 1983); and Mary Blewitt, *Men, Women, and Work: Class, Gender, and Protest in the New England Shoe Industry, 1780–1910* (Urbana: University of Illinois Press, 1988).

13. Seidman, *Needle Trades,* 30–49 (see chap. 1, n. 5); "Minutes of Baltimore District Council No. 3," Papers of the Joint Boards and Local Unions, ACWA Papers (see chap. 2, n. 39); Senate, *Report on Condition of Woman and Child Wage-Earners,* 2:51–4, 180–94, 206, 442–5. Ethnicity, of course, created further variations in the sexual division of labor. In Baltimore before World War I, Italian women rarely operated sewing machines; Bohemian women (and Italian men) nearly always did.

14. Barron, interview by author; Sadie Goodman to Dorothy J. Bellanca, June 24, 1925, Box 30, Folder 2, Bellanca Papers, ACWA Papers. See also Eisenstein, *Give Us Bread,* and Glenn, *Daughters of the Shtetl,* 122–30.

15. See Mary P. Ryan, *Womanhood in America* (New York: New Viewpoints 1979); Nancy F. Cott, *The Grounding of Modern Feminism* (New Haven, Conn.: Yale University Press, 1987); Carroll Smith-Rosenberg, "The New Woman as Androgyne: Social Disorder and Gender Crisis, 1870–1936," in *Disorderly Conduct: Visions of Gender in Victorian America,* ed. Carroll Smith-Rosenberg (New York: Knopf, 1985); Paula Fass, *The Damned and the Beautiful* (New York: Oxford University Press, 1977); and Glenn, *Daughters of the Shtetl,* esp. 213–6. For discussions of ethnicity and class in the "New Womanhood," see Peiss, *Cheap Amusements,* and Elizabeth Ewen, *Immigrant Women in the Land of Dollars: Life and Culture on the Lower East Side, 1890–1925* (New York: Monthly Review, 1985).

16. For feminism and suffrage, see Cott, *Grounding of Modern Feminism.* For discussions of domestic feminism and "municipal housekeeping," see Daniel Scott Smith, "Family Limitation, Sexual Control and Domestic Feminism in Victorian America," in *Clio's Consciousness Raised,* ed. Mary Hartman and Lois W. Banner (New York: Harper & Row, 1974), 119–36; Karen Blair, *The Clubwoman as Feminist: True Womanhood Redefined, 1868–1914* (New York: Holmes & Meier, 1980); Linda Gordon, ed., *Women, the State, and Welfare* (Madison: University of Wisconsin Press, 1990), particularly the essays by Gordon, Paula Baker, and Gwendolyn Mink; and Sandra Schackel, *Social Housekeepers: Women Shaping Public Policy in New Mexico, 1920–1940* (Albuquerque: University of New Mexico Press, 1992). On Gilman, see Argersinger, *Toward a New Deal,* 128, 152, 153, 161, 167; on Ellicott and Hooker, see Crooks, *Politics and Progress,* 79–81, 82, 172, 176, 181, 235 (see chap. 1, n. 22).

17. *Baltimore American,* Dec. 18 and 21, 1909.

18. *Baltimore Sun,* May 9, 1910; *Weekly Bulletin of the Clothing Trades* (New York), May 27, 1910.

19. *Baltimore Sun,* May 12, 1910.

20. *Baltimore American,* Feb. 2–5, 1913; *Baltimore Sun,* Feb. 2–3, 1913.

21. *Baltimore American,* Feb. 2, 1913; *Baltimore Sun,* Feb. 3, 1913.

22. *Baltimore American,* Feb. 4, 5, 18, 21, and 24 and Mar. 3 and 4, 1913; *Baltimore Sun,* Feb. 4 and Mar. 3 and 4, 1913.

23. *Baltimore Sun,* Mar. 4, 1913.

24. Helen Marot to Margaret Dreier Robins, May 18, 1911, National Women's Trade Union League of America Papers, Library of Congress (hereafter referred to as NWTUL Papers); Elizabeth King Ellicott to Margaret Dreier Robins, May 21, 1911, Margaret Dreier Robins Papers, University of Florida Libraries (microfilm edition of the Papers of the Women's Trade Union League and Its Principal Leaders, Robins Papers, Reel 22); *Labor Leader* (Baltimore), May 20 and Nov. 4, 1911; *Life and Labor* (Chicago), Dec. 1912, 380, Feb. 1913, 61, and July 1913, 215. For a valuable study of the Women's Trade Union League in New York, see Nancy Schrom Dye, *As Equals and as Sisters: Feminism, Unionism, and the Women's Trade Union League of New York* (Columbia: University of Missouri Press, 1980).

25. *Life and Labor* (Chicago), Apr. 1912, 124; *Baltimore Evening Sun,* Feb. 16, 1912. For Rose Schneiderman and the WTUL, see Alice Kessler-Harris, "Rose Schneiderman and the Limits of Women's Trade Unionism," in *Labor Leaders in America,* ed. Melvyn Dubofsky and Warren Van Tyne (Urbana: University of Illinois Press, 1987), 160–84.

26. Anna Bercowitz to Stella Franklin, May 29, 1914, NWTUL Papers; *Baltimore American,* May 25 and 26, 1914. For a useful account of Chicago's WTUL and its influence, see Colette A. Hyman, "Labor Organizing and Female Institution-building: The Chicago Women's Trade Union League, 1904–24," in *Women, Work, and Protest: A Century of U.S. Women's Labor History,* ed. Ruth Milkman (Boston: Routledge & Kegan Paul, 1985), 22–41.

27. *Baltimore Evening Sun,* Jan. 25 and 26, 1912; *Baltimore American,* Mar. 16, 1911; *Labor Leader* (Baltimore), Mar. 18, 1911; Bercowitz to Franklin, May 29, 1914, NWTUL Papers. See also Crooks, *Politics and Progress,* 170, and "History of the Consumers League, 1900–1917," Vertical File, EPFL.

28. Although I have a slightly different interpretation of how the working-class variant of "new womanhood" interacted with the ACW's "new unionism," I am nevertheless indebted to the insights offered by Glenn in *Daughters of the Shtetl,* esp. 216–22.

29. See the letters of Dorothy Jacobs Bellanca in her papers at the ACWA (see chap. 2,

202   n. 39) and her speeches reprinted in the *Advance*. Blumberg and other leaders thought that the organization of women constituted a "special problem"—as opposed to the special opportunity Jacobs saw among women. See Blumberg to Schlossberg, May 17, 1916, Box 9, Folder 2, Schlossberg Correspondence, ACWA Papers. Similar dynamics occurred within Baltimore's smaller women's garment industry, which was dominated even more by women workers. And because it was "a girl's trade," reported the journal of the International Ladies' Garment Workers' Union, organization was "of course . . . rather difficult . . . and the local is now in search of a woman organizer to help them along" (*Ladies' Garment Worker*, Jan. 1916, 18).

30. For a sympathetic and comprehensive treatment of Jacobs, see Asher, "Dorothy Jacobs Bellanca" (see chap. 2, n. 7).

31. Jacobs to Schlossberg, Nov. 5, 1916, Box 8, Folder 26, Schlossberg Correspondence, ACWA Papers; *Advance,* July 16, 1917.

32. *ACW Documentary History, Special Founding Convention, 1914,* 100.

33. "Minutes of the Baltimore District Council No. 3, January 3 to Dec. 16, 1916," Papers of the Joint Boards and Local Unions, ACWA Papers; Blumberg to Schlossberg, Oct. 20, 1917, Box 9, Folder 2, Schlossberg Correspondence, ACWA Papers; H. Eisen to Hillman, May 18, 1915, Box 45A, Folder 2, and David Wolf to Schlossberg, Feb. 3, 1916, Box 45A, Folder 4, Papers of the Joint Boards and Local Unions, ACWA Papers; Madanick to Hillman, June 17, 1915, Box 3, Folder 37, Hillman Correspondence, ACWA Papers. See also Asher, "Dorothy Jacobs Bellanca," 80–94.

34. Blumberg to Schlossberg, June 8, 1916, Box 9, Folder 2, Schlossberg Correspondence, ACWA Papers.

35. "Minutes of the Baltimore Distict Council No. 3, January 3 to Dec. 16, 1916," Box 37, Folder 20, Papers of the Joint Boards and Local Unions, ACWA Papers; Blumberg to Schlossberg, May 17, 1916, Box 9, Folder 2, Schlossberg Correspondence, ACWA Papers.

36. "Minutes of the Baltimore District Council No. 3, January 3 to Dec. 16, 1916," Box 37, Folder 20, Papers of the Joint Boards and Local Unions, ACWA Papers.

37. Jacobs to Hillman, Mar. 30, 1915, Box 45A, Folder 2, Papers of the Joint Boards and Local Unions, ACWA Papers. For the issue of the WTUL's connection to the Amalgamated women, and the anger it generated in the UGW and the BFL, see also *Labor Leader* (Baltimore), Apr. 24 and May 1 and 8, 1915. For oblique comments on its impact on the Baltimore WTUL itself, see *Life and Labor* (Chicago), Oct. 1916, 160. For similar developments at the national level, see Elizabeth Anne Payne, *Reform, Labor, and Feminism: Margaret Dreier Robins and the Women's Trade Union League* (Urbana: University of Illinois Press, 1988), 94–5, 102, 103, 106. Emma Steghagen, the secretary-treasurer of the NWTUL, later visited Baltimore in an effort to heal the rift between the Baltimore WTUL, still focused primarily on women garment workers, and "the men's unions" of the BFL. See Steghagen to Executive Board Members, Mar. 19, 1917, NWTUL Papers.

38. As the correspondence among Baltimore's women of the ACW indicates, they rarely deviated from their optimism and idealism about creating a union of brothers and sisters, and they were persistent in pursuing that goal as well. Jacobs frequently spoke of the need to educate not only women but men as well, and Sara Barron recalled that Jacobs often reminded them "not to forget the boys" in their educational programs. See, for example, Jacobs to Schlossberg, Nov. 5, 1916, Box 8, Folder 26, Schlossberg Correspondence, ACWA Papers; Barron, interview by author.

39. For examples of these activities among ACW women in Chicago, Rochester, Cleveland, Indianapolis, and other cities, see *Advance,* May 7, Aug. 27, and Nov. 26, 1920, June 9, 1922, May 18, and Oct. 5, 1923, Aug. 8 and Nov. 7, 1924, Apr. 1 and June 10, 1927. The evidence for Baltimore suggests that the establishment of a separate local represented a mechanism for women to be more active with their union brothers in the union. It was, in large part, a response to male exclusivity. A part of the inclination toward separatism also grew out of a sense of their "new womanhood," their campaigns for the vote, and their larger public presence in the union and the city. Few union women, however, sought a separate institution in order to distance themselves from union men; they wanted fuller integration, more recognition, and more respect. See, for example, Mamie Santora, "Women Workers and the Amalgamated," *Advance,* Jan. 14, 1921. The case for Baltimore, then, does not correspond to the interpretation of separatism offered by Glenn in *Daughters of the Shtetl,* which attributes separatist impulses to the few and asserts that most Jewish women were "content to follow men's leadership" (237). The distinction is discussed more fully later in this chapter.

40. *ACW Documentary History, Fourth Biennial Convention, 1920,* 94.

41. Kessler-Harris, *Out To Work,* esp. chaps. 3–6. In addition to reading all issues of the *Advance,* I read all the resolutions passed by all ACW locals from 1914 to 1940 to understand the priorities of local unions and to get a sense of the ways in which locals framed particular issues and located union concerns within larger, national developments. The Jacobs quotation is from *Advance,* June 29, 1917.

42. "Minutes of the Baltimore District Council No. 3, January 3 to Dec. 16, 1916," Box 37, Folder 20, Papers of the Joint Boards and Local Unions, ACWA Papers; Jacobs to Schlossberg, Nov. 8, 1917, Box 45A, Folder 7, Papers of the Joint Boards and Local Unions, ACWA Papers; Madanick to Hillman, June 17, 1915, Box 3, Folder 37, Hillman Correspondence, ACWA Papers; *Advance,* Aug. 9, 1918. For similar concerns among UGW officials, see *Labor Leader* (Baltimore), Sept. 14, 1918.

43. *Baltimore Sun,* Aug. 18, 1917; *Advance,* Apr. 6, June 22, and Sept. 14, 1917, Feb. 15, 1918; "Minutes of the Baltimore District Council No. 3, January 3 to Dec. 16, 1916," Box 37, Folder 20, Papers of the Joint Boards and Local Unions, ACWA Papers.

44. Jacobs to Potofsky, Oct. 30, 1917, and Jacobs to Schlossberg, Nov. 8, 1917, Box 45A, Folder 7, Papers of the Joint Boards and Local Unions, ACWA Papers.

45. Blumberg to Schlossberg, July 19, 1919, Box 9, Folder 2, Schlossberg Correspondence, ACWA Papers; Mildred Rankin to Potofsky, Aug. 4, 1920, Box 45A, Folder 10, Papers of the Joint Boards and Local Unions, ACWA Papers.

46. Jacobs to Hillman, Mar. 30, 1915, Box 45A, Folder 2, Papers of the Joint Boards and Local Unions, ACWA Papers; *Advance,* Aug. 24, 1917.

47. *Advance,* Sept. 28, 1917.

48. Asher, "Dorothy Jacobs Bellanca," 93–4; Edelman, interview by author; Barron, interview by author; "Oral History Interview with Barron."

49. Asher, "Dorothy Jacobs Bellanca," 106–8.

50. These observations are drawn from the speeches delivered by Mamie Santora and Dorothy Jacobs Bellanca at the ACW's biennial conventions and from the resolutions put forth by Amalgamated women and women's locals at those conventions. Also particularly helpful was the separate Women's Page in the *Advance.* See, for example, *Advance,* June 15 and 29, Sept. 14, and Oct. 19 and 26, 1917, Nov. 7, 1924, Feb. 13 and 20, 1925.

51. Margret S. Owen, "Women in the Workshop of the World: A Study Course in the

204 Work of Women," Series No. 26, YWCA (New York: Women's Press, 1925), pamphlet in the American Labor Education Services Papers, Affiliated Schools for Workers, Box 71, State Historical Society of Wisconsin, Madison.

I also detected in ACW writings and speeches a transition toward what Elizabeth Faue calls a "gendering of solidarity" in *Community of Suffering and Struggle: Women, Men, and the Labor Movement in Minneapolis, 1915–1945* (Chapel Hill: University of North Carolina Press, 1991), esp. chap. 3. Whereas Faue locates this development in the 1930s, it appeared in Baltimore in the 1920s during a period of depressed economic conditions in the garment industry and backlash against women in the local Amalgamated. Moreover, women drew their own lessons from the male-dominated rhetoric and still used the romanticized imagery and the notion of solidarity to define their own place in the union. The image of the union as "home" figured prominently among women organizers and leaders.

52. "Minutes of the Baltimore District Council No. 3, January 3 to Dec. 16, 1916," Box 37, Folder 20, Papers of the Joint Boards and Local Unions, ACWA Papers; *Advance,* Feb. 3, 1928; Barron, interview by author; Jacobs to Schlossberg, Nov. 5, 1916, Box 8, Folder 26, Schlossberg Correspondence, ACWA Papers.

53. Jacobs to Schlossberg, Nov. 26, 1917, Box 8, Folder 26, Schlossberg Correspondence, ACWA Papers; *Advance,* Apr. 20, June 15, Aug. 3, Oct. 26, and Nov. 9, 1917, Feb. 1, 1918, Jan. 28 and Apr. 22, 1921, Mar. 10, 1922, May 23 and 30, June 6, and Aug. 8, 1924.

54. *Advance,* Sept. 28, 1917.

55. Blumberg to Schlossberg, June 2 and Oct. 20, 1917, Box 9, Folder 2, Schlossberg Correspondence, ACWA Papers.

56. "Minutes of the Baltimore District Council No. 3, January 3 to Dec. 16, 1916," Box 37, Folder 20, Papers of the Joint Boards and Local Unions, ACWA Papers; Jacobs to Schlossberg, Nov. 26, 1917, Box 8, Folder 26, Schlossberg Correspondence, ACWA Papers; Barron, interview by author; *Advance,* June 15, July 27, Oct. 26, and Nov. 9, 1917.

57. *Advance,* Apr. 20, June 29, July 6 and 13, Aug. 3 and 24, Sept. 14 and 28, Nov. 2, 9, and 16, and Dec. 7, 1917; Jacobs to Potofsky, Oct. 30, 1917, Box 45A, Folder 7, Papers of the Joint Boards and Local Unions, ACWA Papers.

58. "A Tribute to the Amalgamated Clothing Workers of America," *Ladies' Garment Worker* (Feb. 1917), 7–11, 18; "A Trying Time in Baltimore," *Ladies' Garment Worker* (June 1917), 14–5; *Advance,* June 22, Sept. 14, Oct. 26, Nov. 23 and 30, 1917, Jan. 18 and Feb. 15, 1918.

59. Barron, interview by author; "Oral History Interview with Barron"; *Baltimore American,* Jan. 4 and Nov. 16, 1917. Sara Barron disclosed in my interview with her that she had insisted on being called shop "chairlady" instead of "chairman" by the foremen at Sonneborn's and, for this, had been ridiculed by them; one foreman had even nicknamed her "Queen of Sheba."

60. Lee McCardell, "New Hope in Men's Apparel Here," n.d., clipping in Vertical File, EPFL; Maryland State Board of Labor and Statistics, *Thirty-first Annual Report, 1921.* See also Kahn, *Stitch in Time,* 136–88 (see chap. 1, n. 5), and Fraser, *Labor Will Rule,* 166–8 (see intro., n. 8).

61. *Baltimore Sun,* Mar. 1, 9, and 10 and Apr. 1 and 5, 1917; *Labor Leader* (Baltimore), Mar. 22, 1919. See also Olson, *Baltimore,* 298–301 (see chap. 1, n. 1), and Brugger, *Middle Temperament,* 442–3 (see chap. 1, n. 12).

62. The strikes and lockouts are discussed fully in Chapter 5. See, for example, *Baltimore Sun,* Dec. 21, 1919, Dec. 19 and 24, 1920, June 30, 1922.

63. "New Babies Fund" and "Immediate Release," Feb. 11, 1921, ACW Publicity Department, and "Mrs. Vorse's Report on the Proposed Plans for the Children's Party To Be Held January 1 at 3 O'Clock," Jan. 1921, Box 122, Mary Heaton Vorse Papers, Reuther Library (see chap. 3, n. 1). See also *Advance*, Jan. 28, Feb. 18, Mar. 25, and Apr. 15 and 22, 1921.

64. *Advance*, Mar. 10, 17, and 31 and May 5, 1922.

65. Ibid., Jan. 14, July 22, and Aug. 19, 1921, Sept. 28, 1923, Apr. 1, 1927, Nov. 22, 1929. It was Dressner, moreover, who was responsible for persuading Bryn Mawr College president M. Carey Thomas to grant labor an equal role in the school, making it truly a cross-class organization, like the WTUL, which supported it. See Rita Heller, "Blue Collars and Blue-stockings: The Bryn Mawr Summer School for Women Workers, 1921–1938," in *Sisterhood and Solidarity: Workers' Education for Women, 1914–1984,* ed. Joyce L. Kornbluh and Mary Frederickson (Philadelphia: Temple University Press, 1984), 107–45, esp. 118.

66. Mary Heaton Vorse, "Amalgamated Women of Baltimore," *Advance,* Apr. 22, 1921.

67. *Advance*, Feb. 24, 1922; *Baltimore Evening Sun,* Feb. 16, 1922; *Baltimore Sun,* Feb. 17, 1922.

68. Agnes Nestor to Elisabeth Christman, Mar. 17, 1922, Edith Houghton Hooker to Elisabeth Christman, Feb. 14, 1922, Minutes of the Meeting of the Executive Board of the NWTUL, Feb. 27, 1922, Elisabeth Christman to Members of the Executive Board, Mar. 18 and 23, 1922, and Schlossberg to Samuel Rudow, Mar. 2, 1922 (copy), NWTUL Papers; *Baltimore Sun,* Mar. 16, 17, 1922.

69. Cf. Dye, *As Equals and as Sisters,* 151.

70. *Advance*, May 23, June 6, Aug. 8, and Dec. 5, 1924; *ACW Documentary History, Sixth Biennial Convention, 1924.*

71. *Advance*, Nov. 7, 1924, Jan. 16, Feb. 13, and Mar. 13, 1925.

72. Santora to Bellanca, Sept. 2 and 16, 1924, Box 32, Folder 9, Bellanca Papers, ACWA Papers. See also *Advance,* letter to Dorothy Jacobs Bellanca, Nov. 7, 1924. Privately, Santora denied that Crystal was "the right kind of a union man." See Santora to Bellanca, Aug. 3, 1925, Box 32, Folder 9, Bellanca Papers, ACWA Papers.

73. Santora to Bellanca, Sept. 2 and 16, 1924, Box 32, Folder 9, Bellanca Papers, ACWA Papers.

74. Santora to Bellanca, Sept. 2, 1924, Box 32, Folder 9, Bellanca Papers, ACWA Papers. In the mid-1920s, there was also strong sentiment among ACW women to elect a woman Joint Board manager. Ultimately, however, they decided against such a move, for they believed, according to Sara Barron, that a male leader of the city's organization would command more respect among the union locals and the city's employers. See "Oral History Interview with Barron."

75. See *Advance,* July 14, 1922, July 25, 1924, for vote totals by local. Voting by Baltimore's Polish locals, #100 and #114, fell between the extremes reported above, offering modest support to both Santora and Bellanca in 1924. The 1924 voting results also reflected the decline in the number of women ACW members. In 1922, when a much larger proportion of the members of the Jewish Local #36 were women, it had voted strongly for Santora. The Bohemian local retained an active women's contingent. See *Advance,* Mar. 10 and July 14, 1922.

76. *Baltimore Sun,* June 29, 1922; Argersinger, "To Discipline an Industry" (see chap. 1, n. 6).

77. Santora to Bellanca, Sept. 5 and Oct. 14, 1924, Box 32, Folder 9; Bessie Malac to Bellanca, Mar. 29, 1925, Box 31, Folder 17, Bellanca Papers, ACWA Papers.

206   78. Barron, interview by author. Also see letters in the *Advance* and in the Bellanca papers, March–August 1925, and Schlossberg to Bellanca, Nov. 12, 1925, Box 31, Folder 18, Bellanca Papers, ACWA Papers.

79. *Advance,* Nov. 7, 1924, Mar. 13, Apr. 3, May 8, and June 26, 1925.

80. Barron, interview by author; Malac to Bellanca, Mar. 29, 1925, Box 31, Folder 17, Bellanca Papers, ACWA Papers.

81. Bellanca to Malac, Feb. 26 and Mar. 9, 1925, Bellanca to Santora, Apr. 10, 1925, Box 31, Folder 17, Bellanca Papers, ACWA Papers.

82. *Advance,* Mar. 13 and Apr. 3, 1925; Malac to Bellanca, Mar. 18 and 29, 1925, Box 31, Folder 17, Bellanca Papers, ACWA Papers. Dorothy Jacobs Bellanca expressed serious reservations about the Women's Activity's persistence and chastised Malac for allowing gender-based divisions to spill over onto the shopfloor. See Bellanca to Malac, Mar. 9 and Apr. 6, 1925, Box 31, Folder 17.

83. Bellanca to Santora, Aug. 25, 1925, Box 31, Folder 17, Bellanca Papers, ACWA Papers.

84. Barron, interview by author; Santora to Bellanca, Aug. 5, 1925, Box 31, Folder 17, Bellanca Papers, ACWA Papers. For indications of the extent of the disillusionment, see Malac to Bellanca, Mar. 18 and 29, 1925, Bellanca to Malac, Apr. 2, 6, and 26 and Sept. 2, 1925, and Bellanca to Santora, Apr. 10, 1925, Box 31, Folder 17, Bellanca Papers, ACWA Papers.

85. *Advance,* June 15, July 27, Sept. 14, and Oct. 26, 1917; "The Amalgamated Spirit," by Ann and Heber Blankenhorn, May 17, 1953, Box 1, Folder 24, Ann Blankenhorn Papers, Reuther Library; Edelman, interview by author. The Rozner quotation is from Glenn, *Daughters of the Shtetl,* 233–4. Rozner, a confidant of both Santora and Dorothy Bellanca, took a keen interest in the struggle over the Women's Activity in Baltimore in 1925. See Santora to Bellanca, Aug. 12, 1925, Box 32, Folder 9, Bellanca Papers, ACWA Papers.

86. Glenn, in *Daughters of the Shtetl,* 227–38, offers many valuable insights, yet my evidence suggests that women supported separate locals in the same way they called for special entertainments and organizational activities. They saw them as mechanisms to become more fully integrated—and accepted—within the union. The issue was not so much resenting male leadership as overcoming male exclusivity. Certain aspects of their separatist campaigns, however, suggested more competition than cooperation, as they demanded an equal place in the union. They were not unaffected by the political, social, and economic changes that had enabled them to become more visible in the public arena. Glenn concedes that the "minority who advocated separatism tended to see it not as an institutional expression of female difference" but as a method of becoming more fully integrated in the union. While I agree with that assessment, my evidence suggests that there were women—indeed the same women—who also saw separatism as an expression of "cultural difference." After all, both men and women regarded women members as "different." Even Dorothy Jacobs, who put the union above issues of gender, still defended the "special character of women" as an enriching contribution to the union movement and called for special—and separate—activities for women that would make them more comfortable and active within the union. Moreover, when five hundred women called for the election of a woman to the city's top position in the union, as they did in Baltimore in 1925, there was clearly a recognition of the importance of gender, power, and separatism.

87. *ACW Documentary History, Eighth Biennial Convention, 1928,* 236–7.

1. *ACW Documentary History, Third Biennial Convention, 1918,* 51; *Baltimore Evening Sun,* May 15, 1918.

2. *Advance,* Jan. 25, 1918; *ACW Documentary History, Third Biennial Convention, 1918,* 51.

3. *Baltimore Sun,* Dec. 21, 23, and 24, 1919. For a discussion of the ACW's 1920 national convention, see Fraser, *Labor Will Rule,* 166–7 (see intro., n. 8).

4. *ACW Documentary History, Third Biennial Convention, 1918,* 51.

5. *Baltimore Sun,* Dec. 21, 23, and 24, 1919; Maryland State Board of Labor and Statistics, *Twenty-ninth Annual Report, 1919, and Thirtieth Annual Report, 1920.* See also Kahn, *Stitch in Time,* 135–6 (see chap. 1, n. 5), and McCardell, "New Hope in Men's Apparel Here" (see chap. 4, n. 60).

6. *Baltimore Sun,* Dec. 20 and 24, 1920; *Advance,* Aug. 12, 1921.

7. Fraser, *Labor Will Rule,* 166; ACW Research and Publicity Department, untitled pamphlet, Dec. 18, 1920 (the ACW issued a 19-page pamphlet of questions and answers about the industry, the union, and labor-management cooperation that was designed to counter congressional fears about the Amalgamated's "radicalism" and its purported "negative" effect on business), Box 122, Folder titled "Textile Industry: ACW Press Releases, 1920–21," Mary Heaton Vorse Papers, Reuther Library (see chap. 3, n. 1).

8. ACW untitled pamphlet, 18–9; *Baltimore Sun,* Dec. 24, 1920.

9. *Advance,* May 13 and Aug. 12, 1921, May 12, 1922.

10. Ibid., Aug. 12, 1921.

11. *Baltimore Sun,* Dec. 22 and 23, 1919.

12. Ibid., Dec. 20 and 22, 1920. Baltimore's *Jewish Times* proved an exception to this tendency in the local press; see, for example, its issue of December 19, 1919.

13. Jacob Edelman, interview by author, June 18, 1983; *Advance,* July 25, 1924, Apr. 3, 1925; Imberman, "Men's Clothing," 20–1 (see chap. 1, n. 5). In adopting these tactics, of course, Baltimore's clothing manufacturers conformed to patterns elsewhere in the industry. In calling for a "readjustment" of labor power in the postwar era, for instance, the *Garment Manufacturers' Index* raised the alarm of "sovietism, Bolshevism," and urged the nation's clothiers to attack "radical unionism" in order to reduce both wages and inefficiency. See *Garment Manufacturers' Index* (New York), Jan. 1921, 24.

14. ACW untitled pamphlet; *Baltimore Sun,* Dec. 22 and 24, 1920.

15. *Baltimore Sun,* Dec. 19, 21, 24, and 27–31, 1920, Jan. 4 and 9, 1921.

16. *Advance,* July 18, 1924; *Baltimore Sun,* Dec. 24, 1920, July 18 and 19, 1922; *ACW Documentary History, Fifth Biennial Convention, 1922.*

17. *Advance,* June 30, 1922, July 18 and 25 and Aug. 15, 1924; "Memo on Baltimore," n.d. (from the ACW General Office), Box 45A, Folder 11, Papers of the Joint Boards and Local Unions, ACWA Papers (see chap. 2, n. 39); *ACW Documentary History, Fifth Biennial Convention, 1922.*

18. *Baltimore Sun,* June 29 and 30, 1922; *Advance,* July 7, 1922.

19. *Advance,* June 9 and 30 and July 7, 1922.

20. *Advance,* July 14 and Aug. 4, 1922; *Baltimore Sun,* July 1, 1922; *Baltimore Evening Sun,* July 18, 1922.

21. *Advance,* July 14, 21, and 28 and Aug. 4, 1922.

22. Ibid., July 28, 1922; *Baltimore Sun,* July 1, 2, 4, 6, 18–21, and 23, 1922; *Baltimore Evening Sun,* July 18 and 19, 1922.

23. *Advance,* July 21 and 28 and Nov. 3, 1922, Jan. 19 and Oct. 19, 1923.

24. *Baltimore Sun,* July 21 and 22, 1922; "Memo on Baltimore," n.d. See also Asher, "Dorothy Jacobs Bellanca: Women Clothing Workers and the Runaway Shops," in *A Needle, A Bobbin, A Strike,* ed. Jensen and Davidson, 195–226 (see chap. 1, n. 20).

25. *Baltimore Sun,* Mar. 6, 7, and 9, 1923; *Advance,* Mar. 9, 1923. See also Imberman, "Men's Clothing Industry," 20–5.

26. *Advance,* Mar. 9 and Nov. 30, 1923.

27. *ACW Documentary History, Sixth Biennial Convention, 1924,* 66–9; *ACW Documentary History, Seventh Biennial Convention, 1926,* 108–9. See also *Advance,* Mar. 9, 1923, Jan. 16, May 15, and Aug. 14, 1925.

28. "Baltimore Locals, A.C.W. of A., Average Dues Paying Membership since February 1920," [1925], Box 45A, Folder 11, Papers of Joint Boards and Local Unions, ACWA Papers; "Memo on Baltimore," n.d. For a typical appeal of the Baltimore Joint Board for members to pay their dues, see *Advance,* Oct. 19, 1923.

29. *Advance,* July 25, Aug. 15, and Sept. 5, 12, 19, and 26, 1924; Imberman, "Men's Clothing"; McCardell, "New Hope in Men's Apparel Here." These comparisons are based on data from the U.S. Bureau of Labor and Statistics.

30. *ACW Documentary History, Seventh Biennial Convention, 1926; Advance,* Dec. 5, 1924, Feb. 20, 1925; Sara Barron, interview by author, Feb. 17, 1986. For a typical example of press coverage, see *Baltimore Sun,* Dec. 29, 1920.

31. Edelman, interview by author; Santora to Bellanca, Sept. 2, 1924, Box 23, Folder 9, Bellanca Papers, ACWA Papers.

32. "Ulisse DeDominicis," ACWA Biographical File, Box 242, Folder 1, ACWA Papers; *Baltimore Sun,* July 19, 1922; *Advance,* May 2 and Sept. 26, 1924, Feb. 20, 1925. Giacomo Matteotti, a Socialist member of the Italian Chamber of Deputies, was assassinated on June 10, 1924, as he prepared an address denouncing fascism.

33. *Advance,* Apr. 3 and May 29, 1925; "Coat Pressers Claim" (memorandum), Schloss Brothers, July 10, 1925, Harry Crystal to Blumberg, June 17 and Apr. 2, 1925, Schloss to Blumberg, June 17, 1925, "Understanding Between the House and the Union Regarding the Elimination of Cloth Trimmings on 'S' Work," Apr. 2, 1925, Louis Leiderman to Blumberg, Mar. 28, 1925, Blumberg to Leiderman, July 23, 1925, and Blumberg to Crystal, July 24, 1925, Box 45A, Folder 11, Papers of the Joint Boards and Local Unions, ACWA Papers.

34. Barron, interview by author; *Advance,* Aug. 14, 1925, Jan. 14, 1927.

35. *Advance,* Jan. 14 and 28, 1927. For leadership problems, see esp. *Advance,* Dec. 7, 1923, and Mamie Santora to Dorothy Bellanca, Sept. 2, 1924, Box 32, Folder 9, Bellanca Papers, ACWA Papers.

36. *Advance,* Jan. 14, Apr. 1 and 15, and July 22, 1927.

37. Ibid., June 15 and 22 and Oct. 5, 1928. For the union's continuing weakness among Baltimore's Lithuanians, see also *Advance,* June 21 and Aug. 30, 1929.

38. *ACW Documentary History, Fifth Biennial Convention, 1922; ACW Documentary History, Sixth Biennial Convention, 1924; ACW Documentary History, Seventh Biennial Convention, 1926; ACW Documentary History, Eighth Biennial Convention, 1928.* See also *Advance,* Aug. 8, 1924, May 25, 1928.

39. *Advance,* May 15, July 24 and 31, Aug. 7, and Dec. 5 and 11, 1925, Jan. 14, 1927.

40. Ibid., Jan. 16, 1925.

41. See Zaretz, *The Amalgamated* (see intro., n. 8); George Soule, *Sidney Hillman: Labor Statesman* (New York: Macmillan, 1939); Earl Strong, *The Amalgamated Clothing Workers of America* (Grinnell, Iowa: Herald-Register, 1940); Schaefer, "Educational Activities," 124–37 (see intro., n. 8).

42. Fraser, *Labor Will Rule,* 178.

43. *Advance,* Feb. 20, 1925.

44. Herbert Harris, "Hillman and the Amalgamated," *Common Sense,* Box 123, Folder titled "Textiles-1937," Mary Heaton Vorse Papers, Reuther Library; Nathan Shaviro, "Labor Leader: Hillman of the CIO," *Survey Graphic* (June 1937), in the Herman Wolf Collection, Box 13, Folder titled "Textile Workers," Mary Heaton Vorse Papers, Reuther Library.

45. *ACW Documentary History, Eighth Biennial Convention, 1928.* See also *Advance,* May 11, 1928.

46. *Advance,* June 30, 1922; Imberman, "Men's Clothing."

47. Imberman, "Men's Clothing"; Minutes of the General Executive Board (hereafter referred to as GEB Minutes), Aug. 25–8, 1931, Box 165, Folder 15, ACWA Papers.

48. GEB Minutes, Nov. 27–9, 1930, Box 15, Folder 14, ACWA Papers; *BJB Minutes, 1932–1935* (see chap. 2, n. 39).

CHAPTER 6: REMAKING THE UNION

1. Philip Scranton, "The Transition from Custom to Ready-to-Wear Clothing in Philadelphia, 1890–1930," *Textile History* 25 (1994): 267.

2. Jacob Edelman, interview by author, June 18, 1983.

3. Imberman, "Men's Clothing" (see chap. 1, n. 5); Argersinger, "To Discipline an Industry" (see chap. 1, n. 6).

4. GEB Minutes, Aug. 25–8, 1931, Box 165, Folder 15, and Aug. 30–Sept. 1, 1932, Box 165, Folder 17, ACWA Papers (see chap. 2, n. 39).

5. Imberman, "Men's Clothing"; GEB Minutes, May 8–10, 1930, Box 165, Folder 13, Nov. 27–9, 1930, Box 165, Folder 14, and Aug. 25-8, 1931, Box 165, Folder 15, ACWA Papers.

6. GEB Minutes, May 8–10 and Nov. 27–9, 1930, Aug. 25–8, 1931.

7. GEB Minutes, Aug. 30–Sept. 1, 1932, Box 165, Folder 17, ACWA Papers.

8. Imberman, "Men's Clothing"; Sara Barron, interview by author, Feb. 17, 1986.

9. GEB Minutes, Aug. 25–8, 1931.

10. *Advance,* Oct. 1932.

11. *Baltimore Sun,* Sept. 12 and 13, 1932; GEB Minutes, Aug. 30–Sept. 1, 1932; *ACW Documentary History, Tenth Biennial Convention, 1934.*

12. *Advance,* Oct. and Nov. 1932.

13. *Advance,* Oct. 1932.

14. Ibid.; "Oral History Interview with Barron" (see chap. 2, n. 1); Barron, interview by author; Edelman, interview by author; *Baltimore Sun,* Sept. 13, 1932.

15. *Baltimore Post,* Sept. 13, 1932; *Advance,* Dec. 1932, Jan. 1933; Jacob Hollander, *Report to Honorable Howard W. Jackson on Working Conditions in the Garment Industry* (Baltimore: n.p., Oct. 13, 1932); Hollander, *Report of the Hearing of Strikers from the Schoeneman Shops in Connection with an Investigation of Conditions in the Clothing Industry Held at City Hall* (Baltimore: n.p., Oct. 13, 1932).

16. Hollander, *Report of the Hearing of Strikers; Advance,* Nov. 1932.

210

17. Hollander, *Report to Honorable Howard W. Jackson.*

18. *Baltimore Post* quoted in *Advance,* Nov. 1932; Hollander, *Report of the Hearing of Strikers.*

19. *Advance,* Oct. 1932.

20. *BJB Minutes, 1932–1935* (see chap. 2, n. 39); Barron, interview by author; "Oral History Interview with Barron."

21. GEB Minutes, Nov. 6 and 7, 1933, Box 165, Folder 19, ACWA Papers.

22. Imberman, "Men's Clothing"; Newman Jeffrey to J. S. Potofsky, Sept. 7, 1939, Box 57, Folder 7, Papers of the Joint Boards and Local Unions, ACWA Papers.

23. Barron, interview by author; *BJB Minutes, 1932–1935.*

24. GEB Minutes, June 5, 1933, Box 165, Folder 18, ACWA Papers.

25. *Baltimore Sun,* June 27 and 29, 1933. See also Argersinger, *Toward a New Deal,* 146–7 (see chap. 4, n. 4). For a careful analysis of Hillman and the NRA, see Steve Fraser, "From the 'New Unionism' to the New Deal," *Labor History* 25 (summer 1984): 405–30.

26. Imberman, "Men's Clothing"; *Baltimore Sun,* June 27 and 29, 1933; *Advance,* July 1933, May 1934; Robert Connery, *The Administration of an NRA Code* (Chicago: Public Administration Service, 1938), 9–18.

27. NRA Violations, Box 249, Folder 2, ACWA Papers; "Other Cases Involving Discharge of Employees in Violation of Section 7(a)," *Monthly Labor Review* 39 (Nov. 1934): 1155; Arthur Hungerford to Donald Richberg, Aug. 18, 1934, National Emergency Council, Record Group 44, Box 180, Washington National Records Center, Suitland, Md.; *BJB Minutes, 1932–1935.*

28. Minutes of the Baltimore Joint Board, Aug. 28, Sept. 11 and 25, Oct. 23, and Nov. 13, 1933, Mar. 12 and June 11, 1934, *BJB Minutes, 1932–1935.*

29. *Maryland Leader,* Sept. 16, 1933; "Report on the Activities of the Baltimore Labor Relations Panel, to August 17th, 1934," "Report on the Activities of the Baltimore Labor Relations Panel, August 17th, 1934 to September 1st, 1934," and folders marked "Monthly," "Weekly," and "Daily" reports, Administrative File, Baltimore, Papers of the National Labor Relations Board, Record Group 25, National Archives, Washington, D.C.

30. "Violations of Men's Clothing Code: Baltimore," [April–June 1934], Box 249, Folder 2, NRA Violations, ACWA Papers. A series of state investigations into Baltimore's men's garment industry also found that firms maintained irregular or no records as to employee hours and paid women workers "miserably low sums." See *Report of Investigation of Strike Existing in Men's Garment Industry Made by J. Knox Insley, Aug. 4, 1933, Report of Investigation of Strike Existing in Men's Garment Industry in Baltimore by J. Knox Insley, Aug. 12, 1933,* and *Report of Investigation of Strike Involving the Goldman Company by J. Knox Insley, Sept. 11, 1933,* Folder titled "Correspondence-Labor," Executive Papers of Governor Albert C. Ritchie, Maryland Hall of Records, Annapolis.

31. Minutes of the Baltimore Joint Board, Sept. 11 and Oct. 9 and 23, 1933, Mar. 12, Apr. 9, and June 11, 1934, *BJB Minutes, 1932–1935; Advance,* Nov. 1933, Aug. and Dec. 1934; *Maryland Leader,* Apr. 21 and June 16, 1934.

32. *Advance,* July 1933.

33. *Baltimore Sun,* July 19, 26, 28, and 30 and Sept. 2, 1934; *Advance,* Aug. 1934; *Maryland Leader,* July 21, 1934; Connery, *Administration of an NRA Code,* 69. See also Argersinger, *Toward a New Deal,* 149, and Charles Kimberly, "The Depression and New Deal in Maryland" (Ph.D. diss., American University, 1974), 122–4.

34. *Baltimore Sun,* July 19, 26, 28, and 30 and Sept. 2, 1934; Connery, *Administration of an NRA Code,* 74–5; Biweekly Report, Sept. 26, 1935, National Emergency Council, Record Group 44, Box 412, Washington National Records Center, Suitland, Md.

35. Minutes of the Baltimore Joint Board, May 17, 1935, *BJB Minutes, 1932–1935.*

36. Imberman, "Men's Clothing"; J. W. Hathcock, "The Men's Clothing Industry," Work Materials No. 58 (Washington, D.C.: Office of National Recovery Administration, Division of Review, 1936), 8–9, 125–6, 151.

37. Imberman, "Men's Clothing"; GEB Minutes, Feb. 1–3, 1932, Box 165, Folder 16, and June 5, 1933, Box 165, Folder 18; Argersinger, "To Discipline an Industry."

38. GEB Minutes, June 5, 1933; *BJB Minutes, 1932–1935.*

39. Imberman, "Men's Clothing"; Minutes of the Baltimore Joint Board, Jan. 13, 1936, in *Baltimore Joint Board Minutes, Jan. 1936 to Dec. 1938,* Regional Office, UNITE, Baltimore (hereafter referred to as *BJB Minutes, 1936–1938*).

40. The *BJB Minutes, 1932–1935* records repeated efforts at enforcement; see the minutes for Dec. 18, 1933, Jan. 18, 1934, and Sept. 11, 1935, for examples. For the organizational campaigns, see the minutes for Mar. 26 and Apr. 9 and 23, 1934, in *BJB Minutes, 1932–1935* and Sara Borinsky to Jacob Potofsky, Feb. 6, 1935, Dorothy Bellanca to Sara Barron, Jan. 13, 1939, Potofsky to Mildred Jeffrey, Jan. 27, 1939, Mildred McWilliams [Jeffrey] to Bellanca, Jan. 19, 1939, McWilliams to Potofsky, Jan. 26, 1939, Potofsky to P. Epstein, Mar. 7, 1939, and Newman Jeffrey to Potofsky, Apr. 5, 1939, Box 57, Folder 6, and Potofsky to DeDominicis, Aug. 18, 1939, Box 57, Folder 7, Papers of the Joint Boards and Local Unions, ACWA Papers; Jeffrey, interview by author, April 14, 1988.

41. Dorothy Bellanca to Ulisse DeDominicis, Aug. 24, 1939, Box 57, Folder 7, and Jacob Potofsky to Newman Jeffrey, July 7, 1939, and Mildred McWilliams [Jeffrey] to Dorothy Bellanca, Jan. 19, 1939, Box 57, Folder 6, Papers of the Joint Boards and Local Unions, ACWA Papers; Jeffrey, interview by author.

42. Barron, interview by author; "Oral History Interview with Barron"; Hyman Caplan to Jacob Potofsky, n.d., Box 122, Folder 24, Potofsky Correspondence, ACWA Papers; *Advance,* Oct. 1932.

43. For Jacobs, see also Asher, "Dorothy Jacobs Bellanca: Women Clothing Workers and the Runaway Shops," in *A Needle, A Bobbin, A Strike,* ed. Jensen and Davidson, 195–226 (see chap. 1, n. 20).

44. "Oral History Interview with Barron."

45. Argersinger, *Toward a New Deal,* 8–10; *Baltimore Sun,* Sept. 17, 1930.

46. "Oral History Interview with Barron"; Barron, interview by author; Minutes of the Baltimore Joint Board, Apr. 23, 1934, *BJB Minutes, 1932–1935.*

47. *Advance,* July 1933; *BJB Minutes, 1932–1935;* Edelman, interview by author; "A.C.W.A. Organizers Staff Meeting, New Howard Hotel, Baltimore, Md., July 23, 1934," Box 3, Folder 5, Edith Christenson Papers, Reuther Library (see chap. 3, n. 1).

48. Minutes of the Baltimore Joint Board, Sept. 11, 1935, *BJB Minutes, 1932–1935,* and Feb. 24, 1938, *BJB Minutes, 1936–1938;* Dorothy Bellanca to Nettie Mehaffry, Aug. 22, 1939, Box 57, Folder 7, Papers of the Joint Boards and Local Unions, ACWA Papers; *Maryland Leader,* Aug. 24, 1935; Jeffrey, interview by author.

49. Maryland Commissioner of Labor and Statistics, *Forty-fifth Annual Report* (Baltimore, 1936), 6; Minutes of the Baltimore Federation of Labor, Sept. 15, 1937, Feb. 9 and Apr. 13, 1938, Baltimore Office of the Metropolitan Council AFL-CIO Unions; *Balti-*

212 *more Sun,* July 15, 1938; Argersinger, *Toward a New Deal,* 157, 171.

50. *Baltimore Evening Sun,* Mar. 9, 1937; *Labor Herald,* Apr. 9, 1937. For the La Follette Committee, see Jerold S. Auerbach, *Labor and Liberty: The La Follette Committee and the New Deal* (Indianapolis, Ind.: Bobbs-Merrill, 1966).

51. *Maryland Leader,* July 22 and Dec. 9, 1933, Feb. 10, June 16, and July 28, 1934, Mar. 30 and Aug. 31, 1935, Mar. 21 and Apr. 11, 1936; *Baltimore Sun,* May 21–3 and Sept. 25, 1936; Edelman, interview by author. The *BJB Minutes, 1932–1935* and *BJB Minutes, 1936–1938* also note the monthly expenditures on legal fees, all of which went to Edelman's firm during the 1930s.

52. Newman Jeffrey to Dorothy Bellanca, Sept. 8, 1939, and Bellanca to Nettie Mehaffry, Aug. 22, 1939, Box 57, Folder 7, Papers of the Joint Boards and Local Unions, ACWA Papers; Minutes of the Baltimore Joint Board, Mar. 14 and May 3, 1935, *BJB Minutes, 1932–1935*; letter to the author from Broadus Mitchell, Sept. 19, 1975.

53. Minutes of the Baltimore Joint Board, Jan. 13 and Sept. 14, 1936, *BJB Minutes, 1936–1938*; "Industrial Disputes," *Monthly Labor Review* 42 (May 1936): 1305 and 48 (May 1939): 1119; *Baltimore Sun,* Aug. 14 and Nov. 7, 1935.

54. *Baltimore Sun,* Nov. 7, 1935; *Labor Herald,* Aug. 28 and Sept. 4 and 11, 1936; Minutes of the Baltimore Joint Board, Mar. 20, 1936, *BJB Minutes, 1936–1938.*

55. Minutes of the Baltimore Joint Board, Aug. 16, 1937, *BJB Minutes, 1936–1938; Advance,* Oct. 1937.

56. Barron, interview by author; Dorothy Bellanca to Sara Barron, Jan. 13, 1939, Box 57, Folder 6, and Jacob Potofsky to Ulisse DeDominicis, Aug. 18, 1939, Box 57, Folder 7, Papers of the Joint Boards and Local Unions, ACWA Papers.

57. *Labor Herald,* Sept. 3, 1937; *Maryland Leader,* Aug. 19 and Sept. 2, 1933; Ira De A. Reid, *The Negro Community in Baltimore: A Social Survey* (New York: National Urban League, 1934); Newman Jeffrey to Potofsky, Apr. 5, 1939, Box 57, Folder 6, Papers of the Joint Boards and Local Unions, ACWA Papers.

58. Argersinger, *Toward a New Deal,* 157–63. For the division within the national labor movement, see Walter Galenson, *The CIO Challenge to the AFL* (Cambridge, Mass.: Harvard University Press, 1960).

59. "Oral History Interview with Barron"; Argersinger, *Toward a New Deal,* 158; Ulisse De-Dominicis to Sidney Hillman, Oct. 30, 1939, Box 57, Folder 7, Papers of the Joint Boards and Local Unions, ACWA Papers; *Advance,* Jan. 1938, Mar. 1940; Barron, interview by author.

60. Mildred McWilliams to Potofsky, Jan. 26, 1939, and Potofsky to McWilliams, Mar. 3, 1939, Box 57, Folder 6, and Dorothy Bellanca to Mildred Jeffrey, Sept. 20, 1939, Box 57, Folder 7, Papers of the Joint Boards and Local Unions, ACWA Papers; Jeffrey, interview by author.

61. *Advance,* Apr. 1939; Newman Jeffrey to Dorothy Bellanca, Sept. 8, 1939, Box 57, Folder 7, Papers of the Joint Boards and Local Unions, ACWA Papers. For a useful description of this process, emphasizing the constraints manufacturers faced, see Philip Scranton, "The Transition from Custom to Ready-to-Wear Clothing in Philadelphia, 1890–1930," *Textile History* 25 (1994): 265–9.

62. Copy of letter titled "AETNA Shirt: Amalgamated Union Committee," July 13, 1939, Box 57, Folder 6, Papers of the Joint Boards and Local Unions, ACWA Papers.

63. Minutes of the Baltimore Joint Board, Aug. 7, 1933, *BJB Minutes, 1932–1935.*

64. Minutes of the Baltimore Joint Board, May 28, Sept. 21, and Oct. 8, 1934, Mar. 11 and May 13, 1935, *BJB Minutes, 1932–1935*; Minutes of the Baltimore Joint Board, June 9, 1936, Feb. 24, 1937, *BJB Minutes, 1936–1938*. See also *Executive Board Minutes, Local 15, 1932–1940* (2 vols.), UNITE, Baltimore.

65. Minutes of the Baltimore Joint Board, Feb. 18 and 24 and Sept. 19, 1938, *BJB Minutes, 1936–1938*; Calvin Sutherlin to Potofsky (1937) and Potofsky to Sutherlin, Aug. 25, 1937, Box 122, Folder 26, Potofsky Correspondence, ACWA Papers.

66. Minutes of the Baltimore Joint Board, Oct. 9 and 23, 1933, *BJB Minutes, 1932–1935*; Minutes of the Baltimore Joint Board, Nov. 26 and 29, 1937, Jan. 31 and Mar. 7, 1938, *BJB Minutes, 1936–1938*.

67. Minutes of the Baltimore Joint Board, Feb. 17, 1936, *BJB Minutes, 1936–1938*.

68. Schaefer, "Educational Activities," 149–58 (see intro., n. 8); Minutes of the Baltimore Joint Board, Aug. 28, 1933, Oct. 14, 1935, *BJB Minutes, 1932–1935*; Minutes of the Baltimore Joint Board, Jan. 13 and Feb. 17, 1936, Nov. 29, 1937, *BJB Minutes, 1936–1938*.

69. Barron, interview by author; Edelman, interview by author.

70. *Advance*, Oct. 1932, Jan. 1938; Barron, interview by author; Schaefer, "Educational Activities," 192–8; Minutes of the Baltimore Joint Board, June 30 and Nov. 1, 1937, Oct. 31 and Nov. 7, 1938, *BJB Minutes, 1936–1938*.

71. Schaefer, "Educational Activities," 192–8; Argersinger, *Toward a New Deal*, 162–3. For a valuable study of New Deal programs for worker education, see Joyce L. Kornbluh, *A New Deal for Workers' Education: The Workers' Service Program, 1933–1942* (Urbana: University of Illinois Press, 1987).

72. Minutes of the Baltimore Joint Board, Aug. 28, 1933, Feb. 12, 1934, *BJB Minutes, 1932–1935*; Minutes of the Baltimore Joint Board, Jan. 13 and Feb. 13, 1936, Nov. 29, 1937, *BJB Minutes, 1936–1938*; "What New Members Must Be Taught" (1937), Box 18, Folder 4 (Pamphlets—1937), Katherine Pollak Ellickson Papers, Reuther Library; *Advance*, Oct. and Dec. 1935, Mar. 1936, June 1937, Oct. and Nov. 1938; Barron, interview by author.

73. "Movies for the C.I.O.," n.d., Box 110, Folder titled "Labor, General Miscellaneous Notes," Mary Heaton Vorse Papers, Reuther Library; Schaefer, "Educational Activities," 161–2, 192–8; Minutes of the Baltimore Joint Board, Aug. 30, 1937, Oct. 31 and Nov. 7, 1938, *BJB Minutes, 1936–1938*; *Advance*, Oct. and Dec. 1937, Nov. 1938, Nov. 1939.

74. *Advance*, Oct. 1932, Nov. 1936; *Baltimore Sun*, Oct. 18 and 22, 1936; Minutes of the Baltimore Joint Board, Sept. 14 and Nov. 16, 1936, *BJB Minutes, 1936–1938*; Minutes of the Baltimore Federation of Labor, July 29, 1936, Baltimore Office of the Metropolitan Council AFL-CIO Unions.

75. Mary Dewson to Millard Tydings, Sept. 2 and 22, 1936, Box 81, Women's Division, Democratic National Committee Papers, Franklin D. Roosevelt Library, Hyde Park, N.Y.; *Baltimore Sun*, Oct. 18 and 22, 1936; "Oral History Interview with Barron."

76. Minutes of the Baltimore Joint Board, Nov. 16, 1936, Feb. 27, 1937, *BJB Minutes, 1936–1938*.

77. Minutes of the Baltimore Joint Board, Mar. 28 and Sept. 19, 1938, *BJB Minutes, 1936–1938*; *Advance*, Feb., Apr., and Oct. 1938. For a fuller discussion of the 1938 senatorial contest, see Argersinger, *Toward a New Deal*, 196–9.

78. Minutes of the Baltimore Joint Board, Feb. 24, Apr. 5, and Nov. 26, 1937, Nov. 7, 1938, *BJB Minutes, 1936–1938*; *Advance*, May 1937, Jan., Mar., and June 1939; Edelman, in-

214 terview by author. For Edelman's career, see Argersinger, "Baltimore's Clothing Industry," 98 (see chap. 1, n. 6). For the growing ties between the ACW and the Democratic Party on the national level, see Fraser, *Labor Will Rule* (see intro., n. 8).

79. Minutes of the Baltimore Joint Board, Jan. 13, Feb. 17, Sept. 14, and Nov. 16, 1936, Apr. 5, Aug. 30, and Nov. 29, 1937, Oct. 31 and Nov. 7, 1938, *BJB Minutes, 1936–1938; Advance*, Oct. 1935, Mar. and May 1936, Jan. 1938, June 1939; *Labor Herald*, June 12, 1936, Sept. 3, 1937; *Baltimore Sun*, Aug. 14, 1935, Nov. 29, 1939.

80. Minutes from the Baltimore Joint Board, Aug. 16, 1937, *BJB Minutes, 1936–1938; Advance*, Nov. 1937, Jan., Feb., Apr., and Oct. 1938.

81. *Advance*, Jan. 1939.

82. Minutes from the Baltimore Joint Board, Aug. 16, 1937, June 6, 1938, *BJB Minutes, 1936–1938*.

Epilogue

1. *Baltimore Sun*, Nov. 14, 24, and 27, 1942, Jan. 1, 1943. For a summary list of Baltimore manufacturers' production and employment during World War II, see Kahn, *Stitch in Time*, 222–3 (see chap. 1, n. 5).

2. *Advance*, May 1, 1952, Mar. 1, 1960, Aug. 1, 1964; *New York Times*, Mar. 9, 1950, 39; *Baltimore News-American*, Mar. 11, 1979; Kahn, *Stitch in Time*, 182–5.

3. *Advance*, Nov. 15, 1950, Dec. 15, 1951, Jan. 1, Feb. 1, and May 1, 1952, Oct. 1, 1959, May 1, 1961.

4. Ibid., Feb. 1, 1961; *Baltimore Sun*, Jan. 19, 1961.

5. *Baltimore Sun*, Apr. 18 and Aug. 21, 1984; Asher, "Dorothy Jacobs Bellanca," 275–8 (see chap. 2, n. 7); *Advance*, July 1, 1962.

6. *Advance*, Mar. 1, Apr. 1, and May 1, 1961.

7. Ibid., June 15, 1959, May 1 and June 1, 1961, Dec. 1, 1962, June 15, 1963, Apr. 15 and Dec. 1, 1964. By 1974 Nocella and the Baltimore Amalgamated had created what the local media touted as "the largest private day care program in the country" and what a Labor Department official dubbed "the Cadillac of daycare centers." Funded by seventy employers and manufacturers from a now five-state area represented by the Baltimore Regional Joint Board, the center featured a low teacher-child ratio, nurses, pediatricians, extensive hot-meal services, and many educational and recreational activities. See *Advance*, Feb. 1974, Jan. 1975.

8. Ibid., June 15, 1963, Apr. 15 and May 1, 1964.

9. Ibid., Dec. 1, 1961, Jan. 15, 1964, July 15, 1959.

10. Ibid., July 15, 1959, May 15, 1964, Sept. 1975.

11. Ibid., Dec. 1974. The Baltimore ACW attempted to draw on other potent symbols to make its point in a demonstration the following year. In conjunction with a Bicentennial celebration, Paul Mignini, who had replaced Sara Barron as the Joint Board's business agent, dressed in "colonial attire" to warn against the "invasion" of imported apparel and to urge all consumers to insist on the union label "and drive these invaders from our shores." See *Advance*, Oct. 1975.

12. Foster Rhea Dulles and Melvyn Dubofsky, *Labor in America: A History* (Arlington Heights, IL: Harlan Davidson, 1984), 155.

13. Philip L. Quaglieri, ed., *America's Labor Leaders* (Lexington, Mass.: Lexington Books, 1989), 154–9; Robert H. Zieger, *American Workers, American Unions* (Baltimore: Johns Hopkins University Press, 1994), 193–4; *Baltimore Sun*, Oct. 29, 1995.

14. *Baltimore Sun,* Oct. 29, 1995. See also *Baltimore Sun,* Aug. 9, 1996.

15. Ibid., Aug. 8, 1994; Kahn, *Stitch in Time,* 221.

16. *Baltimore Sun,* Mar. 30, 1997.

17. Ibid., Aug. 8, 1994, Mar. 30 and Apr. 3, 1997.

18. Ibid., Aug. 8, 1994.

ESSAY ON SOURCES

Most of the papers of the Amalgamated Clothing Workers of America (ACW) are in the Labor-Management Documentation Center of the Martin P. Catherwood Library of the New York State School of Industrial and Labor Relations at Cornell University, Ithaca, New York. Particularly important for this study are the Papers of Joint Boards and Local Unions, which contain detailed information about the Amalgamated in Baltimore; the Papers of Sidney Hillman, which reveal his careful attention to both industrial and union developments in Baltimore; the Dorothy Jacobs Bellanca Papers, which are uniquely valuable for understanding the complex role of gender within the union; the Papers of Joseph Schlossberg; the Jacob Potofsky Papers; the Minutes of the General Executive Board; the ACWA Biographical File; and the *Documentary History of the Amalgamated Clothing Workers of America,* which includes complete accounts of the ACW's biennial conventions.

Additional records of the Amalgamated in Baltimore are preserved in the Regional Office, Union of Needletrades, Industrial, and Textile Employees, Baltimore. Especially significant are the minutes of the Baltimore Joint Board for the 1930s and the bound volumes of the Executive Board Minutes of Local #15.

Several useful manuscript collections are in The Archives of Labor History and Urban Affairs, Walter Reuther Library, Wayne State University, Detroit. The Mary Heaton Vorse Papers, Ann Blankenhorn Papers, Katherine Pollak Ellickson Papers, Herman Wolf Collection, and Edith L. Christenson Papers all provide insight into the programs and activities of the Amalgamated, particularly those related to education and organizing. Two collections in the State Historical Society of Wisconsin, Madison, also shed important light on the educational programs of the Amalgamated: the Papers of the American Labor Education Service and the Papers of the Textile

218 Workers Union of America. Letters of Broadus Mitchell in the Samuel Chiles Mitchell Papers, Southern Historical Collection, University of North Carolina, Chapel Hill, illuminate his role in workers' education and the Amalgamated in Baltimore.

The National Women's Trade Union League of America Papers, Library of Congress, and the Margaret Dreier Robins Papers, University of Florida Libraries (microfilm edition), both provide critical information on Baltimore's women garment workers and their interests in woman suffrage and other reforms. Correspondence in the Women's Division, Democratic National Committee Papers, Franklin D. Roosevelt Library, Hyde Park, New York, reveal their continuing involvement with political issues.

The Papers of the National Labor Relations Board, Record Group 25, National Archives, and the Papers of the National Emergency Council, Record Group 44, Washington National Records Center, Suitland, Maryland, provide evidence of the Amalgamated's attempt to use government agencies to establish an effective rule of law in the garment industry in the 1930s.

The Minutes of the Baltimore Federation of Labor, in possession of the Baltimore Office of the Metropolitan Council of AFL-CIO Unions, contain some information on the activities and interests of the Amalgamated in Baltimore. Records of state investigations into strikes, working conditions, and the ACW's role in Baltimore's garment shops are preserved in the Executive Papers and Governor's Correspondence of Governor Albert C. Ritchie, Maryland Hall of Records, Annapolis.

The Jewish Historical Society of Maryland has extensive records on the garment industry and its workers in Baltimore. The Papers of Rudolph Sonneborn indicate some of the interests and concerns of the city's most important manufacturer. An impressive collection of oral histories includes careful interviews of Henry Sonneborn, Jr., and Jacob Edelman, the latter especially forthcoming on ethnic issues.

My understanding of the complex issues of ethnicity and gender in Baltimore's ACW was further shaped by my own formal interviews and informal conversations with Jacob Edelman, Sara Barron, and Mildred Jeffrey, three remarkable individuals. Another valuable oral history is "Oral History Interview with Sara Barron by Barbara Wertheimer, June 4, 1976, Baltimore Maryland," New York State School of Industrial and Labor Relations, New York City Division of Cornell University.

Newspapers and periodicals were crucial to this study. Of most importance was the Amalgamated's own *Advance,* which frequently printed lengthy accounts (often written by Sara Barron) of the union's activities in Baltimore, as well as columns by Dorothy Jacobs Bellanca, reports by Mamie Santora, and other pieces of either direct or indirect relevance to the issues faced by the city's garment industry and workers. Various Baltimore labor journals, including the *Critic,* the *Labor Leader,* the *Labor Herald,* the *Baltimore Trades Unionist,* and the *Baltimore Federationist,* all reported regularly on clothing workers or the Amalgamated and its place in the city's labor movement. The *Maryland Leader,* the official organ of the state's Socialist Party, is especially valuable for the 1930s. Baltimore's *Jewish Times* was frequently sympathetic to the Amalgamated. The city's daily newspapers, including the *Baltimore Sun,* the *Baltimore Evening Sun,* the *Baltimore American,* and the *Baltimore Post* all furnished important information, usually on the union's most spectacular strikes.

Journals published outside Baltimore also often proved helpful. The *Weekly Bulletin of the Clothing Trades* (New York), published by the United Garment Workers of America, and the *Ladies' Garment Worker* (New York), published by the International Ladies' Garment Workers' Union, occasionally surveyed the workers in the city's men's garment industry. The *Garment Manufacturers' Index* (New York), *Manufacturing Industries,* and *Apparel Manufacturer* all offer insight into management's perspective. *Life and Labor,* published in Chicago by the Women's Trade Union League, reported on that organization's activities in Baltimore.

Finally, government documents provide a wealth of information. Working conditions, wage rates, manufacturing statistics, workers' ethnicity, strikes, and other features of Baltimore's garment industry are examined in U.S. Census reports; bulletins of the U.S. Bureau of Labor Statistics; congressional documents; annual reports of Maryland's variously named Bureau of Industries and Statistics; and an exceptional study sponsored by the Works Progress Administration: Abraham Imberman, *Report on Men's Clothing Industry* (Baltimore: State Printers, 1945). Of particular value are *Report on Condition of Woman and Child Wage-Earners in the United States,* vol. 2, *Men's Ready-Made Clothing* (Senate Document 645, 61st Cong., 2d sess., Washington: Government Printing Office, 1911) and *Reports of the Immigration Commission: Immigrants in Industries,* pt. 6, *Clothing Manufacturing* (Senate Document 633, 61st Cong., 2d sess., Washington: Government Printing Office, 1911), in both of which Baltimore's men's garment industry is the focus of detailed investigation.

INDEX